BETWEEN EXILE AND RETURN

SUNY Series
in Modern Jewish Literature and Culture

Sarah Blacher Cohen, Editor

BETWEEN EXILE AND RETURN

S. Y. Agnon and the Drama of Writing

Anne Golomb Hoffman

State University of New York Press

Published by
State University of New York Press, Albany

Printed in the United States of America

For information, address State University of New York
Press, State University Plaza, Albany, N. Y., 12246

Production by Diane Ganeles
Marketing by Fran Keneston

Library of Congress Cataloging-in-Publication Data

Hoffman, Anne Golomb, 1946-
Between exile and return : S. Y. Agnon and the drama of writing / Anne Golomb Hoffman.
p. cm.—(SUNY series in modern Jewish literature and culture)
Includes bibliographical references.
ISBN 0-7914-0540-0 (alk. paper). -- ISBN 0-7914-0541-9 (pbk. : alk. paper)
1. Agnon, Shmuel Yosef, 1888-1970--Criticism and interpretation. 2. Kafka, Franz, 1883-1924--Criticism and interpretation. 3. Jabès, Edmond--Criticism and interpretation. I. Title. II. Series.
PJ5053.A4Z614 1991
892.4′35--dc20 90-35371
CIP

10 9 8 7 6 5 4 3 2 1

To the memory of my father,
Maurice Golomb

Contents

Acknowledgments

My parents, Rita Pick and Maurice Golomb, led me first to European literature and to Hebrew; my interests reflect some of the patterns of their lives. Thanks go to David Patterson and Isaac Barzilay, with whom I first read and began to write about Agnon. In recent years, I have welcomed the critiques and collegiality of Gershon Shaked. This project has brought with it the friendship of Emuna Agnon Yaron and Hayyim Yaron; I hope they will feel that I have added something to the reading of Agnon. Naomi Sokoloff has shared her critical insights generously. I am grateful to Rafael Veiser of the Jewish National and University Library in Jerusalem for his help with archival sources. The libraries of Columbia University and the Jewish Theological Seminary of America, as well as the Research Branch of the New York Public Library, have been of great assistance. Research for this book was funded in part by grants from the National Endowment for the Humanities, the Fordham University Research Council, and the Lucius N. Littauer Foundation. The College at Lincoln Center of Fordham University has offered research support and collegiality. The International Center for University Teaching of Jewish Civilization provided a hospitable setting in Jerusalem, in which to share ideas. Various colleagues and friends read all or part of this work and and offered helpful comments. I am grateful to Patricia Clough, Yael Feldman, Maris Fiondella, Nurit Gertz, Avraham Holtz, Alan Mintz, Gershon Shaked, and Naomi Sokoloff. My husband, Leon Hoffman, has been a companionable and rigorous reader, whose interest and support I have always been able to count on. My daughters, Miriam and Liora, sustained me with their enthusiasm and love of books, while reminding me to keep my priorities in order.

Earlier versions of portions of chapters 5, 6, and 7 appeared in the following publications: *Prooftexts* 2:265–82, *Hebrew Annual Review* 11:153–71, and *S.Y. Agnon: Texts and Contexts in English Translation,* ed. Leon Yudkin (New York, 1988). Permission to reprint is gratefully acknowledged.

Chapter

1

Introduction: "Like a Man Who Is Exiled From the Palace of His Father"

S. Y. Agnon: Modern Jewish Writer

Each of these terms—"modern," "Jewish," "writer"—provides structure to this inquiry. S. Y. Agnon, the subject of my study, ranks with the major modernists of this century, but differs from his European peers in his intense engagement in a universe of sacred language. The modernism of the early part of this century consisted of a revolt against inherited norms and conventions, along with a self-conscious search for new forms of expression. The literary experiments of Shmuel Yosef Agnon are the more striking within this context, insofar as they appropriate and transform elements of the ongoing religious and cultural traditions of Judaism.

Agnon's is a restless writing that resists easy classification. He has been read by some as a pious storyteller, by others as a modern ironist. He is both and more. Shifting between exile and return, Agnon's writing cannot simply be identified with the ideological enclosures of traditional world views; nor is it characterized by the complete absence of inherited structures. Because Agnon writes in Hebrew, the very language that he uses maintains a connection to the language of Scripture and commentary; that relationship is made inescapable by the many ways in which the writing uses Jewish themes and sources. Sharply modern disjunctions within self, social world and tradition are all the more startling for their interaction with a deeply rooted mystique of the wholeness inherent in sacred language.

Agnon explores structures that are not so much those of European history and society as they are those of traditional eastern European culture surrounding sacred Jewish texts, whose study and elaboration had been the binding force of the people in its dispersion. The modern Jewish imagination, with its collective memory of dispersion and the experience of return, carries the history of a people inscribed in its language. On the eve of the return to a physical homeland through the Zionist movement in which Agnon participated, we find the writer engaged in fictions that oscillate ambivalently between old world and new, filial rebellion and a return to the father (and the identity of the "father" is not constant), and between extreme positions in relation to the texts at the center of the community's identification of itself.

Images of books and writing express a central tension and offer a rich starting point for a study of Agnon's modernism. These images offer an emblem of the writing's link to a text-centered tradition; at the same time, they make visible the displacement of authority and the decentering of the text that is the writing's break with tradition.

My study approaches the fertile field of writing that is Agnon's art to examine questions of authority and voice, self and other, text and language. The deep allusiveness to Jewish sources in texts that call themselves into question prompts my inquiry into the nature of textuality and the place of the modern, secular text in a tradition of sacred writing. I use the term "textuality" to suggest that issues of boundary and transgression, exile, and return are acted out within the domain of the writing itself.

This is a study *of* writing *in* the writing of S. Y. Agnon. "Writing" here can be understood as a process of signification, or communication in language, a multi-leveled process with conscious and unconscious components to it. Agnon's writing brings into the foreground dimensions of the text that might otherwise go unnoticed by the reader, signaling a revision of relations among writing, text, language, and subject.

Language becomes the issue and writing the scene of the action in the dramas of signification that I propose to discuss. I am less interested in a representational approach that ignores or suppresses the writing in the interests of examining the purported external reality to which it refers. In making this claim, I do not mean to overlook the impact of political or historical factors on texts. I propose rather to examine historical and cultural trends and developments through their inscription in the text. They are part of the writing, not external to it.

Periods of cultural breakdown and renascence produce intensified self-consciousness in literary works, as if the processes involved in the production of the text and the relationship of the text to its historical-cultural context have come up for question and so make themselves more strongly felt in our reading. "Modernity . . . is about the loss of narrative," observes Alice Jardine [1985, 100]; modernist writers valorize the loss, making it the occasion for moves in new directions. The modernists of the first part of the twentieth century, among whom Agnon has a place, take on the project of renewing literature out of the disclosure of new territories in language. For some, this process involves exploration of territory that is as much psychological as topographical and in which the unconscious exerts a disruptive force. Joseph Conrad goes upriver into the heart of darkness to uncover a bestiality that is not only the horror of colonialism, but is also just as much the lawlessness buried in the depths of civilized men. Thomas Mann takes hyper-disciplined Gustave von Aschenbach on a southward journey that undoes repressive constraints, allowing for emergence of an Eros that destroys the careful structures of an Apollonian consciousness. Franz Kafka explores the penal colony, crumbling the distances between archaic and modern, primitive and civilized, that his European traveler relies upon.

In each of these modernist fictions, language discloses multiple referents for the journey that is occurring. Landscape and setting become charged with implication that cannot be located simply in the point of view of a particular character. As a result, the reader suffers a loss of privilege; no longer can the reader assert the vantage point of a superior knowledge or claim the text for the territory of a particular set of beliefs.[1]

One might compare S. Y. Agnon to James Joyce. If Joyce's project is the absorption and reformulation of the English language, his texts make us aware of the languages within language, the play of polysemy in any verbal utterance. The mythic and the mundane are made to interact through the medium of language. In a revolutionary transformation that is comparable in scope but different in substance, Agnon blurs the boundaries of sacred and secular, enlarging the domain of the literary, and implying a claim for writing that approaches the collective.

Agnon writes during the period of the renewal of Hebrew as a language of daily use. In the context of political and social upheavals that the nineteenth century brought to European and Russian Jewry, we find a coalescence of some currents of Jewish life into a nationalist movement in which the revival of Hebrew constituted a significant feature of national identity. The precipitous pace of events of the last century, including not only the rise of Jewish nationalism but also the Nazi effort at genocide, has made of modern Jewish identity less a stable set of concepts than an ongoing field of forces. Agnon's texts are inscribed within that cultural-political upheaval. Registering the impact of the competing tendencies of modern Jewish thought, including questions of language choice and use, nationalism, piety, and skepticism, the writing gives access to the main currents of this last century of Jewish modernization and modernism. At the same time, Agnon's writing sustains a detachment from the immediacy of solutions or the urgency of contemporary pressures, allowing itself an exploration of the ways in which cultural constructs and ideologies derive from deeper levels of subjectivity and collectivity.

The conflict between sacred and secular has proved in many ways to be an energizing source for the modern Hebrew writer. Agnon's writing responds to the question of secularization of a sacred tongue and can be studied in relation to other texts of the modern period for its treatment of issues surrounding that effort. Mendele Mokher Seforim prepared the way with novels and tales that put traditional sources to parodic use in biting social satires. Mendele's writing registers the impact on the eastern European Jewish community of Enlightenment expectations and their frustration, nationalist aspirations, and the rise of state anti-Semitism. In H. N. Bialik's essays, as well as his poetry, we find indications of profound cultural dislocation; the writer experiences language as a realm of promise as well as terror. (See, for example, Bialik's exploration of mundane and poetic langauge in "Revelation and Concealment in Language" and more recent discussions by Scholem, 1972; Hartman, 1985.) For Agnon, as for Bialik, language forms a charged field of operations.

While Agnon's strength as a writer was heralded early on by Y. H. Brenner, full acknowledgment of his importance to modern literature came in the 1930s with Dov Sadan's emergence as a critic; Sadan directed readers to the psychological dimensions of the writing and demonstrated the complexity of Agnon's relationship to the past. During the 1940s, Baruch Kurzweil explored many of the conflicts central to Agnon's fiction; following Sadan, Kurzweil (1970, 76) made a particular claim for the surrealistic *"Sefer hama'asim"* ("The Book of Deeds") as the "psychological key" to Agnon. In 1968, Arnold Band provided an overview of the life and work that constituted an important initiative in the study of artistic development. Since the late 1970s, Gershon Shaked has led the way in examining theme, structure, and intertextuality through close reading of texts. The present study brings current literary theory to bear on a reading of Agnon in a comparative context. In doing so, it builds upon previous work, while drawing on more recent developments in post-structuralist thought.

To enter Agnon's fictive universe, one must acknowledge the very central place occupied by Torah as the fabric of the world that both contains Creation and binds God to Israel. At the mythic center of Agnon's fictive universe, Torah constitutes a text of presence where word and thing join. Within this emblematic geography, two sorts of movement can be discerned, movement away from or toward the source. More interesting than any simple linear movement of departure and return is the expression of both movements simultaneously in the text. "Like a man who is exiled from the palace of his father": the phrase, which forms the title of this introductory chapter (taken from a 1934 story called "*Ḥush hareaḥ*" or "The Sense of Smell"), signals the ambivalence that informs the relationship of text and writing to a rich linguistic patrimony.[2]

Mystical and rabbinic approaches to language and writing constitute an attractive source for Agnon, insofar as they retrieve a relationship to the letters of a holy alphabet out of which the world was formed. The Midrash tells us, for example, that "God consulted the Torah and created the world" [Genesis Rabbah I.1]. As the blueprint for Creation, Torah is understood to be literally the world-forming text, one indication of a "mystique of language" [Scholem 1972, 70] that pervades Judaism. A sense of the rich inherence of meaning in the text, as well as the infinite interpretability of that text, manifests itself in the talmudic conviction that all Torah was given to Moses at Sinai [Avot 1:1].

Through his own formative immersion in Jewish sources, Agnon gains access to this linguistic domain and uses it as a primary source for his art. There are moments in reading Agnon that suggest a restoration of presence in text and word. The text evokes the horizon of a golden age that it can only point to, so that the reader is made to feel loss, while glimpsing a wholeness that cannot be achieved. Like Kafka, Agnon writes for a restoration he knows to be unattainable in writing. His writing activates both a sense of the inherence of meaning in language and the testimony to loss of a prior plenitude. In a geography of language and text, his writing moves between exile and return.

This study of the tensions that inform Agnon's literary art begins by comparing Agnon to two other twentieth-century Jewish writers, in order to identify some central questions concerning inscription, utterance, and authority. The chapters that follow examine the production of an autobiographical myth in the writing, as well as stories of writing that play with the relationship of later texts to their predecessors; the book concludes with readings of several major novels that both raise and subvert some fundamental cultural assumptions. While not intended as a survey of Agnon's art, this study does demonstrate the diverse moves of texts in relation to inherited or traditional structures, as well as the range of the writing through the significant components of modern Jewish experience. The thematic continuity of my work is supplied by a focus on representations of writing and books, considered as components of an ongoing drama of textuality, and also by an approach to reading and writing as related processes in the production of meaning.

To introduce this drama of writing and text in Agnon, the opening section of this study situates Agnon in relation to Franz Kafka and Edmond Jabès, in order to explore their common interest in problems of communication, as well as their different uses of Jewish sources. Kafka and Agnon merit comparison for the ways in which each calls into question the relationship of writing to authority and to the body. Thus, chapter 2, "Scribal Fictions," compares two stories of Agnon and Kafka in order to examine scenes of writing and the dramas that surround "inscription." These stories *of* writing show writing to be a charged field of intersubjective relations in language. Chapter 3, "Dramas of Signification: Edmond Jabès, S. Y. Agnon, Franz Kafka," examines how texts work in making problematic the communicative processes they represent. From the perspective of the comparative study of modern Jewish writing, Franz Kafka and Edmond Jabès offer strong contrasts to each other and to S. Y. Agnon. Each of the three writers both represents and subverts structures of communication. Two of them—Agnon and Jabès—do so in ways that explicitly evoke traditional Jewish themes and contexts. Voices of rabbis in Jabès, a Moses figure in Agnon, and hunger in Kafka supply the points of departure for a study of signification, or the production of signs, as it is represented in texts.

Building on this comparative approach to the thematics of writing in Agnon, the second major section of this book examines autobiographical myths and stories of the writer. Chapter 4, "Autochthon of the Book," examines Agnon's autobiography as it is to be found in the writing, enmeshed in a relation to language. This shaping of a life in, among, and through texts produces a persona of the writer that is itself a literary construct. Ancestors—personal and national—are defined through a relationship to Torah, in a post-romantic myth of the artist created through his work.

The notion of a life in the writing or of fiction as a form of autobiography provides the transition to chapter 5. This chapter,

"Housing the Past," takes up the project of restoration in the major novel, *Oreaḥ natah lalun* or *A Guest for the Night*. This first person narrative allows for dissection of the various, contradictory impulses that enter into the very act of telling. Playing with the relationship of the writer to the collective, *A Guest for the Night* invokes the social tapestry of Europe between the wars. The novel links its narrator's effort at self-renewal to the restoration of the *beit midrash* or House of Study in his eastern European birthplace, as well as to renewal in the larger Jewish community; through this set of parallels, the novel plays with the possibility of the text itself as a life-giving instrument. Nevertheless, *A Guest for the Night* undermines its own project of restoration through its exploration of the contradictory impulses bound up in the activity of narration; themes of rebirth and renewal disclose opposing tendencies that subvert claims to progress. To cite just one example, the novel plays with variations on the theme of the infant in the womb who knows the entirety of the Torah. This fantasy of an intrauterine state of pure knowledge not only expresses the attraction of a return to Torah, but also poses the threat of regression to the integrative project that the narrator has undertaken.

Agnon enjoyed a variety of roles in relation to classical Jewish texts, as collector, student of the sources, and anthologist. He played a major role, for example, in the society known as *Mekitze nirdamim* (Awakeners of the Sleeping), a group devoted to the retrieval, preservation, and dissemination of old Jewish manuscripts. Typically, Agnon's address on the one-hundredth anniversary of the society describes the impact of his encounter, as a youth of twelve in a Hasidic *kloyz* with a book published by *Mekitze nirdamim* [1976, 348–49]. He incorporates that early reading into an account of the formation of the writer that gracefully subordinates storytelling to the project of retrieving the texts of the past.

In Agnon's writing, however, we find no simple relation to sacred texts, but rather the complex unfolding of a multi-faceted relationship. Agnon is a "bookish" writer, not only in his allusiveness, but also in his use of books, manuscripts, and a variety of representations of texts in his narratives. I have selected three such dramas of textuality for study in chapter 6, "Inclusion and Exclusion." These stories illustrate the movement of the writing between exile and return, as it both includes itself in and excludes itself from a geography of texts surrounding the Torah. These three short stories enact varieties of relationship to predecessor texts, which are themselves fictions of the writing. Two of the three stories draw on the model of the wonder-working deeds and writings of holy men, in playful attempts to join present-day narrative to its more potent predecessors. Using writing as theme, the Agnon text plays out issues of authority, autonomy, affiliation, and utterance. It is in this sense that we meet the writer in the text, not so much as a consistent persona who wields the authority of his intentions, but rather as a function of the writing, subject to the play of discourses in the text.

The third major section of this book moves from close study of writing and writer to the broader cultural canvas of two major novels. My reading attends to the ways in which these novels jostle some major cultural myths or constructions, concerning gender, the dissociation of culture from the body, and formative passage of the subject through the Oedipus complex. Chapter 7, "Inscription and Madness," considers the function of a random writing on the back of a dog in *Only Yesterday (Tmol shilshom)*, Agnon's novel of the Second *Aliyah* (wave of immigration to Palestine, 1905–14). It begins by looking at the puzzling relationship of the novel's two plots, the story of Yitzhak Kummer, would-be pioneer, and the wanderings of the dog Balak. The relationship of these two plot lines was apparently a source of difficulty for Agnon in the composition of the novel and has continued to trouble readers in search of interpretive coherence. Using the writing on the dog as a point of departure, this chapter examines the meeting of a young man and a dog in a moment of writing, and considers the wanderings or dissemination of the dog Balak as a "text" cut loose from its putative author. The young man's writing can be read as a gesture of Oedipal defiance that makes manifest the madness inherent in any writing. The end result of that defiance is a form of filial sacrifice that is both savage and conciliatory in its move to restore a primitive paternal authority.

Chapter 8, "The Wound and the Book," turns to *Shira*, an unfinished masterpiece that is an antimonumental work. *Shira* is a response to the distinctions between self and other, male and female, flesh and spirit that inhabit culture. The novel's setting in the German-Jewish academic community of Jerusalem brings in the historical moment at which the destruction of German Jewry became clear. In its anatomy of culture, the novel implicates Germany's designation of a diseased Jewish "other" in service of a myth of racial purity. The novel takes the perspective of that "diseased other," the German Jew who is the product of the very culture that rejects him. Hence, the novel's texture, which is informed by a degree of explicit cultural reference, rare in Agnon's writing.

Shira raises questions as to the relationship of body and book in culture, with particular attention to the German-Jewish book as a problematic object. Signs of the emergence of a repressed body can be discerned in the novel's recurring preoccupation with images of disease in the body. These thematic concerns displace plot and signal a turn away from metaphysical oppositions. The effect is to alter the reader's sense of texts as bounded entities that can be described objectively.

While I am less concerned with tracing development in Agnon than with following some of the rich explorations that the writing makes available to the reader, the concluding portion of my study makes a particular claim for *Only Yesterday* and *Shira*, two vast and dissonant texts that offer narrative dissections of cultural processes. Along with *A Guest for the Night*, these are texts of our time whose writing discloses the persistent and opposing tendencies that inhabit our constructions of self, gender, authority, and text. Moving toward this larger territory of the writing in which uncertainties of definition and boundary are enacted, this study accepts the invitation that the writing offers to enter an encounter in and through the text.

Language, Literature and Subjectivity

No longer the transparent medium in which story is given, language has become visible in the texts of our modernity. For writers and anatomists of various persuasions, from the linguist to the psychoanalyst, and the literary critic, language is the dense medium of cultural expression in which subjectivity takes shape. As a preface, I would like to suggest some theoretical coordinates for the questions that structure this study of textuality in Agnon. Realizing that this brief discussion risks offering too much to the novice and too little to the more experienced reader, I would also simply direct readers to the body of the book, where theoretical issues come out of the readings themselves.

Agnon's texts make manifest problems in communication that involve the transmission and decoding of messages. In order to enter the domain of signification in which signs are produced, I make use of a model of communication that situates the sender of the message in relation to the addressee and notes also the code in which the message is communicated. The notion of "message" is complicated, however, insofar as literary or poetic language defies our ability to detach any simple "message" from the text we read. The poetic aspects of language acquire communicative function of their own, directing our attention to the play of language. This self-referential quality constitutes the poetic function of language [Jakobson, 1960, 356].

Extending this notion of the reflexive nature of poetic language, I argue that the effect of self-reference is intensified in texts that contain within them representations of writing, books, and structures of communication. My starting point in reading Agnon is to look at representations of structures of communication in order to see what they have to tell us about the texts in which they are to be found, about ourselves as readers, and about the nature of the experiences we call "literary."

As readers and critics, we can draw upon linguistics and psychoanalysis to investigate the ways in which texts call into question concepts of identity, self, and ego as unitary fictions. This is particularly a feature of modernist texts such as Agnon's, where voice and utterance, the relationship of an "I" to a "you," become major sites of conflict and supply the dramatic material of plot. This study demonstrates the ways in which Agnon's writing posits varieties of wholeness, which it then calls into question. Agnon's writing calls our attention not only to narration as an ordering activity aimed at producing coherence, but also to self as a construction out of disparate impulses. By reminding us of the constructedness of story and character, the writing demonstrates the often tenuous nature of the coherence that such concepts allow.

We should note at the outset that use of the terms "subject" and "subjectivity" reflects the impact of linguistics and psychoanalysis on understanding the nature of the self. The concept of "self," as it is commonly used, suggests the undivided presence of consciousness to itself. This assumption of coherence can be maintained, however, only at the cost of overlooking or erasing difference [Derrida 1982, 16]. Rather than assume the self to be a coherent and integrated entity, we have come to understand that the knowledge of self supplied by consciousness is only part of the story. The term "subject" takes the place of unitary terms like "identity," "individuality," or "person," because it provides greater acknowledgement of the constructedness of the self, as well as of the role of cultural and unconscious factors in its construction of the world [Silverman 1983, 130].

The interaction of psychoanalysis and literature makes possible rich examinations of subjectivity in language. We can understand why this should be so, if we remind ourselves that it is through the acquisition of language that we gain the possibility of subjectivity. By assuming the personal pronoun "I" in relation to the "you" of another person, each of us enters the social realm of language [Benveniste

1971, 224, 227]. Discourse is the arena in which subjectivity takes shape. Nevertheless, no one of us can claim ownership of the pronoun "I." Those pronouns are "shifters": "I" and "you" change their reference with each user. The interpersonal realm of pronouns demonstrates the dependence of a sense of self on another person's corroborative participation in discourse.

Texts do not mirror the subjectivity either of author or of reader, but texts are produced and read out of processes and structures that are inherent to subjectivity. In Jacques Lacan's hypothesis of the mirror stage, for example, we find suggestive indications of "the *méconnaissances* that constitute the ego, the illusion of autonomy to which it entrusts itself" [1977, 6]. In that hypothetical moment, the infant gains a rudimentary sense of self by assuming an absolute identification with its mirror image, overlooking the mediating other in that transaction. Lacan uses the term "imaginary" for this illusory or specular identification of self with other. While the mirror stage constitutes a theoretical moment in development, it suggests also an emblematic account of the achievement of self at the very cost of alienation from self. Lacan's approach to Freud demonstrates the alienation of the subject in the very utterance that affirms his/her subjectivity.

Our experiences with language testify to the workings of the unconscious. In this respect, Lacan's attention to linguistic manifestations of unconscious processes has opened up new possibilities for our reading of texts. Using the Saussurean structure of the sign, J. Laplanche and J.-B. Pontalis [1973, 210] refer to a coalescence of signifier with signified in the imaginary. That illusory coalescence corresponds to the infant's experience of a one-to-one correspondence, or the illusion of perfect fit in the early mother-child dyad. That specular identification or mirroring is disrupted by the intrusion of a third term, the paternal, which brings about the advent to the symbolic order, a pre-existing cultural order or world of signs in which the relation of signifier to signified is arbitrary.[3]

Despite the inevitable move into the symbolic order, the residual effects of the "imaginary" inhabit our use of language and make themselves felt in forms of cultural expression. Myths of a primal language such as the Eden story posit the original unity of word and object, expressive of a magical relationship to environment [Cassirer 1944, 109–10]. These are fantasies of an original and originary presence, fictions of a lost wholeness. While we may be tempted, as readers, to identify this "recollection" of wholeness as Edenic, pre-Oedipal, prelinguistic or imaginary, we should keep in mind that these are verbal tags, retrospective efforts to retrieve in language that to which language attests our loss.[4]

The literary text may bring about experiences of language for the reader that reflect both the imaginary and the symbolic order. In particular, Agnon's writing may activate in the reader a nostalgia for the imaginary coalescence of signifier with signified, as well as a sense of their inevitable separation and dislocation in discourse. Thus, fictional texts provide a unique access to processes of subjectivity, not only in their representations of character, but in the reader's own engagement with the text. While the reader's distance from the text may supply the illusion of safety, we find on closer examination that these borderlines are indeterminate: any reading reflects both text and reader. The reader actualizes the text in a reading that is shaped by conscious and unconscious presuppositions and by cultural codes [Eco 1979].

The linguistic structures of the text betray traces of the cumulative impact of developmental struggles and long lost battles in the formation of subjectivity. These paradigmatic stages and ruptures shape our use of language, and we can try to assess their impact on our reading. Rather than view development as a smoothly continuous process, J. Laplanche and J.-B. Pontalis [1973, 427] regard the abundance of references to ruptures or "splittings" of one sort or another in psychological writings of the last century as indicative of a pervasive sense that human beings are inherently divided within themselves. Indeed, if we survey the territory that Freud and his French followers have disclosed to us, we may be struck by the succession of "splits" or decisive ruptures that begins with the trauma of birth, separation from the body of the mother, and the hypothesis of a primal repression through which the unconscious is formed.

Texts may recall stages in the formation of the subject, not sequentially, but cumulatively, so that we can try to read the register of the unconscious both in texts and in ourselves as readers. Julia Kristeva observes that theory enables us to "'situate' such processes and relations diachronically within the process of the constitution of the subject precisely because they function synchronically within the signifying process of the subject himself" [1986, 96]. These synchronic operations dominate the signifying process in texts, particularly those we call "literary." My reading attends to echoes in the writing of earlier stages in the formation of subjectivity that, contrary to popular belief and everyday functioning, have not been superseded.

The notion of "inscription," in particular, is crucial to my study, insofar as it resonates with the impact of early stages in the formation of subjectivity. "Inscription" denotes the action of writing upon something; more concretely, it indicates that which is inscribed or written into a surface. It carries the sense of a formative writing and has been used as a metaphor for the formation of the unconscious [Freud 1925; Derrida 1978]. "Inscription" suggests something of the incisive impact with which cultural processes shape and gender individuals. My study focuses on inscription in a textual field constituted by male Jewish writers, for whom it has a different significance than it would for a female reader, evoking as it does writing, incision, and a relation to the body. Turning to Agnon and Kafka, I argue that dramas of inscription in literary texts register the impact of difference in our knowledge of ourselves, disclosing as well the uncertainties of our positions in culture.

From the perspective of a female reader, I draw attention to issues in the writing that carry explicitly masculine labels. The order of culture is patriarchal; the terms we use and the positions we occupy are gendered. Nevertheless, "male" and "female" should be understood not as essences, but as mutually dependent terms in an opposition that is constitutive of culture. I would like to think that this study is sensitive to issues of gender in the domain of textuality; that territory, however, is neither exclusively masculine nor feminine, and, in some ways, challenges or resists those classifications.

In *Beyond the Pleasure Principle* [1920], Freud describes the child's game of "*Fort-da*," that is born out of the experience of loss of the mother. (The child overcomes the impact of the mother's absence by constructing a game in which he repeatedly throws away a spool and retrieves it, uttering "*fort*" and "*da*" triumphantly.) The anecdote shows language to be a form of mastery that responds to loss and attests to the absence of the object, even as it asserts its presence in words [Silverman 1983, 169]. This play of absence and presence persists into later language games, including those we call literary. Thus, for example, representations of books and writing in Agnon give access to a drama of presence and absence, attachment and loss. Not at all secondary to the ideas it conveys, writing moves into the foreground as the scene of the action. This book is an effort to render a reading of the writing.

Jacques Derrida calls for a psychoanalysis of literature that would study the "becoming literary of the literal," an approach that would respect the "originality of the literary signifier," rather than privileging "nonliterary signified meanings." This approach undoes the assumption of a fixed distance between sign and referent and directs our attention back to the writing in order to work towards a "psychoanalytic graphology" which would study the relation between writing and repression [1978, 226, 229–30]. Drawing our attention to the ways in which texts subvert their own manifest statements, deconstruction demonstrates that the position of the observer is implicated in the structure it purports to survey. There is no privileged vantage point from which one can arrive at conclusive statements about a text. This loss of privilege opens up new possibilities of reading by directing us to a study of constructions of authority either in the text or in ourselves.

As object and as concept, "book" suggests an authoritative definition of a discursive field that is orderly and bounded. If we look at the development of western literature, we find the "book" as metaphor has a rich history. E. R. Curtius [1953] traces the history of the metaphor of the Book in European culture from its first flowering in Hellenistic Greece (with some earlier appearances), through Rome, attributing to Christianity "a religion of the Holy Book" [1953, 310] and noting a rich history of metaphors of writing and of the book.

We stand to amplify that history with a study of textuality in the history of Judaism. Susan Handelman [1982] offers an important initiative in this area by considering rabbinic methods of exegesis in light of postmodern theories of language and text. In Jewish traditions of interpretation, the sacred text is regarded as both definitive and inalterable and, at the same time, unbounded, in the sense that it already contains all later interpretations within it. Furthermore, rabbinic strategies of interpretation utilize the potential for polysemy in language. Here we see the grounds for the attraction of postmodern theorists to rabbinic exegesis: rabbinic approaches to Scripture appear to anticipate and confirm the postmodern reader's sense of polysemy and indeterminacy in the text. It must be noted that rabbinic exegesis takes the play of language as a manifestation of divine plentitude, while for the postmodernist, polysemy indicates the instability of the text that is the product of multiple discourses. Nevertheless, although a comparison of these two approaches to textuality may risk overlooking significant epistemological differences, it should also be evident that comparison can amplify our readings of both modern and ancient texts.

The Talmud tells us that after the destruction of the second Temple, God was left with the four cubits or ells of the law [Berakhot 8a], a suggestion that the activity of interpretation of the law supplies the architecture of the faith. Simon Rawidowicz, Gershom Scholem, and, most recently, Susan Handelman and José Faur delineate the drama inherent in interpretation and assert its importance to understanding the nature of the text in Jewish tradition. Rawidowicz refers to rabbinic interpretation as "the second house of the Jews," and describes the breaking up and building from within that the process of interpretation involves; he argues that the very structure of the "house" (subordination to the "four ells of the Law") provides the "limitation which leads to expansion" (1974, 50, 52, 100, 102].

Gershom Scholem asserts that "tradition" is itself a revisionary process in which claims of fidelity to prior texts are made for "interpretations" of great originality. He characterizes the biblical commentator in terms of both his awe of the sacred text and the boldness of his intrusion upon it; from the interpreter's stance, the text is not monolithic in its consistency, but shows itself to be "diversified, multifold, and full of contradictions" [1971, 285, 288–90]. Recuperating strategies of interpretation and a focus on the very letters of the sacred text, Scholem examines approaches that belong as much to rabbinic interpretation as to specifically mystical movements. Scholem's work constituted a response to the rationalist enterprise of nineteenth-century German *Wissenschaft des Judentums* (as David Biale, 1979, has shown), which may also help to explain its appeal to poststructuralist thinkers. Jacques Derrida, Harold Bloom and others have used the work of Scholem as access to rabbinic and mystical approaches to interpretation and writing. These theorists incorporate elements of a loosely defined Jewish textuality into the critical enterprise of demonstrating the fierce dramas that occur in and between texts.

Thus, Scholem's work on Jewish mysticism, with its consistent focus on writing, texts, and issues of interpretation, has served as an energizing source for current theorists. They find in his discussions of language and textuality the transitional space in which to consider rabbinic attitudes to textuality together with contemporary theory. This commingling of current literary theory, on the one hand, with, on the other, rabbinic exegesis and mystical approaches to language has proved controversial, to say the least. Nevertheless, the discussion of textuality is a valuable one that should be kept from territorializing attempts on the part of contemporary theorists or from isolationist defenses on the part of rabbinic scholars. Certainly, there is little point to ignoring historical and ideological differences in order to claim the identity of rabbinic and postmodern modes of interpretation. At the same time, however, as long as we remain alert to the dangers of collapsing significant differences, we stand to gain in understanding the linguistic universes we inhabit, by extending our knowledge of the interpretive modes and traditions that have contributed to them.

My study fits into this general area by considering some of the ways in which Agnon's modernist writing draws on a history of interpretive strategies. This approach to Agnon both acknowledges the participation of his writing in traditional structures, but understands that it can never be completely identified with them. I read Agnon with a sense of his participation in a drama of language use that is deeply rooted in Jewish learning, however marginalized and ambivalent his activities in that domain may be.

I have not made the author the focus of study, because it seems to me that is not the task of the literary critic, whose effort it is to understand what constitutes the "literary." While the author is technically the subject of the enunciation as producer of the text, he or she is lost to us as direct speaker; we encounter instead a voice or play of voices in the text. Language speaks through the text in ways the author may not have imagined.[5] I have, however, studied the production of a persona of the author, a "literary" Agnon, who is the production of bits of narrative found in a variety of texts—speeches, interviews, reminiscences, not to mention in the margins of the texts that are properly designated as literary themselves. That "Agnon" is literary insofar as it is a rich "text," constructed over time, open to different readings. It is a construction on the reader's part out of material that the writer has made available over time, material that accumulates to form the larger "text" that is the life of the writer in relation to the community in which he writes.

A last point of reference for this study concerns feminism's further revision of the relationship of the subject to language through recuperation of the lost and fragmented body of the woman, the subtext so long repressed in western culture. That subtext makes itself felt in Agnon in images of relationship to the body that may subvert the ostensible metaphysics of sacred writing. That writing has been, until very recently, a male province in a tradition that developed rules and practices to the specific exclusion of women. Without arguing that Agnon was a feminist, we can examine the ways in which his writing evokes a patriarchal writing, but does not rest within theologically defined structures. It subjects that patriarchal writing to the play that is literature, play that is at least disruptive, if not subversive. My readings are attentive to the Oedipal dramas that shape Agnon's literary art, but I am equally aware of issues surrounding fusion with an archaic maternal body that may disrupt that linguistic order. Those issues of relationship to the female body reflect a level of experience prior to the positioning of the subject in culture that occurs through the Oedipus complex.

Feminist theory argues for recontextualizing knowledge in personal relations and the body. While I agree with the attempt to contextualize knowledge in the personal, it seems to me that such an effort cannot simply discredit or replace the "objective" with a new way of knowing. Rather, it must modify the seemingly objective by incorporating an acknowledgment of the perspective of the observing "I." I have attempted to find a base for discussion in the texts of Agnon that acknowledges the role of the reader in selecting and designating as noteworthy particular elements of texts. Nevertheless, the text remains the primary, though ultimately indefinable, object of study for me. It takes its place in a continuum that runs from author to reader, in a series of interactions whose boundaries cannot be definitively determined.

Criticism must explore that interactive process, thereby modifying the old sense of the text as autonomous artifact and the reader as invisible interrogator. At the same time, critics who attempt to subvert academic discourse and shake its epistemology by writing in the personal, as opposed to the presumably "objective" mode of academic discourse, may forget that any discourse produces its subject, a subject that can never be identical with the subject of the enunciation. If current theorists attempt to move beyond what they criticize as an outmoded humanism, that effort strikes me as an alteration of the focus on the human subject, rather than a repudiation of it.

Ultimately it is reading that interests me. Part of the value of literary criticism is to give access to the workings of the process by which texts are received, assimilated, and reformulated in readers' statements about them. While we may want to ignore the process of reading in order to arrive at statements of meaning, reading is the interaction in which such statements take shape. Reading reflects indeterminacies that are inherent in any communicative process, however much we may need to assume a stable identification of sender, message, and addressee.

Rabbi Nahman and "The Menorah": Toward a Model of Reading

My introduction comes to an end with a brief reference to Rabbi Nahman of Bratslav, whose "Tale of the Menorah," can be read as a depiction of the reading process. Agnon and Kafka find a common source in Rabbi Nahman of Bratslav.[6] Indeed, Rabbi Nahman figures as both a model and a source for modern Jewish writing: he draws interest both for his enigmatic tales, with their parabolic qualities, and for the fiercely experienced contradictions within his personal life, a "highly complex inner dialectic," as Arthur Green [1981, 106] describes it, that gave rise to a new definition of the *zaddiq* or righteous man in terms of "conflict and controversy."

For our purposes, Rabbi Nahman's "Tale of the Menorah" [1981, 239–40; 1983, 231–32] can be read for the ways in which it conceptualizes the variable relationships between artist, created object, and viewer. This is the story of a young man who returns home to his father after a long absence and "prides himself on his mastery of the craft of making a hanging lamp or menorah." He has his father invite to their home all the "masters of this craft," so that he, the son, can demonstrate his mastery to them. But the craftsmen are not impressed with the son's skill. The father approaches each and each admits that he has found fault with the menorah. When the father tells his son that all have found the menorah to be flawed, the son turns to his father and says: "By this I have shown my greatness. For I have shown to all of them their defects. For in this menorah are to be found the defects of each and every one of the craftsmen who are here. [. . .] What one sees as ugly, the other sees as lovely. And vice versa. And I made this menorah of mine from defects alone, in order to show to all of them that they lack perfection, and to each there is a defect: for what is lovely in the eyes of one is a flaw in the eyes of his friend. But in truth I can make a menorah properly."

The parabolic qualities of this short tale lead the reader or listener to play with applications beyond the story itself. For the contemporary reader, "The Tale of the Menorah" is particularly self-reflexive insofar as it offers a depiction and an enactment of the reading process. One could argue that the menorah, as a created work, is analogous to a text that a reader reads in its openness to the reader's construction of it. Considered as a text, the menorah is not fixed or invariable, but rather is shaped by the response of the viewer or reader. (This effect is intensified once we realize that we possess no stable text of the parable itself, which comes down to us through its transmission by the Bratslaver Hasidim.[7])

The flaw that each observer finds in the menorah mirrors the observer to himself, confusing subject and object, and suggesting an important dimension of the process of reading: the reader finds his/her reflection in the text, but with a difference that disrupts the comfort of an easy identification. The menorah or work of art disturbs the observer's comfortable self-assurance and initiates a process of self-criticism. In effect, if the reader were to follow through to complete the interactive process that the text initiates, he/she would be working towards an understanding of subjectivity on the model of self-reflection that the parable prompts. To begin the process of "restoration" is to participate in *tiqqun*, that is, to carry out human action, directed towards return, under the sign of the Father.

Two concepts of the text operate in this short tale. On the one hand, we find indications of radical indeterminacy: the menorah as text is what the viewer says it is. It reflects each viewer to himself. On the other hand, the craftsman's statements assume a notion of the text as invariable. He stands outside the reader-text interaction and comments on it from a privileged vantage point that suggests a higher perspective. His statements imply a judgment of those variable readings according to an unchanging standard that classifies them as flaws. In effect, the craftsman's words raise the ideal of a fully restored menorah (presumably a stable text) that would subsume all variant readings into it.

Whether the reader chooses to identify the craftsman as Creator, as Rabbi Nahman, or simply as the artist, the suggestion is that the role of this craftsman is to make the interaction between viewer and object possible. The menorah as text is stabilized, implicitly, through its participation in a divinely authorized structure. That theological structure nevertheless allows and even provides for individual experiences or readings. Within the larger structure of religious values, variables are termed "flaws" or "shortcomings," a designation which makes viewers or participants aware of a higher standard, while acknowledging the "difference" of each that is his or her humanness.

This is a tale that thematizes its own efforts and opens out towards the reader or listener. It works to engage the reader with the object of which the narrative speaks and to bring about an experience of the text for the reader similar to the viewer-menorah interactions that the story describes. Rabbi Nahman's narrative initiates an elaborate dance of textuality, whose participants define and illuminate each other in their interaction.[8]

While literary criticism involves the effort to articulate the interaction between reader and text, the focus remains on the text itself. Although the roots of any reading are always personal, reading sustains a vital connection with the text that we hold in common, however varied our responses to it may be. The challenge is to make public a reading, demonstrating its derivation from a configuration of texts and a particular angle of approach. I want to emphasize the non-exclusivity of the approach I take, while making a strong case for the importance of a study of writing and textuality to our understanding of Agnon.

We can only use our language, constructs that shape our thought and our relation to the world. No critic stands apart from culture. Nevertheless, while we cannot think outside of the signifying systems, conscious and unconscious, that have formed us, texts do offer a unique medium through which we can read ourselves in culture. Rather than hold up the goal or the promise of a "revolutionary" or revolutionized language, we may agree that our participation in culture is now accompanied by a degree of self-consciousness that enables us to assume the dual stance of participant-observers. The literary art of S. Y. Agnon offers to us complex dramas of textuality and consciousness, through which we may move to interrogate some of the constitutive assumptions in our knowledge of the world.

Part I

Comparative Agnon

Chapter

2

Scribal Fictions: Franz Kafka and S. Y. Agnon

The issue of the relationship of Franz Kafka to S. Y. Agnon has prompted lively critical debates.[1] Questions of influence aside, however, these two twentieth-century writers can be read usefully, one against the other, for their concern with writing and textuality. In the short fiction of Kafka and Agnon, the center of energy shifts from a represented world to problems of perception and interpretation that are shared by reader and characters. Kafka and Agnon situate representations of writing and inscription so as to allow the reader to experience and trace significant variations on a spectrum of possible relations to writing. I turn now to two stories, both originally published in 1919, that start from attention to representations of writing and dramas of inscription. As exotic as they may seem, "In the Penal Colony" and "Tale of the Scribe" are two stories of reading and writing, although, as we shall see, "reading" and "writing" are scarcely innocent processes. I begin with a story about inscription and, from there, go on to a story about a scribe.

"In the Penal Colony": the Writing Machine

Consider Kafka's Traveler in "In the Penal Colony" ("*In der Strafkolonie*").[2] As the first character we meet and the one through whom the story is focalized, the Traveler mediates the reader's introduction to the harsh landscape of the penal colony. (The translation refers to the "explorer," but the original is *der Reisende* or "traveler," rather than *der Forscher* or "explorer," a term that would carry with it more of a sense of goal-directedness.) The reader moves easily into an identification with the Traveler, who offers a comforting familiarity, in contrast to the harsh, alien setting of the penal colony. As we take note of the Traveler's concern for due process and the rights of the accused, we are all the more likely to associate ourselves with this apparent representative of enlightened western views of justice.

Our efforts to decipher the elements of the story conform roughly to the Traveler's efforts at understanding the penal colony, as he is introduced to the old Commandant's system of justice by the Officer who is its chief proponent. The central precept in the old Commandant's system—"Guilt is never to be doubted"—may strengthen the reader's identification with the Traveler; he and we can share a reaction of distaste for an apparently primitive system that is alien to both of us. Nevertheless, the Traveler's illusion of neutrality, as well as his sense of his own advancement relative to the primitive penal colony, are jarred through his reaction to the Officer, the regime of the old Commandant and, most prominently, to the machine.

The process of the story involves a shift in the Traveler's perspective from his declared distance, to an unacknowledged yet tangible sympathy for the Officer. This shift causes the Traveler ultimately to protect the Officer's right to place himself on the machine, although that sympathy is denied in his parting gesture of threat to the condemned man who wishes to accompany him. These shifts in the Traveler's position are more often recorded, rather than commented on in the narrative, so that the reader may experience an unease that reflects the dislocation of an identification that the story elicits so smoothly at the outset. In effect, the text manipulates the reader, moving him/her through a variety of subject positions in relation to the archaic that acquires representation through the machine.

In this respect, the voyage that has brought the Traveler to the penal colony, remote from his presumably European homeland, carries with it a psychological weight not unlike that attached to the map of Africa in Conrad's *Heart of Darkness*. These two great texts of modernism utilize a geography that is traceable not only on the map of European colonialism, but also on the map of psychic structure that Freud, contemporary and kin of the modernists, was charting. For Conrad, for Kafka, and, I think, for Agnon as well, the text moves in two directions at once; it retains its mimetic relationship to the social world, while offering the reader graphic suggestions of unconscious operations.

The reader traces a writing in "In the Penal Colony" that does not so much permit an analysis of character from the outside, as it draws the reader into a drama of inscription that undoes the distance between reader and text and elicits responses from more primitive strata of our mental lives. If it is ultimately the stance of the enlightened, detached observer, the Traveler, that is deconstructed and satirized through the process of the story, then the reader loses at least some of the privilege and distance that the story seemed at first to offer.

The machine, center of attraction from which the Traveler tries so hard to avert his eyes, is of course a writing machine. It produces *die Schrift*, script or writing, but also the term for Scripture [Politzer 1966, 106]. We see the Traveler attempt to focus at first on irrelevant details, apparently in order to avoid confronting the machine and the procedures that the Officer is intent on showing him. The narrative traces subtle shifts in the Traveler's relationship to the machine, from his initial efforts to ignore it through the subtle signs of his gradually awakening interest, as well as his efforts to hold onto his role as representative of scientific advance.

According to the old Commandant's regime, the condemned man is placed on the machine that conforms to the shape of his body. His sentence is inscribed in his body by the needles in the machine so that he "reads it in his body" only at the moment of dying. What can the nature of such a writing be if it "communicates" its message to its addressee only in death?

To understand better the strange fascination of this cruel writing, I suggest an analogy between inscription, as it is carried out by Kafka's machine, and inscription as a term for the dynamic process through which "self" is constituted. Freud's [1925] metaphor of the mystic writing pad sets inscription as the model for the formation of the unconscious; the unconscious is like the child's toy, the "mystic writing pad," where inscription is always already there.[3] Lacan's [1977] discussion of the formation of subjectivity refers to a series of splittings inscribed in the subject, beginning with the hypothesized repression of the signified as the origin of the unconscious. Lacan's emphasis is not so much on the repression of the signified as lost object, as it is on the consequences of that loss as reflected in the play of signifiers that characterizes language. "Inscription" expresses the impact of the successive splittings through which subjectivity takes shape.

The question for the critic is to consider how representations of writing work to recall these primal dramas of inscription. Together with the Traveler, we may see the condemned man who is to be placed on the machine as a subliterate creature. While the Officer describes the enlightenment that will come to this primitive creature, we become aware of a cruel irony: It is only in the moment of death that the condemned man will achieve "literacy" (hypothetically, at least). This "literacy," I would argue, is roughly analogous to entry into the symbolic order. In a strange reversal of the normal developmental path, the condemned man's life ends in the very moment that would make him a participant in the world of language. Despite the irony, I would argue that the reader is positioned to identify with a description that mimics certain features of development.

In the primal story that is the backdrop for Freud's masculine model of development, and to which the male universe of Kafka's penal colony appears to conform, the punishment for rebellion against the father is castration [Freud 1912–13; 1923a]. Oedipal rebellion finds its resolution in the child's acceptance of symbolic castration: by giving up the wish to take the father's place, the child gains entry to the social world whose authority the father represents. The system of the old Commandant forecloses the possibility of any such compromise, filial or scriptural, in its brutal finality. The unmediated primitiveness of the machine suggests the writing of the terrifying Oedipal father, unmodified by any form of compromise.

Whereas the castration complex, through which the Oedipus complex is resolved, allows the subject to survive at the cost of *symbolic* castration, the regime of the old Commandant finds expression in the machine whose inscription is definitive in a way that precludes individuality. This machine reinscribes castration, over and over, fusing the subject with the letter of the Law, in a punishment no "son" can survive. It is a dire language, inscrutable yet awesome in its capacities for a definitive writing.

What is the reader's relationship to all of this? If, according to the old Commandant's theory, the "punishment" that the machine inscribes is a message intended for the condemned man as addressee, then the Traveler and the reader occupy the position of secondary addressees or witnesses, who stand by, listen and watch. Our relative distance does not, however, remove us entirely from the scene of reading and we are not immune to its effects.

The position of the Officer is more ambiguous: he both represents the authority of the sender, the old Commandant, but is also subject to inscription himself. As high priest of a deified machine, to which he will eventually offer himself as sacrifice, the Officer describes for the Traveler and for us a particular relationship to writing and textuality. He lays out the old Commandant's plans for the Traveler to admire, with all the reverence accorded to sacred writing. The Traveler's responses reflect the polite disinterest of the tourist and prompt further exposition from the Officer:

> The traveler would have liked to say something appreciative, but all he could see was a labyrinth of lines crossing and recrossing each

> other, which covered the paper so thickly that it was difficult to discern the blank spaces between them. "Read it," said the officer. "I can't," said the traveler. "Yet it's clear enough," said the officer. "It's very ingenious," said the traveler evasively, "but I can't make it out (*entziffern*)." "Yes," said the officer with a laugh, putting the paper away again, "it's no calligraphy for schoolchildren. It needs to be studied closely. I'm quite sure that in the end you would understand it, too. Of course the script can't be a simple one; it's not supposed to kill a man straight off, but only after an interval of, on an average, twelve hours. . . . So there have to be lots and lots of flourishes around the actual script; the script itself runs around the body only in a narrow girdle; the rest of the body is reserved for the embellishments." [Kafka 1971, 149; 1946, 107].

The description of labyrinthine, crisscrossing lines conveys the intensity that emanates from this writing, both as it is described for us and also in the role it plays in the text. "*Kunstvoll*" and "*Schönschrift*" are the terms that Kafka uses to describe the old Commandant's handwriting, suggesting that it is truly an "artwriting," the writing of art, even the art of writing for Kafka. Heinz Politzer was the first to see in this description of writing an uncanny description of one of Kafka's own manuscript pages, which he describes as resembling "hieroglyphics of an unknown language, beautiful and terrifying at the same time" [1966, 105].

The description of the old Commandant's plans suggests a vortex of inscription. This representation of writing constitutes an emblem of the text we read. It is the writing of writing. The activity of critical reading, like the Traveler's interpretive effort, is an attempt at a deciphering that can never be completed. The Traveler may not move beyond his initial inability to decipher—*entziffern*—the artful script, but he does remain fascinated by and respectful of the machine and its powers of inscription.

Like Conrad's Marlow on the trail of Kurtz, the Traveler pursues the "horror" while maintaining a distance from it that insures his survival. Like Kurtz, the Officer goes so far that he cannot return, nor does he seem to want to. Armchair tourists that we are, we readers follow at a distance the responses of the Traveler and the Officer to the archaic machine to which the Officer serves as guide. These territorial demarcations, so vital to the Traveler and so helpful to the reader, hold, however, only insofar as we resist the process of psychic reinscription that is reading. We may not be able to read the writing on the old Commandant's documents, but we can write the reading that is our interaction with the text and glimpse in that reading traces of our own archaic script.[4]

To "write" such a "reading," we must consider several possibilities, some even mutually contradictory. In its most shocking assertion, the text admits the possibility that the Traveler is *attracted* to the idea of perfect inscription, or a definitive writing, no matter how barbaric he (or we) may find the presentation of that system. As the Officer describes it, the writing transforms body into text in what amounts to an idealized reading experience:

> But how quiet he grows at the sixth hour! Enlightenment comes to the most dull-witted. It begins around the eyes. From there it radiates. A moment that might tempt one to get under the Harrow oneself. Nothing more happens than that the man begins to understand the inscription, he purses his mouth as if he were listening. You have seen how difficult it is to decipher (*entziffern*) the script with one's eyes; but our man deciphers it with his wounds. [Kafka 1971, 150; 1946, 108].

The reading in the body that the Officer describes here stands in strong contrast to the Traveler's inability to *decipher—entziffern—* the script of the old Commandant's plans. *Entziffern* is the key term in both passages. The Traveler gazes at an impenetrable text—the scrawled writings of the old Commandant. That script—archaic writing—is alien to him; he can find no common ground with it. By virtue of his identification with the old Commandant, this same text is clear to the Officer, for whom it offers a clear reading of the guilt and sentence of any man. The Traveler can get only so close to that reading as to acquiesce in the possible validity of the Officer's reading: "Perhaps I am prepared to believe you." The conciliatory gesture in his words suggests an approach to the text that modifies his distance ever so slightly.

The Officer's description of past executions renders the climactic moment as one in which bystanders share:

> Well, and then came the sixth hour! It was impossible to grant all the requests to be allowed to watch it from nearby. The Commandant in his wisdom ordained that the children should have the privilege of always being at hand; often enough I would be squatting there with a small child in either arm. How we all absorbed the look of transfiguration on the face of the sufferer, how we bathed our cheeks in the radiance of that justice, so hard to achieve and so quick to fade! [Kafka 1971, 154; 1946, 112–113].

This access to participation, made possible by contiguity, suggests communal share in religious experience, and the attempt to achieve an experience so powerful that it dissolves distinctions between audience and celebrant.[5]

The Officer refers to a moment that is "so hard to achieve and so quick to fade" (*dieser endlich erreichten und schon vergenhende Gerechtigkeit*). The wording is characteristic of Kafka in extending and withdrawing a possibility within a single phrase. And indeed a carefully constructed narrative structure allows for the description of the moment, but simultaneously discredits it in the possibility that the Officer's description may not be reliable. The Officer is giving a retrospective account of executions from the time of the old Commandant as part of a pitch for their resumption. Therefore, his "description" may be more a wishful utterance than an "historical" account. Nevertheless, the felt impact of experience in the language works more persuasively than do doubts about the Officer's reliability. The language of the text constitutes a reality in the utterance that allows for an alarming possibility, *idealizing* the moment of inscription for subject and for audience.

It is perhaps the central paradox of the story that this account of a fatal inscription of the subject is conveyed to us as a moment of radiant fulfillment. One wonders if Kafka's text does not manage to have it both ways. Does the radiance on the face of the victim suggest participation in a fusion that is lost with access to language and the formation of subjectivity? From the perspective of the Officer, the condemned man achieves an identity with the text that is to be envied—"a moment that might tempt one to get under the harrow oneself," which is what the Officer *does* do in a final gesture of fidelity and submission to the old Commandant. This may suggest to the reader the recapture of a kind of fusion that the advent of language, not to mention reading, precludes. This moment in the text is constituted out of the conjunction of impossibilities: a return to oneness and identity with the text, but at the same time, the affirmation of the authority of the paternal in the machine, together with an obliteration of self.

The machine's very literal inscription suggests a masochistic yielding to the power of the Father, and we may be tempted to read this as the Officer's longing for the Father. Then comes the joke, however: we witness the butchery of the Officer that is the outcome of his submission to the machine and his anticipation of enlightenment. The Officer's expectation goes awry. Far from achieving identity with writing through the experience of becoming text (a process suggesting self-immolation on the altar to the Father), the Officer ends up with a spike through his head and a blank stare of noncomprehension on his face. The reader is forced into complicity with this brutal joke on the ideal textuality that the text both envisions and derides. We are made to see it both ways in the two images of body and text that the story juxtaposes: the *dead corpse* versus the *illuminated text*. From this angle, "In the Penal Colony" can be read as an elaborate dance of approach and avoidance, intrusion, entry and withdrawal, that takes place in and around the body of the text or the text as inscribed body.

It is the Traveler who survives in the ambivalence of his reading, an ambivalence that combines elements of attraction with civilized horror in reaction to the writing machine. He offers the middle ground for a range of subject positions in relation to the writing machine; these range from the virtual noncomprehension of the condemned man to the off-the-scene new Commandant whose interests are so far removed from the old order that he is only interested in "harborworks," or links to the world beyond the penal colony. In between, we have the Traveler whose high degree of cultural literacy keeps him from the kind of primitivity the story depicts, yet does not keep him from being attracted to it. Opposite to the Traveler is the Officer who attempts to mediate a return to the unmediated and on whom the contradictions of the text are most obviously carried out.

"Tale of the Scribe": Falling into the Writing

Inscription in "In the Penal Colony" can be compared with the ideal of writing in "Tale of the Scribe" (*"Agadat hasofer"*), a story that culminates in a grotesque, neoromantic fusion of Scribe, Torah scroll and wife's wedding dress.[6] While one could say that these two stories of Agnon and Kafka are *about* the function of inscription in subjectivity, each dismantles the distance implied in the relation of narration to its object, in the sense that a story is "about" something other than itself.

The central text in Agnon's story is explicitly identified as the Torah, with all the socio-historical weight that the designation carries. Unlike the indeterminate and suggestively unnamed writing (*die Schrift*) of Kafka's story, the identification of the Torah in Agnon invokes the status of that text as a divinely inspired writing. Nevertheless, the Torah in Agnon's story is less a fixed and determinate text as it is the charged field for erotic and thanatotic drives, as well as social tensions.

Ecstatic fusion with text in "Tale of a Scribe" parallels fusion or "reading" experience in "In the Penal Colony." A relationship analogous to that of Kafka's Officer and machine can be discerned in the move of Agnon's Scribe toward erotic fusion with the Torah scroll. In "Tale of the Scribe," we see enacted in relation to the Torah an array of subject positions not unlike that found in Kafka's story. They include (1) the controlled, eloquent and essentially distant piety of the narrative voice; (2) the position of members of the community who wish to purchase a share in *mitsvot* (deeds of merit) by using Raphael, the Scribe, as mediator between themselves and the Torah scrolls he inscribes; (3) the ambiguous and ambivalent combination of erotic and ascetic tendencies that marks the relationship of Raphael and his wife to one another and to the sacred texts that adorn their walls; (4) the position of the childless Miriam, for whom the Torah scroll becomes interchangeable with a child.

Raphael the Scribe completes the Sefer Torah he is inscribing, but as he concludes the writing, he falls into the mirror, Narcissus-like, completing the final letters of the scroll himself, isolating himself from the community with whom he might have shared the *mitsvah* (deed of merit). (His childless wife turns green and dies.) Erotic images of text and writer come together in a *Totentanz*, a dance of death in which the structure of realistic narrative and distinctions between subject and object collapse. In effect, one could say that it is the posture of the writer as faithful scribe that is deconstructed through the text's disclosure of the complex play of drives that enter into the writing process.

Raphael the Scribe is like Kafka's Officer in his extreme devotion to a regime of writing and a fidelity to the Father that exceed social norms. "All day he sat in his house communing with his soul in solitude, completely within the frame of Torah. He did not mingle with other human beings and was thus saved from any of the transgressions between man and man, and remained holy in his speech, thought, and deed, and was spared all temptation and distraction" [Agnon 1970, 9; 1968, 2:133].[7] The narrator situates Raphael "within the frame of Torah," a phrase that appears to affirm structure. A translation that is closer to the Hebrew phrase "*sagur umesugar betokh dalet amot shel Torah*" would be "closed up within the four cubits of Torah." This wording carries talmudic resonances that strengthen the sense of enclosure of the individual within the sacred text. (See Berakhot 8a for a sample source text.) This phrasing acquires more force as we realize that it concretizes Raphael's vocational activities of inscribing Torah scrolls.

The vocational structure in which Raphael is so securely housed appears here to be defined, quite literally, by the name of God:

> He sat secluded and isolated and no one was with him except His Name, may He be blessed, and he studied a portion of the Talmud in order to tie together the oral teachings with the written ones, and concentrated on all the sacred meanings hinted at in Scripture. He was careful never to write the Holy Name without first having purified his body. For this reason he often wrote an entire sheet of parchment but left blank the spaces for the Holy Name, and later he wrote the Name in the blank spaces only after having immersed himself again in the purifying bath. [Agnon 1970, 9–10; 1968, 2:133]

The activity of transcription that the Scribe carries out is central to the transmission of Torah. Despite the importance of that writing to tradition, however, it is still transcription, a mediated writing. The intensity that surrounds Raphael's scribal practice expresses the effort to obviate the distance and displacement that characterize any mediation. The description of ritual in this passage expresses an effacing of individuality that would transform the Scribe into a vehicle for the writing that is his labor. His is a writing to get out of writing or, put differently, a writing that moves in the direction of the definitive writing, signified here by the Holy Name.

In Agnon's art, an originary loss is often presented as the stimulus for verbal activity, as for example, in the oft-cited passage "The Secret of Writing Stories" [in "The Sense of Smell" 1968, v. 2]. That passage pictures the writer, after the destruction of the Temple. No longer able to join the priests in song, he sits at a distance writing songs of lamentation for the lost glories of the Temple. (See chapter 6 for a discussion of this passage.) In such presentations, art is predicated on loss; it can never recapture the sense of participation in the sacred that the priestly song expresses. Agnon tends to depict the very activity of the writer as the effort to regain an identity with the source (or source text) that linguistic practice, or the condition of being in language, does not permit. In "Tale of the Scribe," the zeal of the Scribe expresses the urgency of such an effort at return and hints even at the cessation of desire through restoration of a lost object: Raphael is described as "*nitsul meta'avah veḥemdah*" or "saved from desire and appetite" through his scribal activity.

The drive to return to the source or to recapture a lost fusion may make itself felt within narrative, but its success would endanger the very structure that gives it expression. Narrative is predicated on differentiations of a sort that Raphael, in effect, tries to undo. Out of this tension, Agnon's story records a series of encounters between text, mirror, and eye, as it moves towards a neoromantic denouement. The carefully constructed home of Raphael and Miriam, with its partitions between marriage bed and workspace, maintains a distinction between Eros and God's work, supporting the ascetic purity of Raphael's scribal activities.

The interactions of husband and wife disclose a structure within which desire is both stimulated and deflected. Most interesting is the role that a text and its reflection play in the complex space of their interaction. On the east wall is a hanging Miriam embroidered, with the inscription, "'The earth is the Lord's and the fullness thereof'" [cf. Ps. 24:1]. In each of the four corners of the embroidery there is a square which contains the words: "'I have set the Lord always before me'" [Agnon 1970, 12; cf. Ps. 16:8]. On the opposite wall hangs a mirror. Within this highly emblematic structure, a drama of the gaze is enacted:

> When Miriam visits the bathhouse Raphael remains in the House of Study. When she returns home she dresses in fine clothes like a bride on her wedding, and stands before the mirror. [. . .] and at that moment the thought enters her mind to make herself beautiful for her husband. But then she sees reflected in the mirror the east-wall embroidery with its scenes and those two lions with their mouths open; immediately she is startled and shrinks back: "The earth is the Lord's and the fullness thereof."
>
> And when Raphael returns home after the prayers and sees his wife in her true beauty reflected in the mirror, he is immediately attracted to her. He goes toward her to make some pleasing remark. But when he is near her, His Name, may He be blessed, flashes before him out of the mirror. Immediately he stops and recites devoutly and in holiness: "I have set the Lord always before me," and shuts his eyes before the glory and awe of the Name. Both turn away silently [Agnon 1970, 15–16; 1968, 2:133].

For Raphael and Miriam, the play of images reflected in the mirror suggests a drama of desire in the gaze of each. Miriam's reflection in the mirror gives her back an image of her own desire, but that desire is deflected as her gaze encounters not only her image but the reflection of the stern scriptural saying that appears to appropriate all desire to the Father. Eros is deflected by the scriptural text, stern paternal law supplanting the erotic relation to the Sabbath queen. Even more graphically, Raphael's erotic gaze is interrupted by the reflection of God's name and his own immediate response to it. Neither husband nor wife can complete the move to appropriate the desire that the mirrored image of the other initiates. The trajectories of desire meet and cross in the gaze, but never reach consummation.

As a result, structures of desire and procreation repeat themselves in the activities of husband and wife without coinciding. Miriam's prayers and activities parallel Raphael's devotion to the Torah scroll he is inscribing: she fashions baby clothes as he shapes a text; she prays for fertility, as he sanctifies himself for writing. Miriam identifies her own activities with the story of Reb Gadiel, "the infant who had been born by virtue of his father's having taught Torah to Jewish children" [Agnon 1970, 11; 1968, 2:134]. The comparison implies a wish for procreation through the text that elides the role of woman. Miriam plays a double role, then, as the *object* of desire, and in providing an ironic *analogue* to Raphael's scribal activities. Her presence clarifies the nature of desire by allowing for elaboration of its operations; at the same time, it obscures the question of the object of desire, in a confusion of Torah scroll, holy writing, and the body of the woman. In light of her double function in narrative structure, it is interesting to note that Miriam's role came into prominence only late in the history of revisions of "Tale of the Scribe."[8]

With an effect similar to the tension produced by Miriam's amplified role, the epigraph to the story invokes another woman, whose title supplies an ironic counterpoint to the narrative. If we pause momentarily to take note of that epigraph, we see that the dedication of the story to the author's wife, Esther, inserts at least a note of irony into this story of a scribe's (or writer's) turn away from social life into textuality. (The epigraph in the Hebrew is slightly more flowery and even more ironic in its tribute to "the mistress of my house.") The epigraph charts a space that is proximate to, but not quite part of the text proper. Like Kafka's bachelor parables, which can be traced back to his diaries where they appear to originate in a drawn-out debate over writing versus marriage, Agnon's epigraph makes a commitment to marriage that the story reveals to be an ambivalent gesture. While the epigraph provides affirmation of the social realm that includes marriage, the conclusion of "Tale of the Scribe" turns away from sociality, allowing the full emergence of instinctual rhythms that might otherwise remain bound within syntax and the structure of predication.

While the story appears to take at face value Raphael's devotion to his work, there are subtle indications that his excess is not simply to be understood as piety. One must read through what appears to be the narrator's approval of Raphael to realize that the text also makes available to us constructions that may undermine that apparent endorsement. The reflexive piety (e.g., "may He be blessed") that characterizes the narrative voice may lull the reader's tendencies to suspicious reading and strengthen the impression that we are reading a pious tale of pious deeds. Thus, for example, when the desire that Raphael and Miriam experience as their gazes meet in the mirror is disrupted by the scriptural sayings on the wall, the reader may simply accept those sayings as a pious endorsement of Raphael's asceticism, or more accurately, of his deflection of desire into scribal activities. Nevertheless, that reading is subjected to the possibility of an irony that emerges once those emblematic writings on the wall are restored to their scriptural context. If the reader gets past the seamless web of pious narrative, the text invites some intertextual comparisons that complicate a simple reading of Raphael's piety.

The drama of mirror, gaze and text that engages Raphael the Scribe appears to produce a yielding to the Father, however perverse a reading of the law of the Father that may be. Two later interactions involving mirror and gaze, however, complicate such a reading. First, in the process of writing a Torah scroll in memory of his wife after her death, Raphael reaches the point at which he must immerse himself in a ritual bath in order to purify himself before writing the Divine Name. Because the bathhouse is closed, Raphael breaks the ice in the river so that he can immerse himself; this gesture carries with it the pious fervor of the man who, as the narrator puts it, in a traditional phrasing, "stands in icy water on a snowy day" [Agnon 1970, 20; 1968, 2:141].[9] At the same time, however, breaking the ice to immerse himself in the river can be read as the moment of the narcissistic fall: Raphael goes back into the mirror, drowning into himself in a moment of icy ecstasy.

This double reading of his immersion is confirmed almost immediately. On the verge of completing the Torah scroll, Raphael leaves a few verses in outline so as to be able to permit a group of Jews the *mitsvah* of filling them in, but as he is about to go in search of a *minyan* or quorum for prayer, he pauses to look in the mirror:

> Raphael pulled aside the end of the sheet, looked into the mirror, and saw his own face, and the east-wall embroidery across the room, and the scroll he had written, with the hollow, outlined letters at its end. At that moment his soul stirred and he returned to the table, took the quill, and filled in the letters in the scroll he had written in memory of his wife's soul. When he completed the task he rolled up the scroll, raised it high dancing with great joy, and he

> leaped and danced and sang in honor of the Torah. [Agnon 1970, 21–22; 1968, 2:142].

Literally captivated by this specular unity of text and self, Raphael turns away from the *mitsvot* of social life and falls into the hollow letters of the Torah.

At the story's conclusion, the frame collapses and the narrative voice records something to which it is external and which it cannot fully explicate for the reader, who stands at an even further remove. Barriers between past and present, writer and text, dead and living, subject and object dissolve in a fusion toward which the narrative does not take a stand:

> The lamp flickers. Raphael is wrapped in his prayer shawl, a Torah scroll in his arm, and the scroll has a mantle of fine silk on which the name of Miriam the wife of Raphael the scribe is embroidered. The house becomes filled with many Torah scrolls, and many elders dancing. As they dance they neither lift their feet nor bend their knees, but move as if they had no joints. They dance without motion, revolving their bodies, and Miriam stands in the center, her face covered, dancing with her shoulders, her arms raised into the emptiness of the room. She approaches Raphael's scroll. She takes off her veil and covers her face with her hands. Suddenly her hands slide down, her face is uncovered, and her lips cling to the mantle of the Torah scroll in Raphael's arms. [Agnon 1970, 25; 1968, 2:144–45].

This hallucinatory moment actually repeats Raphael's memory of the Simhat Torah celebration when Miriam kissed the white cover of the Torah he was carrying and dropped a candle that burned his robe; this double defilement led to their eventual betrothal.[10] If the text has thus far defended itself, however unpersuasively, against that identification of text (Torah scroll) and body, those narrative defenses here give way. In effect, the conclusion collapses at the most literal level the *meḥitsah* (religiously imposed separation) that defines the home of Raphael and Miriam in its delineation of masculine and feminine space and its apparent relegation of sexuality to the sphere of marriage, subordinate to holy writing. Raphael dies into the text whose invitation, we now see, is that of the body of the woman.

Writing, too, has its Eros, as becomes fully evident. In the erotic fusion of the ending, the sexuality of the text, or more accurately perhaps, of Raphael the Scribe's relation to it, emerges fully. We witness the demonic fusion of Miriam's wedding dress, which is also her shroud, and the covering for the Torah scroll: "Suddenly a tongue of flame leaped up and illumined the room. Its light framed the face of Raphael the scribe who sank down with his scroll. His wife's wedding dress was spread out over him and over his scroll" [Agnon 1970, 25; 1968, 2:145]. That enigmatic movement of sinking with the scroll marks in effect the disappearance of Raphael and the end of the story. While Raphael's act of filling in the outlined letters of the Torah scroll appeared to express his appropriation of the text for himself, we see now his disappearance into it. But that "it" can no longer simply be identified as the scroll; the text of the Father is enshrouded in the garment of the woman, signaling the mingling of that paternal writing with an archaic matrix.[11]

The Body of the Text

Available to Agnon in his writing are the many ways in which Jewish mysticism invokes the relation to the text of Torah, which reveals itself to be fluid, literally engaging and world-enclosing. Gershom Scholem has shown how the relationship to the writing of the sacred text plays a very central role in Jewish mysticism, so that ecstatic states are achieved through immersion in a holy alphabet.[12] In effect, the ecstatic fusion with which "Tale of the Scribe" ends dissolves the structure of narrative, which rests on a sustained system of intersubjective differences.

In Kafka's story, the depiction of the comparable moment occurs in the Officer's *description* of a past execution. The moment is mediated and attenuated by the fact that it is retrospection and by the structure of differences among narrator, teller (Officer), listener (Traveler and reader). That the moment depicted is nevertheless so intense in its impact testifies to the defining impact of inscription in the formation of subjectivity.

Clayton Koelb [1989] has argued that in "In the Penal Colony," Kafka depicts a kind of reading that consists of the penetration of the reader by the text, at the risk of obliterating the reader. He contrasts this with the type of reading that allows the reader to pass through the text unharmed—in a manner like that of the Traveler, we could say. Koelb reads "In the Penal Colony" as sexualization of the first type of reading: the machine, identified through such adjectives as "erect" and "stiff," rapes the condemned man, who becomes the female "stuff" to be written on [1989, 70–73]. In fact, despite a passing reference to the sentimentality of female spectators, the penal colony is effectively a world without women; the repressed body of the woman resurfaces in the intersubjective drama of writing.

If Koelb is correct in interpreting the machine as high-tech rapist of the condemned man whose position is essentially female as the "stuff" that is written on, then we can see here an indication of the ambiguous sexualization of the writing process. Writing includes *both* the exaggeratedly masculine activity of the machine's multiple needles and the equally exaggerated masochistic posture of the feminized body that is inscribed. Both of these positions belong to writing as Kafka portrays it, and neither is to be found without the other.

In Agnon's story, the female is very much present, in a gendered dichotomy that evidently became more pronounced as Agnon put the original tale through revisions over the years. The outcome, as we have it, is a full and explicit identification of woman with the impurity of the body, but one that demonstrates the futility of the masculine effort to achieve the ideal of a writing that will exempt itself from and purify itself of that body. The erotic fusion of Raphael the Scribe with Torah and wedding dress that brings the story to its literal and figurative climax collapses the distinctions by which Raphael has attempted to sustain his scribal identity. The Scribe is consumed by the text of the Father that has become fused with the body of the woman. The gender of writing as a masculine engraving of a female body is undone in each of these stories through dramas of inscription that demonstrate the fluctuating positions of the participants, precluding any stable identification of them.

In both Kafka and Agnon, narrative traces the desire to become text, to achieve the perfect reading or writing, to be boundary-less. In their devotion to a severe paternal standard that takes the form of an authoritative writing, Officer and Scribe share an eagerness to submit to the paternal machine. They die into the text in an ecstasy (or attempted ecstasy) that constitutes the failure-to-come-to-be of the writer. To become the writer involves both the appropriation of and the submission to the discourse of the Father, a balanced tension that we may reasonably attribute to each of the unseen authors. In each of these stories, the subject disappears back into the writing of the Father, in a dissolution that carries with it a sense of return to the body of the woman.

For Agnon, writing exists in a sociocultural context that is informed and structured by Judaism. To a certain extent, the reader can assess Raphael's scribal practice against an inherited communal norm. Kafka's text has less to do with an identifiable tradition. Efforts, for example, to link the regimes of old and new Commandants with Jewish or Christian analogues are defeated by crucial inconsistencies in details.[13] (Sokel, 1973, and Robertson, 1985, argue for approaches to Kafka in terms of the contrast between eastern European Jews as the authentic primitive and western European Jews as inauthentic pretenders, a historicizing that enriches our reading without supplanting it.) One might argue that Kafka taps into a stratum of being, a level of subject-object relationship that is prior to the identification of any particular conceptual order. In fact, I would suggest that Agnon joins him there, despite the overtly Jewish content of his texts, to engage in a comparable exploration of subject-object relationship through the text.

Paradoxically, perhaps, these stories give access not only to writing as splitting, but also as its opposite: these dramas of inscription are shot through with glimpses of a lost fusion, a prelinguistic oneness with the object that is lost with access to language. Each of these stories poses an ideal of text production: inscribing a Torah scroll in "Tale of the Scribe"; reading one's punishment in one's body, in a moment of enlightenment in "In the Penal Colony." But while the texts of Agnon and Kafka express the urge to achieve that fusion, through a move into the writing, they also parody it and subject it to irony. The joke is *in* the text and *on* the text, insofar as the writing both shapes ecstatic impulses and yet displaces and distances itself from them.

That ambivalence is here the essence of the literary: moving in two contradictory directions at once, the text marks a border that is variable and indeterminate. Here we can agree with Julia Kristeva, who argues that "textual experience represents one of the most daring explorations the subject can allow himself, one that delves into his constitutive process" [1986, 117]. For both Kafka and Agnon, reading and writing involve participation in a process of inscription that is potentially definitive or destructive of the individual (all the more so in that each invokes the weight of a definitive writing, that is Scripture). The text we read demonstrates its susceptibility to fantasies of return, of presence, of an archaic writing. Indeed the text may exert a pull on the reader's susceptibility to the invitation of an enclosing inscription. And yet both text and we survive to differ. The reader sustains at least a double position, entering the text in an engagement that allows for readings of inscription such as I have traced, but maintaining at the same time a detachment that the very position of reader brings with it.

Chapter

3

Dramas of Signification: Edmond Jabès, S. Y. Agnon, Franz Kafka

I turn now to a reading of S. Y. Agnon in relation to Edmond Jabès and Franz Kafka. Each of these three writers elicits the reader's participation in structures of communication that are thrown into question, subjecting the reader to a dislocation in language. The texts we shall consider show processes of communication to be thwarted, questionable or incomplete, so that struggles to produce an utterance or to receive a message acquire dramatic intensity. Agnon, Jabès, and Kafka use language not simply to represent action in the world, but to enact or bring into play the sense of drama *in* language—the play of significations in a word or phrase, in the relation of the subject to language, in the release of voices in the text that destabilizes character and plot. While my focus is on images of texts and processes of signification, I shall also compare and contrast the uses each writer makes of Jewish themes, topics, and sources. Agnon is the pivot for my discussion that begins with Jabès, moves to Agnon's "*Pat shlemah*" ("A Whole Loaf"), and concludes with Kafka's "*Ein Hungerkünstler*" ("A Hunger Artist").

Edmond Jabès: Dialogue in the Text

In a journey that has taken him through the seven books of *Le Livre des questions* (*The Book of Questions*) and the three books of *Le Livre des ressemblances* (*The Book of Resemblances*), Jabès has arrived at a mode of literary production that is neither fiction nor autobiography, although it contains elements of each; nor is it narrative in that it does not sustain a single level of character, setting, and plot. Jabès invents rabbinic voices that engage in distorted imitations of talmudic dialogue, however remote from it they may be. These voices interact with what appear to be fragments of autobiographical personae to produce a text that is a fabric composed of black letters and white spaces, voices and silences.

Characters appear more as transient figurations in the language, "*moments charnels*" ("moments of flesh"), to use Jabès' phrase [1980a, 142] than as persons.[1] The word does not remain flesh for Jabès, however; the language of the text engages in an enticing alternation between the solidity of apparent configuration that brings the promise of meaning and dissolution into a play of signifiers. "The book reflects us, double mirror; reflects the mirror," observes Jabès [1980b, 42]; the statement mimics the form of a palimpsest and suggests that the relationship of reader, text, and writer resembles a set of mirrored reflections in which it becomes impossible to determine point of origin. The texts of Jabès open self-consciously out toward the reader and push onto us representations or distorting reflections of our own engagement with the text: "*Tu lis. Tu te lies à ce que se délie—à ce que délie dans ton lien*" [1976a, 17]. ("You read [*lis*]. You tie [*lie*] yourself to that which unravels [*délie*]—to that which unravels [*délie*] in your relation [*lien*]." Play with sound, spelling, and word roots carries out the move of the writing to draw the reader into the space of the text.

What we have in Jabès is a writer who releases the power of multiple voices in the text.[2] Unconstrained by an overriding authorial voice, the voices in the text resist the reader's efforts to establish the monologic consistency of a single narrative line:

> "You build walls, I the space between."
>
> —Reb Arim
>
> "My God, I am nothing but a word. I approach You and retreat."
>
> —Reb Zaradel
>
> "The word rocks me as a wet nurse the child of her milk."
>
> —Reb Baran
>
> [Jabès 1977, 61; 1964, 66]

If there is drama here, it comes close to the very notion of utterance. This short piece of dialogue contains images that suggest a kind of birth and nurturing of the speaker in the word. The effect is to indicate a subjectivity that derives from, but is not sustained by participation in language. The origin of language in God is both posited and negated.

Dialogue in Jabès is subjected to disruptions of form on all levels. The "rabbis" who speak in the passage just quoted—Reb Arim, Reb Zaradel, Reb Baran—are forms of wordplay themselves. Each is designated with the title "Reb," indicating their role as teachers. But their names suggest varieties of anagrammatic wordplay rather than indicating proper nouns attached to persons. The effect is to make a tapestry of the dialogue in which these rabbis are more verbal threads than characters.

Amplifying this sense of an inclusive textuality even further, the interaction of these "rabbis" incorporates into the message the physical elements of the text. White space, typography, layout on page, use of italics, parentheses, segmentation: all of these work to defeat our capacity to find one primary level of signification. Voices or scraps of texts do not come to rest on one level, but rather splinter the possibility of any narrative line to create a polytopic universe of language fragments. The message is concretized as a result; it cannot be abstracted from its physical presentation. The reader is called upon to participate more actively in production of the text, rather than simply receiving it.

Without overstating the kinship, I would simply note that Jabès fashions a dialogue whose unfolding of allusion and citation, association and interpretation models a relation to Judaism by evoking the dialogical dimension of rabbinic thought, however distorted its relation to that model may be. While recent scholars of rabbinics have been emphasizing the necessity to differentiate between rabbinic interpretation and contemporary theories of the text, their discussions have also helped to clarify and to delineate the dimensions of rabbinic textuality that have proven so attractive to current theorists.[3] Rabbinic texts are inherently dialogical: rather than the "monologic" effect of a text controlled by an overriding consciousness, an utterance responds to another utterance, proceeding by a process of citation and interactive interpretation, in which the "rabbis" are names of the utterances.[4] On the subject of midrashic interpretation, David Stern observes that: "Midrash became a kind of conversation the Rabbis invented in order to enable God to speak to them from between the lines of Scripture, in the textual fissures and discontinuities that exegesis discovers" [1988, 153]; a process that Daniel Boyarin [1988] calls "re-citing" the Torah.

Jabès is responding to this interpretive process that extends the boundaries of the text, when he tells us that "The book is but a space bounded by the word open to the words" [1987, 5]. *Du Désert au livre* identifies the interrogative stance as that of the writer, suggesting a kinship with rabbinic attitudes to the text. Jabès speaks of the "true-false rabbis of my books" [1980a, 105], designating the rabbis as "privileged interpreters of the book. For them, to find God is to find him *in* the book, through the word that hides itself behind the word, as if there had always been a book in the book" [1980a, 74].

However, we find the crucial point of difference insofar as dialogue and interactive interpretation in Jabès lack the structure, hierarchy, and authorization that characterize classical Jewish texts, where the utterances of the rabbis are understood to form part of Torah, as spoken by Moses and derived from God [Stern 1988, 139, 141, 147–48].[5] In Jabès, it is more a question of language cut loose from its moorings in a universe of text and interpretation. Splintered suggestions of that universe may remain, but without the capacity to provide a sustaining or hierarchical structure.

As Jabès uses them, the "rabbis" signal the permeability of the text. "Then being Jewish," he observes in *Aely*, "means following God on the road of whiteness and turning what seems a divine trace into a letter worn away as soon as it appears" [1983, 175; 1972, 337]. Jabès names a relationship to the text through the rabbis and in so doing appropriates their voices for his own. For Jabès, the rabbis are fictions of interpretation that speak out of the white spaces in the text, foregrounding the opening of the text that is reading. As such, they serve to provoke questions about the process of reading and the status of the text we read in relation to its predecessors, real or imagined.[6]

S. Y. Agnon: Citations and Subversions

If we turn to Agnon, there can be little question as to the relationship of the writer to an identifiable set of traditions and texts. I propose to examine the question of relationships between texts and representations of communication in a particularly famous story, "*Pat shlemah*" or "A Whole Loaf," one of the stories in "*Sefer hama'asim*" or "The Book of Deeds."[7] This particular story concerns the first person narrator's efforts to obtain a meal for himself after a Sabbath during which he has eaten nothing. As he starts out in search of a restaurant, however, he meets Dr. Yequti'el Ne'eman who asks him to mail an important packet of letters at the post office. The story's structure is built around the narrator's conflict between satisfying his hunger and fulfilling Dr. Ne'eman's request.

Any reading of "A Whole Loaf" follows in the wake of Baruch Kurzweil's identification of Dr. Yequti'el Ne'eman as a Moses figure. Dr. Ne'eman is credited with authorship or at least transmission of a famous book that initiates a process of *tiqqun*, or positive change, in the lives of its readers, a set of signals that points us toward the Torah and the question of its authorship and transmission. Kurzweil identified Dr. Ne'eman as a representation of Moses at Sinai, noting that (1) Moses is traditionally called the "faithful servant" (*ne'eman* means "faithful"); (2) Yequti'el is a name given to Moses; (3) Dr. Ne'eman's book is said to have changed people's lives for the better, a description applicable to the Torah; (4) while authorship of Ne'eman's book is disputed by some (as is the authorship of Scripture), the book is said to have been transcribed from "the Lord (. . . .)," whose four-dot name may be said to stand for the Tetragrammaton [Kurzweil 1970, 92–93].

We should note that the capital "L" in Lord is the translator's decision (perhaps under the influence of Kurzweil's persuasive reading), since Hebrew does not use capitalization. Thus, the original *adon* retains more ambiguity and could be read either as "Lord" or "lord." On the other hand, the four dots of ellipsis were originally three in an earlier version of the story. As Avraham Holtz [1971] points out, the shift from three to four in later editions suggests Agnon's growing awareness of the suggestive possibilities of his material. (Kurzweil's reading is so persuasive that it seems simply to consolidate the cues that Agnon developed in the process of writing and revising the story.)

The narrator of "A Whole Loaf" describes the ethical tradition that Dr. Ne'eman's book established: "Indeed one thing I must say, that from the day it became famous in the world the world changed a bit for the good, since a few human beings mended their ways and changed their natures and there were those who directed their limbs to carry out all that was written in the book" [Agnon 1970, 81–82; 1968, 6: 145]. Thus, this book as a spiritual guide can be seen as a sort of supreme narration of existence.

Like any written text, Agnon's story is itself a communication from author to reader. At the same time, it offers us representations of structures of communication:

author
/
———————
[sender—message—receiver]
———————
/
reader

Within the text, this model of communication is complicated by questions of authorship and authority over the "messages" that are communicated. I refer specifically to questions concerning Dr. Ne'eman's transcription of his famous book, with the authorization of the Lord (. . . .) behind him:

> Most opinions were divided about that book. There were Wise Men who said that all that was written in it had been written by Yequti'el Ne'eman from the mouth of the Lord (. . . .) and he had not added to his words and he had not taken anything at all away from his words. And there were those who said, no, that Ne'eman had written it from his own mouth and had credited his words to a Lord whom nobody had ever seen. [Agnon 1970, 81; 1968, 6:144–45]

On the horizontal axis, it begins to look something like this:

Sender	message	intermediary	message	receiver(s)
Lord(. . . .) —	book —	Dr. Ne'eman —	book —	readers

Dr. Ne'eman then repeats and extends this process of transmission of a text when he gives to the narrator, who will serve as intermediary, a packet of letters that are necessary to an addressee whom the narrator later imagines to be desperately ill.

Inasmuch as Dr. Ne'eman's book and possibly his letters initiate a process of *tiqqun*, they form part of a hierarchical and ethical structure clearly evocative of the social structure of Judaism, organized around reception and transmission of a central text. Unlike the contents of the Torah, however, the messages contained in Dr. Ne'eman's book and letters remain unavailable to us. The letters occupy a central place in the story insofar as they are pitted against the narrator's hunger and his uncompromising desire for "a whole loaf." The letters function more as opaque physical objects than as message-bearing communications; we cannot read them, as we can the Torah. Within the story as well, they are signifiers whose signifying function is blocked. Subjected to the drama of the narrator's ambivalence about his mission they end up grimy, soiled, and unread. The "muck and mire and wine" that stain the letters in the course of the story give substance to their existence as physical objects, contributing to the assault on the communicative values associated with their designation as "letters."[8]

A drama of signification occupies "A Whole Loaf" on all levels, with varying outcomes. The speaker of the story never does get to mail Dr. Ne'eman's letters, nor does he find the "whole loaf" he seeks. At the end of the story, the narrator finds himself hungry and still in possession of the soiled and grimy letters. In fact, the movement of the story can be charted via those unread and undelivered letters, whose associative link with the Torah can never be too far from the reader's mind. (Our awareness of this level of communal significance is underscored at the end of the story as the narrator imagines that the doors of the post office are shutting; the root *n-'-l* ["to lock"] forms the noun *ne'ilah*, the name of the closing prayer of the Day of Atonement when it is believed that the gates of heaven are locked and one's fate for the coming year is sealed.)

In addition to *representations* of texts, however, Agnon's text also houses citations of other texts, intertextual fragments that it appropriates or incorporates into itself. The identification of Dr. Ne'eman as Moses is a striking signal that can lead, as Avraham Holtz [1971] has shown, to a universe of citations, an "encyclopedia of references" [Eco 1979, 54]. Holtz's work reconstructs the code of allusions to traditional Jewish sources on which a full reading of Agnon's story relies; in effect, it brings intertextuality to bear on a narrative that itself concerns the transmission of texts.[9] Following is an analysis of the operations of the text that draws on Holtz's [1971] identification of sources.

The semantic space of Agnon's story is enlarged as the reader becomes aware of some possible citations in the background of the text. For example, to "dust oneself with the dust of their feet" in the talmudic tractate Avot refers to the feet of the sages and one's relation to them: "Jose. B. Jo'ezer used to say: Let thy house be a house of meeting for the sages and suffer thyself to be covered by the dust of their feet, and drink in their words with thirst" [Avot 1]. Agnon's story takes the crucial phrase, "to cover oneself with the dust of the feet of" and assimilates it in its new context to the dust of horses' hooves, a particularly compelling example of a reversal of the original passage. In the story, this occurs as the narrator overturns the carriage of Mr. Gressler (a figure of dubious morality) and they both tumble into the street: "Woe was me, Mr. Gressler kept on laughing, as though he found pleasure *in dusting himself with the dust of the horses' feet* and fluttering between life and death" [Agnon 1970, 89; 1968, 6:151; emphasis added]. "A Whole Loaf" is the focal text that takes in and undermines the citation from Avot, turning upside down the relationship to the sages that the passage in Avot prescribes.

Keeping in mind that the rabbinic sages exist in their utterances, we can say that the Talmud encourages its readers to emulate the teaching of the passage, that is, to "dust themselves with dust from the feet of the sages," by studying the text that houses those utterances. In its use of the talmudic phrase, "A Whole Loaf" shows its receptiveness and confirms its *own* relationship to the text of Avot, but it does so with a difference that subverts the citation, substituting a dusty melee among horses' hooves for the dust of the feet of the sages.

The Mr. Gressler, who so diverts the narrator, crops up within an atemporal and highly patterned presentation of the narrator's conflict. (His name, as Arnold Band observes, is of Yiddish/German origin, suggesting "crassness" [1968, 194].) The narrator opens the story saying, "I was a lone man during that period" [Agnon 1970, 79; 1968, 6:143] and repeats the phrase when he meets Mr. Gressler, recalling that he had last seen him when he was in a similar state: "I was a free man in those days and he was available to me at all times" [Agnon 1970, 88; 1968, 6:149]. His words suggest that to be a "lone" or "free" man is to find oneself in the company of Mr. Gressler. Mr. Gressler is also said to have been the indirect cause of a fire that destroyed the narrator's house, a circumstance that is described in a way that refers to a talmudic verse on the dangers that beset a house in which Torah is not heard. (See Sanhedrin 92a; Eruvin 18b.) Mr. Gressler's role in the plot is underscored, then, by the significance of his name and the recurring motif of which he forms a part. Given the identification of Dr. Yequti'el Ne'eman and the pointed suggestiveness of the Lord(. . . .), we have here a layered and encrusted text all of whose levels reinforce isotopically the central issue of authority over a text.

The process by which one text takes in and assimilates a fragment of another produces a lively dialogue in which repressed citations struggle to be heard. (Riffaterre [1987] draws a provocative analogy, when he suggests that intertextuality is the "mimesis of a repression.") The Agnon text takes in its citations and imposes unity on them by absorbing them into its narrative line: as the focal text, Agnon's story gives utterance to citations that can no longer speak for themselves. Nevertheless, the citations do not completely lose their transitivity [Jenny 1982, 45]: they resist in a struggle whose site is the text. Were the citation to disappear with less discernible trace into the focal text, we would lose this microcosmic drama of signification.[10] Modern Jewish writing can be said to constitute itself out of a cultural crisis that involves, to varying degrees, questions of relationship to predecessor texts and traditions. The richness of the Agnon text consists of its exploitation of the ambiguities of that relationship.

Now, if linearization is the process by which a citation is absorbed into a focal text, then Jabès can be said to stage a reversal of the process of linearization by introducing an artificial intertextuality—the invented dialogue of rabbis who are not rabbis—that calls attention to itself. Insofar as there is no linear narrative to incorporate into itself those voices, the energies of the text are displaced from any recognizably mimetic story onto textuality itself. In both Agnon and Jabès, albeit in very different forms, texts enact relationships to other texts, pulling the reader into those communicative circuits. The particular suggestiveness of Jewish signifiers in each writer extends and reshapes a relationship to Jewish traditions; these are varieties of modern writing that simultaneously imitate, repudiate, reflect, and transform their predecessors.

Franz Kafka and the Language of Hungering

In reading Kafka and Agnon, the reader responds to resonances of language, the articulation of a vocabulary that is open-ended. Umberto Eco notes that suggestive elements of Kafka's writing, such as "trial," "castle," "waiting," and "door," demand to be taken in more than an "immediate literal sense," and yet lead to "no confirmation in an encyclopedia, no matching paradigm . . . to provide a key to the symbolism" [1979, 53–54]. By contrast, suggestive terms and phrases in Agnon generally *do* find "confirmation in an encyclopedia," although that confirmation does not signal absolute faithfulness to the source, nor does it establish a stable referent or set of meanings.

Intertextuality enlarges and complicates the semantic space of the Agnon text, drawing in references to Jewish sources that make of tradition itself an arena for conflict. In the Kafka text, the words themselves take on a suggestiveness that does not so much lead to an intertextual dialogue, as it does to one that is *intra*-textual. In Kafka's "A Hunger Artist," "*Ein Hungerkünstler*," the verb *hungern* and its variants set up an internal code, a cluster of terms specific to the text that constitutes the language of "hungering." This story presents the Hunger Artist, who used to excite audiences with extended displays of "hungering," but who is left to "hunger," unnoticed, as audience tastes shift with time. In general, Kafka's English translations introduce a more varied vocabulary that loses the effect of the original. *Hungerkünstlern*, for example, becomes "professional fasting" and *Hungerzeit* is rendered as "during his fast".[11] I refer here to Kafka's assumption of a lexical constraint—a limitation of vocabulary that makes the words themselves the focus of energies that might otherwise retain a higher degree of reference to a world outside the text.[12]

In Kafka's story, the activity of "hungering," a putative art form, is a form of spectacle that implies some communicative value. But while the story describes nostalgia for past feats of hungering that captivated audiences, that portrayal of the relationship between artist and audience is made to turn back upon itself. Indifferent to his audience's admiration and even less interested in their comprehension, the Hunger Artist is the "sole completely satisfied spectator of his own fast" [Kafka 1971, 270] *"nur er also gleichzeitig der von seinem Hungern vollkommen befriedigte Zuschauer sein"* [1946, 129]. The joke at the end, moreover, subverts even that possibility of satisfaction: the dying Hunger Artist's admission that he simply never found the food he wanted deflates the claim of art.

Not unlike Gregor Samsa in "The Metamorphosis," Kafka's Hunger Artist wastes away and is eventually thrown out with the trash. Hillel Barzel notes the resemblance of the posture of the dying Hunger Artist to the crucified Christ and associates the 40-day limit of his fast with Moses, Elijah, and Christ [1972, 313]. As with Gregor Samsa, who submits to the apple that lodges in his back and dies out of love for his family, Kafka allows for the association of his protagonist with Christ, but demonstrates the absolute blockage of that communicative value within the story. The religious connotations suggested by Gregor's self-sacrificing death are supplied by the reader to a narrative that records his loving death, but adds no further comment to it. Suggestive details may strike the *reader's* attention, but are lost within the world of the fiction.

Considered on the axis of communication from author to reader, we can say that the deaths of Gregor Samsa and the Hunger Artist possess a signifying value for the reader. Nevertheless, that value is nowhere in evidence on the horizontal axis that is the representation of communication within the text. Only narrator, reader and possibly Gregor know that he dies out of a selfless love for others. The opacity of these signifiers within the story underscores the irony of the protagonist's failure to achieve a desired communication, however ambiguous that desire and its object may be. Even for the reader, however, they remain possible, rather than necessary, identifications and tend not to find their way into larger networks of signifiers. This split between the reader's interpretive options and the lack of options in the world of the fiction offers a pointed contrast to the situation in "A Whole Loaf": Dr. Ne'eman's letters may remain unread and undelivered, but they retain their association with the redemptive qualities of his famous book for both character and reader. Noticing the religious resonance of an image in Kafka does not exert as decisive an effect on our reading as does the identification of Dr. Yequti'el Ne'eman as Moses in Agnon's story. (Admittedly, this is a relative scale, since one could argue against the *necessity* of identifying Dr. Yequti'el Ne'eman as Moses.)

The place of the Hunger Artist is taken by the leopard, a sleek, healthy beast who simply eats, is satisfied and supplies a gratifying spectacle to an audience of which he is unaware. The leopard closes the gap between desire and demand: he is an unreflecting beast who eats well, unlike the Hunger Artist who is in no way his superior. The continuum of leopard-food-spectator offers a glimpse of a communicative network other than the one of the text we read: It suggests a sublinguistic or subliterary model in which the pieces fit together, and demand, on the level of instinct, achieves satisfaction.

In contrast to the unambiguous solidity of that configuration, the *Kunst* or art of hungering turns back upon itself to reveal internal contradictions that lie close to the heart of literary language. *Schauhungern*, literally "the display of hungering" (translated only as "professional fasting"), conveys just the sense of the impossible *display* of a *lack* that throws into question the substance of art, by suggesting that art is a compensatory activity bound to fail in its effort to supply an indefinable need. *Hungern* and *Kunst* form a compound noun—*Hungerkünstlern*—which defies its status as a word, threatening to fly apart into opposing significations of unanswerable need and valuable spectacle.

In both Kafka and Agnon, "hunger" is an overwrought or overdetermined verb that leads to the open-ended question of its object: *hunger* for what? In both, "hunger" defies the capacity of language to name the object of desire. The Hunger Artist cannot name the food he wants, while Agnon's narrator insists on having a "whole loaf" that expresses not only a yearning for wholeness [Band 1968, 190], but also opens up a universe of citations, as Holtz has shown [1971, 297–98]. Holtz supplies a sampling of intertexts that associate the loaf with such diverse and opposing significations as idolatry and preparation for the Sabbath (e.g., Sanhedrin 92a). At the same time, he shows that the phrase *pat shlemah* has no precise Sabbath referent. In this instance, the "whole loaf" in the text evokes (at least) two citations that are not only incompatible with each other, but also with the narrative function of the phrase. At the same time, suggestive resonances of a "whole loaf" express longing for a "wholeness" that consists not only of bread; in this reading of the story as a drama of signification, we might even say that the phrase suggests the restoration of presence to the word, or fullness to the utterance that modern secular writing cannot hope to attain. This allegorical suggestiveness derives from some of the open-ended ambiguities in the discourse.

Gérard Genette [1982, 54] observes that the "figure . . . is simply a sense of figure, and its existence depends completely on the awareness the reader has, or does not have, of the ambiguity of the discourse that is being offered him." Attempts at a figurative or allegorical reading of the Hunger Artist come from the reader's discomforts with the discourse and sense of its ambiguity. The story uses paradox to seduce the reader into the activity of interpretation, a seduction that the story both initiates and defies: the reader wants to complete the circle of meaning by assigning a significance beyond the narrative to the Hunger Artist, but the concluding joke in the text and on the text completes the defeat of that effort.

The Hunger Artist's admission that he would have stuffed himself like anyone else, had he only found the food he liked subverts the suggestive asceticism and aestheticism of his fasting, although these suggestive qualities cannot simply be eliminated from our reading. Our final glimpse of the narrator of "A Whole Loaf," seated among the refuse of others' meals, as he listens to a sound he identifies as the locking of the post office doors, works somewhat differently. The scene retains its associations to a religious realm, while subjecting them to a grim comedy. These texts utilize phrases that possess suggestive resonances; they permit the evocativeness of those phrases to work their effect, but also undercut their signifying capacities and subject them to irony.

Walter Sokel [1973] and Ritchie Robertson [1985] offer historicized readings of Kafka that are intriguing and even persuasive in their references to conflicts over Jewish assimilation and the impact of migrations of eastern European Jews during World War I, but they do not integrate themselves into our reading in the way that identifying Dr. Ne'eman or understanding *ne'ilah* as the locking of the heavenly gates do in Agnon. Nevertheless, while Agnon's nouns may possess theological significations, these do not impose a religious meaning either on particular elements or on the narrative as a whole. Amplifying the paradigmatic axis, they add in a stratum of significance that complicates the text and enriches the play of reading.

The dialogue of voices in Jabès offers an imitation of intertextuality that forges a relationship with a tradition of interpretation and writing. For Jabès, exile is a pronounced feature of that relationship of text to tradition. Any question of relationship to sacred language or text is mediated through the languages of modern Europe, as he notes in referring to writing "between two translated worlds" [1977, 126; 1964, 132]. In Kafka, suggestive images of source and language bear few discernible traces that would support an affiliation to Jewish texts or traditions; when they seem to, they refer almost as much to Christian as to Jewish significances. Kafka brings into play terms whose suggestiveness is stimulated and then blocked, terms that resist attachment to any one signifying network. In each of these three writers, however, the process of signification becomes the focus, defying limitation to a single level of action. As a communication that the reader receives, the text defies reduction to any simple message and causes the reader to join in its uncertainties of knowing.

Paradoxically, each text suggests as well the elusive possibility of unity and self-presence, as if it is a strategy of the text to displace its manifest content so as to direct the reader toward some prior and lost language.[13] Agnon's writing is most obvious in producing this effect, by way of the text's invocation, however incomplete or contradictory, of traditional sources, but it can be felt as well in the invitations to a theological allegory that the writings of Kafka and Jabès both extend and withdraw. In each of these writers, one traces disharmony in structures of communication that nevertheless still bear traces of the "daydream" of a language that speaks itself and is not alienated in the utterance.[14] The dream of a primal language is a dream of origins, primal in that it is the imagining of language prior to separation, prior to a gap. (This "notion of an original and unqualified wholeness is a cultural dream," observes Silverman [1983, 154].) The reader responds to the experience of language, to the culturally specific terms, that the text makes available.

In the interaction that is reading, Roland Barthes designates the reader as the "space on which all the quotations that make up a writing are inscribed" [1977, 148]. The reader's role is both passive and active, submissive to the text's manipulations and assertive, in return, of particular approaches and interpretive demands. Nevertheless, while the reader's need for coherence may lead him/her to complete what the text makes available, that activity can produce a coherence that is illusory in that it ignores the resistances that are also part of the text's fabric. Just as the capacity to speak of oneself demonstrates not only the formation of subjectivity but the alienation of the subject in the utterance, so, too, the text in representing itself can never complete or come to rest in that representation. A language that speaks of itself, a writing that represents writing has already distanced itself from itself.

Part II

Of Writing and the Writer

Chapter

4

Autochthon of the Book

S. Y. Agnon and Edmond Jabès: The Writer in the Writing

Autochthon: sprung from the land itself. Autochthon of the Book: a product of the text. Edmond Jabès and S. Y. Agnon, "autochthons of the Book" in Jacques Derrida's phrase, take their identity as writers from the rootedness of the Jews, displaced people, in the Book. Derrida [1978] uses the phrase in an essay on Jabès to suggest a likeness of writer and Jew in the condition of exile. Each is the product of a writing; it is the "ground" from which each springs, but that "ground" itself resists stable definition. I adapt Derrida's phrase to study the production of an autobiographical myth in Agnon's writing. My interest is in the fashioning of the persona that is "Agnon," a story told in the writing. I begin with a brief comparison of Agnon and Jabès in order to examine the varieties of "autochthony," or relations of the writer to writing, that can be found in each. This preface introduces the more extended examination of Agnon's autobiographical myth that follows.

In his writing, Jabès refers to a Jewishness acquired through the experience of exile in 1956, although clearly it was there for him in the distinguished history of his family in the Cairo Jewish community. While his writing practices a kind of recovery of relationship to a Jewish hermeneutic, the contradictions inherent in that relationship become for him enmeshed with those of the act of writing itself. By contrast, Agnon's formative immersion in Jewish texts shapes the writer's sensibility to produce a particular kind of exploitation of Jewish sources, an ongoing process in which the Agnon text both makes a place for itself in a tradition of sacred writing and commentary and at the same time enacts its own exclusion from that tradition.

Tradition is a continuity of texts in the lives of the people, sustained by the activities of study and interpretation. The Hebrew word *masoret*, commonly translated as "tradition," means literally transmission; it carries a specific reference to the handing on of traditional materials from generation to generation. (In a similar etymology, "tradition" derives from the Latin *tradere*, "to deliver.") In postexilic Judaism, the structure of the Temple, the Biblical center of faith, is internalized in the consciousness of the people in the practice of ritual and prayer through which the nation sustains its definition of itself. (Geoffrey Hartman refers to the "memory-temple" that the rabbis preserved through ritual and ceremony [1985, 205].) Jabès uses the theme of the destruction and rebuilding of the Temple as a source of metaphor and as a context for exploring the dynamics of writing.[1] The Temple occupies a more central place in Agnon's writing. More obviously identified with the central structure of Judaism, it both houses and expels the figure of the writer whose writing does not necessarily fall within its compass.[2]

Paradoxically, modernist fictions challenge their own generic classification in order to bring about a renewal of form. The relationship to genre is complicated in Agnon by his ambivalent relationship to European culture: renewal cannot be simply thought of in terms of the novel, but must be understood as much in terms of relation to the sacred texts that constitute a model from which secular fiction is excluded. Agnon's fictions encompass a critique of the very forms they use, suggesting an effort at renewal from within, although the outcome of the process is never certain. To take one example, the narrator/protagonist of the quasi-autobiographical novel *Oreaḥ natah lalun* (*A Guest for the Night*) looks at the ruined buildings of his eastern European hometown and observes, "Even now they make books they call novels, just as they still call our town a town" [Agnon 1968a, 46–47; 1968, 4:45]; his statement implies a degradation of the novel form that is bound up with the situation of European Jewry between the two world wars.[3]

Jabès and Agnon share this explicit mistrust of fictional forms that assert their own sufficiency. Thus, in Jabès' *Yaël* we read: "The day that I write a novel, I will have left the book, I will have lost it" [1967, 51; 1983, 36].[4] Jabès opposes "novel" and "book" in a polemical polarization that makes of "novel" a convention-bound entity, while opening "book" up to the process of writing. This mistrust of genre produces an extreme disintegration of form in the writing of Jabès.

By valorizing process and undoing genre, the writing moves away from the kind of mastery over the text that is contained in the very concept of authorship. For Jabès, the dialogue in the text includes both writer and reader and constructs their kinship in a verbal continuum where each figures as a *rassembleur des mots*, one who "gathers together" or "assembles words" [1976a, 89].[5] In Jabès' use of the phrase, there are suggestions of resonances similar to those that attach to the terms Agnon uses to designate the writer, as for example, in the short story "*Ḥush hareaḥ*" ("The Sense of Smell") where the first person speaker refers to himself as the *meḥaber*, the one who composes or pulls together words [Agnon, 1968, 2:296–302]. (This noun can designate both the scribe who insures transmission of holy writings and one who composes original creations.)

Both Jabès and Agnon use first person representations of authorial voice that demonstrate the diminished authority of that voice over the linguistic field of the text. The text constructs the author in order to repudiate narration and enact the disappearance of the author into the writing, staging a return to *le livre* as the Book and *écriture* in the sense both of Scripture and of writing.[6] The term *écriture* signals a move away from a conception of writing as a set of static signs subordinate to a stable, abiding meaning; *écriture* conveys the sense of writing as decentered process, characterized by the deferral of meaning and play of differences [Derrida 1982].

Sefer, sofer vesippur of Agnon and *Du Désert au livre* of Jabès address the question of the text in Judaism and yield a conception of the writer in relation to writing. Jabès' book is itself a dialogue (arranged by Marcel Cohen), consisting of a series of reflections on the Book, that foregrounds the writer and writing. *Du Désert au livre* (*From Desert to Book*) associates the writer's forced departure from Egypt with the exodus of the Jews and exile in the desert. The desert, as the "privileged site" of the writer's "depersonalization," forms him as a writer [Jabès 1980a, 32]. Displacement and exile are the conditions for a writing born out of a void of shifting sands.[7] The writing of Jabès is concerned with an opening of the book, a rupture that occurs through exile and makes utterance possible.

Agnon's *Sefer, sofer vesippur* presents itself as a collection of texts and citations that bear on the nature of the text in Judaism. The title *Sefer, sofer vesippur* (*Book, Writer and Story*), uses the same root (*s-f-r*) for each term. The book or *sefer* of the title is the Book from which all others derive and indeed the text in question collects passages from scriptural, rabbinical, mystical sources that bear on questions of textuality. The first entry, for example, opens into a web of exegetical relationships that exceeds the range of any one utterance. Agnon cites Rabbi Eliazar the son of Rabbi Yossi the Galilean who offers the view that "974 generations before the world was created, the Torah had been written and was resting in the bosom of the Holy

One blessed be He and reciting song with the ministering angels" [Agnon 1978, 17]. Agnon's citation indicates that this picture of a personified Torah is Rabbi Eliazar's expansion ("as it is said") of Prov. 8:30: "Then I was beside him, . . . and I was daily his delight." In this midrashic excursus, not only is the text of Torah given priority over Creation, but that text takes shape and voice as a child at the bosom of the Creator. The image of the sacred text personified and capable of utterance is an apt one, insofar as *Sefer, sofer vesippur* is an intertext that attempts to give voice to its sources.

Agnon's famous library of works from Jewish tradition speaks in the text, claiming its primacy in a world created out of Torah; this collection absorbs into itself questions of writing by citing the sages as to orthography, transmission, even printing of sacred texts. As a collection of passages from a variety of sources, *Sefer, sofer vesippur* gives voice to the rabbis; they in turn give voice to their predecessors by carrying out the activity of citation, grafting onto earlier texts their elaborations and emendations. At the same time, the book itself elegantly suppresses or erases its own author, limiting his role to that of compiler, although as "compiler," his role is perhaps less equivocal that it is otherwise.

The term *sofer* or "writer," from the same root as *sefer* or "book," has a multiple reference. In its modern use, it names the author; in ritual terms, it refers to the scribe who actually writes out the Torah scroll, *tefillin* (phylactories) or *mezuzot* (ritual parchments affixed to doorposts); its traditional usage refers to one who is charged with transmission of traditional teachings. The noun thus suggests a number of communal functions or positions that are defined by their relation to sacred language. In Agnon's writing, this array of positions can be seen in works that range from collections such as *Sefer, sofer vesippur* to a collection or *sefer* of a very different sort, the surrealistic *Sefer hama'asim* ("The Book of Deeds").

The texts of Agnon and Jabès thematize writing in a self-conscious intertextuality that is as much the product of the text, and so its fiction, as it is a facet of its production. Traditional belief in the infinite interpretability of Torah forms part of the impetus for this conception of writing and reading.[8] In *Sefer, sofer vesippur*, Agnon cites the variant of a nineteenth-century rabbi on the old conception that 600,000 souls of Israel received the Torah at Sinai: "600,000 letters in the Torah, for the 600,000 of Israel, who stood at Mt. Sinai, that each one of them was worthy to have a letter written in his name in the Torah" [Agnon 1978, 121]. Six hundred thousand readers are signed into the Torah, a nation of readers defined in the difference of their readings, housed in a text to which no *one* has the key. The texts of Agnon and Jabès make their way into this company, raising questions, however, in the very moment of their entry as to the validity of their membership. "Interpretation is our lot in an indecipherable world," observes Jabès [1983, 116; 1967, 84], consigning reader and writer alike to the impossible task of breaching the threshold—"*franchir le seuil*" [1980a, 30]—of a text one has never left and yet to which one may never gain entry.[9]

Figures of Autobiography

Amid questions of authority and interpretation, in a field of intertextual relations, the figure of the writer takes shape. What follows are some thoughts toward a reading of Agnon's life as literature; examining the public life and persona of the writer yields a construction whose symmetries and juxtapositions generate meaning. One can look for what Jean Starobinski [1980] has called "the contour of a life," a fundamental notion of style that reflects the writer, whether he/she is engaged in storytelling that is ostensibly fictional or autobiographical. For Agnon, the story is that of the writer as Jew, at the margins of community, potentially redeemer or betrayer.

"Agnon" is a fiction constituted by the writing.[10] The historical author (producer of the discourse), who exists apart from the text, disappears; we find ourselves constructing his image, piecing together his story out of the fragments, autobiographical shards, that we gather both in and around the texts. The subject of the utterance—the one of whom the writing tells us—is "Agnon." This is the story of Agnon, who was born on tisha b'Av, made *aliyah* on L'ag B'Omer and came to Palestine a second time in the week of the Torah portion "*Lekh lekha*" [Gen. 12:1–17:27]. Through the accretion of details that possess significance in the history and rituals of the nation, the life of the writer is joined to the life-history of the larger community of Israel.

Paul de Man questions the referentiality of autobiography and argues against assuming an absolute correlation between the life and the work. He suggests that rather than assume that the life determines the autobiography, in the sense that art follows life, we consider the possibility that "the autobiographical project may itself produce and determine the life and that whatever the writer *does* is in fact governed by the technical demands of self-portraiture and thus determined, in all its aspects, by the resources of his medium." Lifelikeness is not so much a matter of correspondence to a referent as it is an "illusion of reference," a fiction which, in turn, "acquires a degree of referential productivity" [de Man, 1984, 69]. Through the figure, then, the life takes shape.

Long before de Man, Montaigne suggested the formative impact of the practice of self-portraiture. In his essay, "Of Giving the Lie," Montaigne observes: "And if no one reads me, have I wasted my time, entertaining myself for so many idle hours with such useful and agreeable thoughts? In modeling this figure upon myself, I have had to fashion and compose myself so often to bring myself out, that the model itself has to some extent grown firm and taken shape. Painting myself for others, I have painted my inward self with colors clearer than my original ones" [Montaigne 1965, 504]. Montaigne develops the essay literally as an *essai*, a bold, yet provisional attempt at a writing that establishes its own particular space for an extended reflection; out of this reflectiveness a new conception of self takes shape.

The project of representing the self belongs to modernity and with it come increasingly dramatic manifestations of a split between those two discursive positions, subject of the enunciation and the subject of the utterance. In reading Montaigne, we are more involved in Renaissance self-fashioning than we are aware of split between the "I" who speaks (the subject of the enunciation) and the "me" who is spoken of (the subject of the utterance). Consciousness of that split comes with the explorations of subjectivity in our century through the disciplines of linguistics and psychoanalysis.

The onset of modernization for the Jews of Europe telescoped the process of the European Enlightenment into a much shorter period of time. One finds the register of some of the conflicts attendant on modernity in the Hebrew writers of the turn of this century whose autobiographical writings demonstrate a fragmentation on the level of theme and of discourse.[11]

While Agnon left us no formal autobiography, we do have evidence of a remarkable process, carried out over most of a lifetime, that amounts to construction of an autobiographical myth—the public name and history of the writer.[12] We can trace the emergence of this figure over time in the accretion of details and correspondences involving dates and events that link writer and writing to Torah, nation, and history. In effect, we can observe the process of figuration, to use de Man's term, that determines the life by producing the illusion of referentiality. While de Man titles his essay "Autobiography as De-Facement," we can adapt this approach to our purposes by referring to the process of *re*-facement, that is to say, the production over time of the public "face" of the writer.[13] In this process, the emphasis falls less on verifiable dates than on structures in language that are linked to larger systems of meaning.

Most striking in this process is Agnon's selection of the 9th of Av as birthday. The 9th of Av is a date with multiple resonances in the history and eschatology of the Jewish people. It is the date of the destruction of the first and second temples; in the memory and the imagination of the people, its significance is reiterated as the date of catastrophes through Jewish history, through the expulsion from Spain. (In the calendar of Jewish ritual, the date is marked by fasting and the reading of *Eikhah* or Lamentations and *Qinot* or special dirges.) There is also, however, the belief that the Messiah would be born on the 9th of Av. Thus, the date signifies not only national catastrophe, but also the hope of redemption. Agnon's designation of *tisha b'Av* as birthdate encodes this layered set of significances, associating the particular life of the writer with a larger historical mythos. Carrying with it suggestions of both destruction and salvation, the date holds an essential tension that contributes to definition of the figure of the writer.

Similarly, Agnon held on to some markers of his early life, referring throughout his career, for example, to several very early poems, one written in response to his father's absence, and a second, "*Gibor qatan*" or "A Little Hero," picturing the boy-savior of his people in rhymes on the occasion of Lag B'Omer. Lag B'Omer is another significant date in the biography of the writer.[14] The occasion and subject of the child's poem is also, according to the writer, the date on which he made *'aliyah* ("went up" to Israel). Thus, in an autobiographical letter, Agnon writes, with Biblical cadence: "On Lag B'Omer [in the year] *t-r-s-t* I attained to ascend to the land of Israel and walked about in the land of life for six years as is the law for a Hebrew slave and in the seventh I descended outside of the land" [Agnon 1976, 9]. The marking of the 9th of Av and Lag B'Omer and the accumulation of details around these dates weaves the story of the writer into the fabric of the larger community. This narrative activity, sustained over time, suggests something like a family romance, in which the young writer's kinship ties are displaced onto the nation.

At the same time, the reader discerns a writerly excess in some of Agnon's citations of dates; we come upon hints of playful amusement at the very symmetries the writing so artfully establishes. It is interesting to note, for example, that Agnon names not only *tisha b'Av*, but 8/8/88 as his birthdate: "I was born in the city Buczacz in eastern Galicia to my father the rabbi Shalom Mordecai Czaczkes haLevi, of blessed memory, on the 9th of Av *t-r-m-h* signifying 'Zion *t-r-h-m'* [Zion will be merciful], and in the numbering of the nations 8.8.88 signifying 8 times 4. Thus, it is written in the passport and I don't know if the foreign date is correct or if it is a sign in the world" [Agnon 1976, 9]. The religious and secular dates that Agnon cites did not coincide that year, as scholars have pointed out. Citing both the 9th of Av and 8.8.88 produces an overload of detail, all the more so since Agnon preserved evidence that undermines the accuracy of the dating.

An address that he gave on Lag B'Omer (collected in *Me'atsmi le'atsmi*) offers engaging evidence of the narrative fertility that produces this sort of autobiographical excess:

> I will recall here some events that happened to me on Lag B'Omer, from among those that have both capital and interest.
>
> Many poems and many stories and plays and new insights into Torah and family trees and a number of other things I wrote in my youth, but my first poem, that was first of the things I published in the holy tongue in periodicals and books, on Lag B'Omer I wrote it. My first *'aliyah* to the Land of Israel occurred on Lag B'Omer. I came under the bridal canopy with my wife, may she live, on Lag B'Omer.
>
> I finished my book *In the Heart of the Seas* on Lag B'Omer. The beginning of the writing of my book *Days of Awe* took place on Lag B'Omer. Even some other external boons happened my way on Lag B'Omer. *And the Crooked was Made Straight* in its Swedish translation reached me on Lag B'Omer. Word that I was awarded a doctorate by the wise men of America reached me on Lag B'Omer. And if I may add here the miracle that happened to me more than fifty years ago at the Lag B'Omer festivities in Meron [near Safed, at the grave] of Rabbi Shim'on bar Yohai: a balcony fell and 27 Israelites were killed and I, who had stood a short time before among all the holy ones, remained alive. Lo, in truth, the merit of the day came my way. [Agnon 1976, 68].

The accretion of details here weaves personal, familial, and literary milestones in the life of the writer together with the date of Lag B'Omer. In the playfully climactic anecdote of this sequence, the writer links his own "salvation" to the celebration held at the gravesite of Rabbi Shimon bar Yohai, the presumed author of the *Zohar*, who is said to have imparted secret knowledge to his followers at the time of his death on Lag B'Omer. Agnon's use of Lag B'Omer reflects not only a diversity of personal significances, but intertwines these with the historical and legendary dimensions of the date; the result is a blurring of the lines between personal and communal, an effect that persists even when it is carried to an excess that amounts to self-parody. (See also Cnaani 1971, 27–28, 60.)

The authenticity of some of the more striking details in Agnon's autobiographical myth, the 9th of Av and Lag B'Omer among them, has been subject to a fair amount of scholarly scrutiny [Bakon 1968]. But what does "accuracy" really mean here? Rafael Veiser points out that while Agnon did construct a mythos of his life, he also held on to documents, the earliest dating from 1908, which have enabled investigators to clarify actual dates and to document discrepancies [Veiser 1980; in Barshai 1988, 102–03]. Agnon's practice holds onto a double meaning and allows for both systems of dating, the "historical" and the "mythical." Why do both? Agnon seems to offer access to the making of the life, as well as to the life that is made. He allows for the myth of the writer, while making visible its construction.

Edmund Wilson characterizes the literary man of modernity as one who is "at once a moralist and an artist, whose genius becomes purer and deeper in ratio to his isolation and outlawry" [1947, 289]; Wilson examines the inextricable linkage of genius and disease, each feeding on the other, in an image of the modern artist. In a study of modern German writing, Erich Heller [1975, 170] describes the dilemma of the artist who lacks the certainty of any abiding order of things and so feels called upon to exercise his creative powers to an extreme, for "the 'real order' has to be 'created' where there is no intuitive conviction that it exists," a Faustian dilemma with catastrophic implications. In contrast to these models, Agnon may be said to offer a special case of the modern writer: he has access to an existing structure and set of values, but creates for himself a very special relation to it. An account of this modern writer must include not only an awareness of the form that the life takes on, but also of the tension with dissolution inherent in that construction.

More recently, Harold Bloom's [1973] model of poetic creation offers a view of the struggle of poet-sons with their paternal precursors in terms of Oedipal conflict. Bloom's model has been criticized for its absorption of writer and poet into an imprecise psychoanalytic schema that merges person with poetic process [Lejeune 1982], a confusion that may reflect a post-romantic fusion of the artist with his work. It was the obsession with the subjectivity of the artist in the romantic era that led M. H. Abrams [1953, 3–29] to depict the poetics of the period in a model that places the artist's expressiveness at the center of the universe of art. Boris Tomashevsky [1971, 47–55] shows how this emphasis on the personal experience of the artist created and fed a demand for biographical material, a demand that produced, in turn, a stereotypical portrait of the artist. The result of this process is the production of a biographical myth that subsumes the data of the life to fit its lineaments.

Agnon is adept at promoting this fusion of writer and writing, this merger of persona with text. Although his portrait does not simply conform to a romantic model, it does invoke and subject to irony some of the characteristic features of the artist as redeemer. Gershon Shaked [1973, 16–19, 25, 28–29, 36, 41; 1989, 46–50] analyzes Agnon's early writings and finds the credo of an artist who wants to redeem the flawed content of reality through the form his art would give it. He traces Agnon's development so that we can see how the mature writer maintains this form-giving impulse but cultivates an ironic detachment toward it; he produces works that are modern rather than romantic, that draw upon the tension between form and content rather than attempting directly to resolve it.

Collected in *Me'atsmi Le'atsmi* (*From Myself to Myself*), we find Agnon's remark on the term *sofer* or "writer" in the modern literary sense: "Even a new word was created and that was the word *sifrut* [literature]. From then on the poet was not the rabbi [teacher] poet or the wise versifier but Mr. So-and-So the *sofer* [writer]." Having established this context, Agnon goes on to admit that "Even I was slated to be a writer." Even to the modern writer some words of the holy tongue are granted, he tells us, and he has done his best not to waste them: "One thing I can say before you . . . and even before the court on High, how much I have tried to protect the divine heritage that it not be lost" [1976, 73–75]. This public statement is characteristic of the writer insofar as it both elevates the mission of the writer as protector of a precious linguistic heritage, and denigrates the capacity of modern writing to carry out that high task. Both moves are essential to the paradox that is "Agnon," a paradox that makes itself felt in Agnon's literary productions and "around" them in the ongoing text of the writer and writing in relation to the community.

Becoming "Agnon"

Consider "'Agunot,'' the first story published under the name Agnon, a name of the writer's own choosing. While "'Agunot" is not the first story that Agnon wrote, it does occupy a special place, not only on literary grounds, but for its significance in the construction of the writer's public identity. Agnon's derivation of his own name from the title of "'Agunot" makes us aware, from a historical perspective, of a space adjacent to the literary text where aspects of the artist's life are drawn into the fictionalizing process and take on a literary cast.

Agnon published "'Agunot" in 1908, when he was twenty years old, but he returned to and revised it in 1921. Subject to revisions over time, "'Agunot" figures as a formative text for the writer during a central period in his development. By deriving his writerly name from the title of his first work, Agnon announces, in effect, the birth of the writer through the text whose author he is. "'Agunot" offers evidence of the "slow gestation of the poet by the poem whose father he is," Derrida's phrase in an essay on Jabès [Derrida 1978, 65].

The very famous opening passage of the story is itself a comment on the question of sacred language and its users. The opening of "'Agunot":

> It is said: A thread of grace is spun and drawn out of the deeds of Israel, and the Holy One, blessed be He, Himself, in His glory, sits and weaves—strand on strand—a prayer shawl all grace and all mercy, for the Congregation of Israel to deck herself in. Radiant in the light of her beauty she glows, even in these, the lands of her exile, as she did in her youth in her Father's house, in the Temple of her Sovereign and the city of sovereignty, Jerusalem. And when He, of ineffable Name, sees her, that she has neither been sullied nor stained even here, in the realm of her oppressors, He—as it were—leans toward her and says, "Behold thou art fair, my beloved, behold thou are fair." And this is the secret of the power and the glory and the exaltation and the tenderness in love which fills the heart of every man in Israel. But there are times—alas!—when some hindrance creeps up, and snaps a thread in the loom. Then the prayer shawl is damaged: evil spirits hover about it, enter into it, and tear it to shreds. At once a sense of shame assails all Israel, and they know they are naked. Their days of rest are wrested from them, their feasts are fasts, their lot is dust instead of luster. At that hour the Congregation of Israel strays abroad in her anguish, crying, "Strike me, wound me, take away my veils from me!" Her beloved has slipped away, and she, seeking him, cries, "If ye find my beloved, what shall ye tell him? That I am afflicted with love." And this affliction of love leads to darkest melancholy, which persists—Mercy shield us!—until, from the heavens above, He breathes down upon us strength of spirit, to repent, and to muster deeds that are

> pride to their doers and again draw forth that thread of grace and love before the Lord. [Agnon 1970, 30–31; 1968, 2:405].

The opening phrase, "It is said in the writings . . ." mimics the invocation of sacred writings that would initiate further exegesis and elaboration of those traditional texts. Agnon's midrashic passage pictures the deeds of Israel as a thread that God weaves into a beautiful prayer shawl in which Israel then wraps itself. When the thread breaks the shawl is flawed, evil winds blow through it and the people of Israel realize they are naked.

Agnon's text makes its way into an exegetical community, drawing on the language of the "Song of Songs" in order to figure the relation of God to Israel in terms of both the collective and the individual. Consider the intertextual fabric here: Agnon alludes to the self-consciousness of Adam and Eve once they realize they are naked; he incorporates into the opening of "'Agunot" a midrash on the "Song of Songs." [See Song of Songs Rabbah I.15, I.16.] Shaked [1983, v. 2: 165–66; 1989, 31–34] has compiled an array of contributing texts that are linked, associatively at least, to Agnon's passage. He has annotated talmudic and mystical sources for the motifs of *beged* or the "garment" as symbol of the soul, and the *ḥut shel ḥesed* or "thread of mercy"; he comments as well on the mystical themes of *'aginut* (state of desertion) and *tiqqun* (spiritual repair) with which the story opens. Thus, Agnon's opening is itself a dense imaginative fabric that extends and transforms its sources.

The passage alludes to the self-consciousness of Adam and Eve once they realize they are naked [Gen. 3:7] and continues the allusion with an untranslatable play on words based on spelling: their "splendor" [*f-'-r*] turns to "dust" [*a-f-r],* the sort of anagrammatic rearrangement of the letters in a word that is a strategy in midrashic hermeneutics [Lieberman 1950, 74]. It is only with a wind from on high, the passage continues, that Israel returns to good deeds that restore the thread and repair the shawl. The question of agency or responsibility for the weaving is left unresolved: God may weave the shawl, but the deeds of Israel determine the strength of the fabric that is produced.

In speaking of deeds that mar the wholeness of the shawl and of deeds that reconstitute it, the opening passage of " 'Agunot" sets up a frame within which human action can be evaluated. This suggestive approach moves the reader's attention in a number of different directions. First, in a quite conventional sense, the opening passage frames the story of thwarted love and artistry that follows. At the same time, however, the text of "'Agunot" is itself also a strand in the fabric that it describes and so implies questions about its own status. The text invokes a frame of reference larger than itself within which deeds are either restorative or harmful to the prayer shawl, the fabric that binds God to Israel.

The opening passage of "'Agunot" may serve as a frame for the story that follows, but it is a frame that blurs the outlines of the text, suggesting playfully that it is impossible to tell where one begins and other leaves off, which is host and which is guest.[15] As the inaugural text in the oeuvre of the writer, "'Agunot" can be read retrospectively for the reflexivity of its images and the self-questioning movement that it initiates. Insofar as the title also supplies a source for the author's name, this approach can be extended to a reading of the writer's lifelong transformation of his life into fiction. Shaked observes that Agnon does not simply imitate Midrash, but uses it for his own often revisionary purposes, in a relationship to source texts that may be parodic or even grotesque [Shaked 1983, v. 2: 166; 1989, 24–28]; he suggests that "'Agunot" can be read as "a form of midrash on the new name of the author" [Shaked, 1986, 287]. As both title and signature, "'Agunot" names the artist, titles the work, inaugurates the oeuvre that is to follow.

In the realm of Jewish law to which the concept of the *'agunah* belongs, the term designates a woman who is not free to marry because her husband has disappeared or left without divorcing her. The *'agunah* is thus the figure of indeterminacy, connected and yet unconnected. It is a fertile figure for the young writer: on the one hand, the youthful artist gives birth to himself, usurping the paternity of his father; at the same time, however, the name that he chooses works to undo that usurpation in its expression of loss and to transform the assertiveness of the writer into the passive status of the one who has been abandoned. At this early point in the writer's career, we find the ingredients of a central mythos, characterized by the longing for completeness amid the awareness of isolation and distance from the source.

The tension between exile and return makes itself felt in narrative portraits of the writer in relation to structure, whether that "structure" is identified as text, house, holy Temple, or *beit hamidrash* (House of Study). There can be little doubt that the impact of experiences of loss and disruption makes a strong contribution to the evolving story of the writer. Agnon lost his house, including library and manuscripts, twice, first to a fire in Germany in 1924, and then again, in Talpiyot during the Arab riots of 1929. These events form part of the signifying shape of the writer's life. Loss or disruption of "house," the inability to find either one's house or the *beit midrash* (the house, in effect, of the community), all form part of a narrative of departure and return. David Cnaani cites Agnon's recurring references to the impact of destruction of a series of homes [1971, 22, 114–16]. (Cnaani's account of his conversations with Agnon is a source not unlike Gustav Janouch's *Conversations with Kafka*: it documents utterances that stage the transition from personal to public.)

Agnon liked to date his return to Palestine in 1924 as coinciding with *parshat Lekh lekha*—the weekly Torah portion beginning with God's command to Abraham: "Go from your country and your kindred and your father's house to the land that I will show you" [Gen. 12:1]. Through this dating, Agnon associates his ascent to the land of Israel with the biblical account of Abraham's response to the divine command. Carrying further the suggestions of an identification with Abraham, we might suggest that the writer makes this 1924 *aliyah* or ascent into the occasion for a move away from the false idols of European culture.[16] These idols or cultural influences are more or less to be effaced in his work after that, although their presence continues to make itself felt in the writing. Identifying with the Abraham of "*Lekh lekha*" expresses filial return and obedience, but it displaces the biological father favor of a higher authority. It also elides the problem of desire. In the biblical text, unruly desire, a pronounced theme, registers conspicuously in characters other than Abraham, whose desire conforms to what God shows him.

Shortly after his return to Palestine in 1924, Agnon extended the use of the name "Agnon" to his personal as well as literary life. Agnon's letters to his wife [1983, 25ff.] during the early 1920s testify to the writer's concern with establishing a home for his family. Between November, 1924 and July, 1925, Agnon shifts in signing his letters to his friend and publisher Zalman Schocken from Sh. Y. Czaczkes to simply Sh. Y. and then to Sh. Y. Agnon. The friendship with Schocken, which can be traced through their letters over the years, served as a crucible in which the cultural identity of each took shape.[17] During the 1924–25 period, Agnon's letters to Schocken express his pleasure at the resumption of his walks through the Old City of Jerusalem, and at the recognition he received, and perhaps most importantly, his letters anticipate Schocken's publication of a complete edition of his works. These cumulative events may have constituted something of an inauguration, heralded once again by the name shift that, on this occasion, extends the domain of "Agnon" to personal as well as professional life, as if to consolidate the assimilation of the writer to his story. It is at this point as well that Agnon resumes the outward practice of orthodox piety in his life. He becomes, in effect, the writer of Jerusalem, the sage of Talpiyot.[18] Agnon has become Agnon.

Pillars of the House

Construction of the life of the writer extends also to the family tree. Ancestral tales figure as the "pillars of the house" and contribute to building a structure that will house the writer within the larger community. *Qorot bateinu* or *The Pillars of Our House* is an autobiographical text, published in part in *Kol sipurav (The Collected Stories)* and completely in a posthumous edition [1979a], in which the writer traces his family tree.[19] (*Qorot* can be translated as "pillars" or "history"; Agnon's title reflects the more concrete sense of the word.) The preface to *The Pillars of Our House* offers a self-portrait of the writer who is bereft of a home and so turns to the past for structure. At the same time, that individual dilemma finds a context in the larger historical situation of post-Holocaust Jewry:

> When I went down to Poland to prostrate myself on the graves of my ancestors and to see my relatives, I found my uncle Rabbi 'Azriel Ya'akov the brother of my father of blessed memory, a student of the wise, old and godfearing. We sat and spoke about ourselves and our fathers (ancestors). After I had told him a bit of my history (*me'ora'otay)* I said to him, Now that the enemies have destroyed my house in the Land of Israel after the fire that burned my house outside of the Land I am left with neither book nor vessel from the inheritance of my fathers, and lo I am bereft of any belongings from the belongings of my fathers. [Agnon 1979a, 63].

In effect, the speaker of this passage, who does not identify himself here as a writer, joins his personal plight to the dilemma of a people. The noun that refers to his personal history, *me'ora'ot*, is used also to refer to the riots in Mandatory Palestine; thus, it brings in the 1929 disturbances in which Agnon's Talpiyot home was destroyed. The eastern European trip to which the passage refers occurred in 1930, at a point at which the destruction caused by World War I was apparent and the imminence of the coming destruction could be felt, but had not yet materialized. This two-page preface carries the date *t-sh-z* or 1946, so that the time of writing is identified as post-Holocaust, while the visit itself occurred some twenty years earlier. In juxtaposing these dates, Agnon constructs a context that endows his visit with a post-Holocaust importance, while allowing him to speak to his uncle, the eastern European student of the wise, in the narrative present of the preface, as if the Holocaust had not yet occurred. The combination of perspectives defines the speaker and his role: bereft in the present, he can draw upon the past, portraying himself as a penitent whose return and retrieval of documents are restorative acts. References to destruction on a personal level, moreover, acquire a larger resonance that attaches them to twentieth-century Jewish history.

This preface to *The Pillars of Our House* modulates the personal into the communal through the agency of the family and its history. By serving as a frame for the genealogical tales that follow, the preface extends an implied invitation to the reader to join in a journey through recent history to the past. There, within a world view that grants priority to Torah, Agnon tells the tales of holy men, a category termed collectively *ziqneinu*—"our elders" or "our ancestors." Agnon fashions a place for himself as the teller who stands at a distance from these figures, whose lives are characterized by the effort to restore wholeness to a flawed world through allegiance to Torah.

The author is occulted: we read the discourse of the narrator who speaks in place of the author. In this first person narrative, Agnon represents himself as the faithful transcriber who only edits here and there to eliminate unnecessary details:

> And in the course of my transcription I corrected the language a bit here and a bit there, in the manner of a son to whom broken vessels come as a part of his inheritance and he fixes them. But in the substance of the words I made no changes. [Agnon 1979a, 64].

Art is muted, but still faintly present in the image of repairing broken vessels, although the Kabbalistic uses of that image lend a mystical aura to that activity. The passage mediates and even attenuates the function of the writer, reshaping his activity more in the direction of the scribe and playing down his assertiveness. These tales speak of the "elders"—*ziqneinu*—who constitute, collectively, the subject of the utterance. By telling the story of their use of the holy tongue, the narrator grants their use of langauge priority over his and moves toward yielding to them his powers of speech.

Thus, he describes his transcription of an old, old manuscript, extending back to a rabbi who sought to bring about salvation through his prayers, while acknowledging that his summary lacks the potency that the words of the original possessed. We can trace the line from world-creating words of Torah, through the magical efficacy of the prayers of the wonder-working rabbis, to the "transcriber" and "editor," who defines his position in terms of distance from the source. (See chapters 4 and 5 for discussions of other narratives of potent writing.)

Looked at from another angle, this history of an ancestral relation to language charts the prehistory of the writer. *Pillars of Our House* is a text devoted to the wholeness of our forebears, *shlemut ziqneinu*, as Agnon puts it, a wholeness that brings together word and deed. This union of word and deed transforms the structure and process of signification into a magical utterance. This is the writer's prehistory insofar as it dissolves the dislocation that characterizes his participation in language. If, as modern linguistics has found, there are no positive terms in language and meaning is generated by differences among signifiers, then here we find in effect a fantasy of language in which full presence is restored to the word.

In effect, these ancestral tales of Agnon's draw upon a mythic relation to Torah: in making the reader feel what the present tense of writing lacks, they alter the frame of reading to include the idea of restoration. Thus, in a culminating cycle of tales, Reb Moshe Mevaqesh (Reb Moshe "the Seeker") times his reading of Mishnayot (passages of rabbinic literature) to coincide with the season in which his younger brother was murdered. The act of study is revealed to possess redemptive qualities insofar as Reb Moshe engages in study at the same time that he rescues souls in Israel. Reb Moshe Mevaqesh may live in a world in which brothers are murdered, but his actions are restorative. Indeed, the story of his life and feats resonates with the language of Agnon's symbolic universe:

> How dear that *mitsvah* was to our ancestor (*ziqneinu*), you will find out in his insistence on time, on every hour that it not be wasted in idleness. Because he sought to conclude a tractate of *Mishnayot* for the period of the year in which he had found his brother murdered, he gave all his time to that *mitsvah*. But by means of it he attained to rescuing a number of souls of Israel and brought a number of the murdered of Israel to burial in the community of Israel and by his hand a number of *'agunot* (abandoned women of indeterminate status) were released from the bonds of *'aginut*. How many were there? In the heavens above they know the number of all of them, for all is written there in true writing. Our ancestor (*ziqneinu*) too had been in the habit of writing in his notebook (his *pinqas* or

> communal record) the name of every murder victim that he found and brought to burial in the community of Israel and the name of every *'agunah* who was released through his hand (intervention) from the bonds of *'aginut*. [Agnon 1979a, 170].

Reb Moshe Mevaqesh carries a name that denotes activity: the root *b-q-sh*, "to seek," suggests the redemptive activity of "seeking" to set things right in God's world. This correspondence between earthly and divine is carried through in his communal record or *pinqas* that approximates the "true writing" found in a higher world. The narrative voice expresses its awe of ancestral strength in its attribution of a level of activity to *ziqneinu* that resonates with the powers of *tiqqun* or repair in a mystical, cosmic sense. In particular, the activity of saving women from the condition of the *'agunah* underscores a dramatic contrast between the name of this strong figure (Moshe the "seeker") and the enforced passivity of those women as *'agunot* or souls in limbo.

There is an inherent tension between the narrator whose words in this memoir register loss and the ancestor whose search is so all-defining and intense that his study of Mishnah is itself a redemptive action, literally equivalent to his rescue of "souls in Israel." Hints of a suppressed narrative make themselves felt here in the relation of the *'agunah* to the strong ancestral figure of *ziqneinu*. Given the name the writer chose for himself, one wonders if the figure of the writer as *'agunah* is not here assimilated to the "pillar of the house" that is his ancestor. From loss to redemption: the *'agunah* as the figure of loss is opposed to Reb Moshe Mevaqesh, the seeker whose actions contribute to redemption. The writer is both and neither of these figures.

In this genealogy of ancestral tales, the writer makes a small place for a portrait of himself as infant in his grandfather's house. That portrait forms part of an account of his grandfather's anger when he finds that a picture of his house, commissioned for the occasion of his daughter's wedding, contained no reminder of the destruction of the Temple. The representation of the house of a Jew, he reminds the artist, must never be complete, as a reminder that the Temple has not yet been rebuilt, a moral-aesthetic criterion that the writer incorporates into his self-portrait:

> When my mother became pregnant my grandfather called the same artist to correct the drawings, so that if mother were to give birth to a boy child the house would be properly repaired (*metuqan*) for

> the son's entry into the covenant with our father Abraham of blessed memory. The artist came and corrected (*tiqayn*) the drawings and on his own left a square cubit and wrote there in black letters, "In memory of the destruction of Jerusalem," and surrounded the writing with a black frame. It was not long before I was born and I still remember that many times when I was nursing from the breasts of my mother I would gaze at those same black letters that were surrounded with a black frame, and it seems likely to me that the more that I tell of the destruction (*ḥurban*) comes to me from those days. [Agnon 1979a, 176].

In an exquisitely crafted miniature, Agnon portrays himself as an infant, in his grandfather's house, nursing and looking at the picture that celebrates the house in the present, but shows the trace of the destruction of the Temple. The completeness of the mother-child union is simultaneously disrupted and amplified by the grandfather's insistence on incorporation of a sign of loss into a portrait of the house that otherwise shelters and sustains its inhabitants. The destruction of the Temple, integral component of a people's identity, becomes associated here with possession and loss on a variety of levels. These range from the mother's breast (irretrievable prototype for all later gratifications, according to Freud [1905]), to the loss and retrieval of an eastern European patrimony, within the context of the memoir as a whole. The effect is to create an emblematic portrait of the writer in an anamnesis that weaves the child's relation to the mother into the larger context of loss and dispersion on the national level, sustaining an intimate balance between the personal and the communal.

Chapter

5

Housing the Past in *A Guest for the Night*

The Grammar of Restoration

Published initially in 1939, *Oreaḥ natah lalun* (*A Guest for the Night*) chronicles the efforts of its first person narrator, a writer, to return to his east European birthplace and repair damages that can be attributed variously to his own youthful rebelliousness, the falling off of faith in the community, and not least of all, the ravages of war. The explicit project of this novel is restoration, on the level of the narrator's own life, as well as that of the Jewish community in the town. The central character, the "Guest" of the novel's title, narrates his own efforts at personal and communal renewal, even as he provides evidence of the contradictions inherent in those efforts that insure their failure.

While the conflict between the past and the present, the world of tradition and modernity, makes itself felt in works such as *Sippur pashut* (*A Simple Story*) and *Tmol shilshom* (*Only Yesterday*), *A Guest for the Night* makes a special claim on our attention because of its autobiographical aspect, its author's manipulation of a narrator-protagonist who so resembles himself. Drawing on Agnon's weeklong stay in 1930 in his hometown of Buczacz in Galicia, *A Guest for the Night* is a fiction that emerges out of Agnon's visit to his past and combines most richly some of the major themes of his life and work, with particular attention to the world of eastern European Jewry in both its physical decline and its preservation of tradition.

The project of restoration organizes the text on a number of levels. A grammar or narrative syntax of restoration positions the narrator as would-be subject of the verb (he who would "restore") and produces a series of predicates in which the object of the verb varies:

> restoring the House of Study (*beit midrash*),
> restoring the self,

> restoring the town,
> restoring the Jewish community,
> and, even, restoring the text as a life-giving instrument.

The nature of the restorative task that the Guest faces in the novel is signaled in the name of the town. "Szybucz," Agnon's fictional name for his hometown of Buczacz, derives from the root *sh-b-sh* meaning "to err" or "make crooked." Baruch Kurzweil was the first to comment on the manner in which the deeply flawed reality of Szybucz announces itself to the Guest in the form of the three figures who greet him on his arrival: a man with a rubber hand, another with a wooden leg, and a third, the town beggar, who snorts "Money! Money!" through a hole in his face where his nose should have been. Kurzweil concludes that these three represent the town that is itself half-living and half-dead [1970, 51–52]. We can go on to say that they also point in the direction of the restoration that the protagonist is about to undertake. The project of restoration is constituted by two cycles: (1) death and rebirth in the natural world: the novel begins in autumn and closes in summer; (2) the Jewish calendar: the novel opens on the eve of the Day of Atonement and closes after *tisha b'Av* or the 9th of Av. *Tisha b'Av* resonates in the novel not only for its significance in Jewish history, but also as the birthdate of both protagonist and author.

The novel invokes classical autobiographical structure by positioning its narrator to tell the story of his return to his hometown as a narrative that will reintegrate the past into the present. According to the model of fictional autobiography, the narrator will tell of a journey that brings his past self together with his present, healing the breaches that were the stimulus to his journey. Reading *A Guest for the Night*, the reader gradually becomes aware of the crisis in the life of the narrator that prompts him to undertake the journey, a move that involves leaving his family, his commitment to the land of Israel, and his vocation as writer. Interspersed in the protagonist's narrative are references to his intention to rebuild his house in Israel and in fact, the destruction of his house is cited as the specific impetus for his journey.

The reader can piece together clues suggesting that the narrator's house was destroyed in the uprisings of 1929—as was Agnon's. It is worth spending a moment on some of the biographical data that are relevant to the novel's construction of its protagonist's life. Agnon's returns to his hometown, after his departure in 1907, were both rare and fraught with significance. After leaving Buczacz in 1907 for

Palestine, he spent the next six years struggling to establish himself amid the community of the Second *Aliyah*. In 1913, he left Palestine abruptly for Germany; called home to the bedside of his sick father, he visited him for a while, but when his father died shortly thereafter, the young Agnon did not manage to arrive home in time for the funeral. He spent the years from 1913–24 largely in Germany, only returning to Palestine after the 1924 fire that destroyed his home in Homburg, Germany, taking with it his library of rare books and the manuscript of an autobiographical novel. In 1930, he once again left Israel, after the 1929 destruction of his home outside Jerusalem. During his stay in Berlin, he oversaw the first printing of his collected works, by the then newly established publishing house of Schocken. Afterwards, he went on to travel through Poland, visiting small towns and noting, as he wrote to a friend, that the inhabitants might well have read his books and modeled their lives accordingly, so closely did they resemble his fictional creations.[1] In the course of that journey, he visited his hometown of Buczacz and remained there for the week that appears to have provided the actual kernel for the novel. In a 1930 letter to his wife, Agnon describes the great to-do that his arrival caused in the town, the endless crowds that accompanied him. With a characteristically playful tone, he portrays himself as the prodigal returned, made much of, feted endlessly, no time even to wipe his nose.[2] But how to go from there to the novel, where the protagonist's role as writer remains hidden and is barely acknowledged more than halfway through the book?

Cumulatively, those losses of house, library, and manuscript make themselves felt in the novel's thematic attention to rebuilding a house, but their inscription in the text is by no means simple. On a personal level, the novel's protagonist or the Guest, as we shall call him, vows that he will return to Israel to build a house there: "and I made a vow that if God would be with me and would return me to the land of Israel I would make myself a house and would not go out of it" [Agnon 1968a, 207; 1968, 4:194].[3] The personal reference of his pledge is already amplified insofar as it echoes vows that are to be found in Gen. 28:20–22 and Deut. 20:6. Through this scriptural mediation, the house that the Guest wants to build (or rebuild) becomes identified with the House of God, transforming what might otherwise be a purely personal mission. Indeed the major "house" structure in the novel is the *beit midrash*, a place where both study and worship are carried out.[4]

The model of fictional autobiography is complicated by this intertwining of the personal in the communal: the first person narrator becomes implicated in the situation of a people, and on a larger scale, in Jewish traditions and history. The novel uses the mutually sustaining relationship of nation to Torah to present the relationships of Guest and townspeople to the *beit midrash* or House of Study where sacred texts are studied:

> The Holy One blessed be He created the world according to his will and chose us from all the nations and gave us his Torah, so that we would know to worship Him. During the time that we study His Torah and perform His commandments, no nation or tongue can harm us. If we don't preserve His Torah, even a little nation harms us. [Agnon 1968a, 29; 1968, 4:32].

In effect, this structure of relationship to Torah gives shape to Jewish history, explaining and moralizing that history in terms of the desires and the capacities of the people:

> The Torah is whole, but the cabinet which holds it is broken. Those longings we long will bring us to receive the Torah a second time, . . . And if our ability is small, lo, our will is great. . . . Lowered is the ability, but the will lives. And we hope that it will heal the broken vessel of our spirit. [Agnon 1968a, 271; 1968, 4:253].

The novel uses recurring citations and images such as these to insert itself into Jewish history and to assert its relationship to the larger community. These issues of community are internal to the novel in terms of its plot, but they also push beyond the borders of the text, arguing for the place of the novel in Jewish life between the two world wars.

Melding autobiographical elements with European history and drawing upon traditional Jewish lore, this is the novel of eastern Europe that ends—unresolvedly—in Palestine. If autobiography utilizes regression to more primitive stages in order to establish the mature self, then *A Guest for the Night* is a failed novelistic autobiography. In what sense is this so? According to the archetypal models that the novel evokes, the protagonist, who undertakes a journey to the past in order to restore a flawed present, must return from that past in order to complete his quest. Whereas "restoration" must involve return from the return, the Guest of Agnon's novel demonstrates an ambivalence that flaws the novel's resolution. Hints in the text may draw the reader's attention to the regressive nature of the Guest's journey by placing it in historical context: he has left the land of Israel, with its hope of homeland and national restoration, for the eastern European village which offers, as its inhabitants themselves know only too well, no future.[5]

To indicate another instance of this deep-rooted ambivalence (one that will be explored in a later section of this chapter), I would like to point to a striking image of relationship to Torah that is enlisted in service of the narrator's project of rebirth. In a recurring image of intrauterine perfection, the novel portrays the Torah as the perfect heritage that every infant possesses in the womb, but loses on emergence into a flawed world. This theme of the wise embryo or infant functions not only as "reminder" of a lost wholeness, but to signal the threat that is posed to the project of restoration by an underlying fantasy of return. The fantasy of perfect embryonic union with Torah demonstrates the attraction of regression and abandonment of a role in the social world. Thus, the project of restoration is defeated as much by the ambivalence inherent in the restorative impulse itself, as it is by obstacles in the social world of the novel.

The question of closure in Agnon's novels has been the subject of considerable critical attention [Miron 1987, 25]. My goal is to disclose the complex and sometimes contradictory structures in the novel and to comment on some of the ways in which the text throws into question whatever closure it achieves. While one can support an argument for closure in the return to the land of Israel, the novel makes possible a number of readings, particularly of its ending.[6] I say this not so much out of a conciliatory pluralism as to take notice of the rich, mazelike structure of this text, and of the consequent diversity of readings it permits.[7]

Agnon's exploitation of a structure in which narrator is protagonist places him within the tradition of the self-conscious novel in European literature. While Agnon's narrator may move further in clocktime than does Tristram Shandy, *A Guest for the Night* is no less complex in its attention to the interaction of narrative time (the time of telling) and the time of events themselves (plot time) than is Sterne's novel. Robert Alter's description of Don Quixote as an "author manqué, . . . at once the creator and protagonist of his own fictions" [1975, 21] applies as well to Agnon's protagonist. The narrator of *A Guest for the Night*, like his illustrious predecessor Don Quixote, undertakes a quest that is as much an attempt to find his place in the story, to establish his own text, as to carry out significant action in the world.

Extending the reach of this search for coherence, *A Guest for the Night* invokes the life of its author through the use of recognizable details from the author's public life, however much these may be interspersed in the text at large. The aura of authenticity that such data produces suggests a move beyond fiction to incorporate a biographical dimension. Gershon Shaked delineates Agnon's use of autobiographical material in the novel, ranging from correspondences such as the whole trip to Galicia to less obvious parallels, and concludes that such "real-life" detail is intended to strengthen our impression of the novel as personal confession, and beyond that, to link it to the collective, that is the Jewish people [Shaked 1973, 265, 270, 276].

But while such details are obviously placed with care by the author, they are not immediately apparent and must be hunted out. Naomi Sokoloff [1984, 105] points out that *A Guest for the Night* demands active reading, in that the "reader, like the narrator, must contend with disorienting phenomena, and the reader's struggle to devise a new strategy of reading—based on parallelisms—corresponds to the Guest's need to create or perceive coherent new patterns of meaning out of social chaos." While the Guest aims at achieving integration on a variety of levels, from the personal to the communal, the text resists that ordering; the reader takes on a more active role in part to account for the excess that defeats the narrator's scheme. This fine doubleness of vision creates a curious complicity between author and reader: we both participate in and become the critical observers of the fiction.

Language as Key

In effect, the text attempts to bridge several crucial gaps and to fuse together the subject of the enunciation with the subject of the utterance. This is the project of regeneration in the discourse. The author is the subject of the enunciation or producer of the discourse that is the novel. The writer Agnon, subject of the enunciation, produces the utterance that is the novel. If we continue this model of linguistic production, we would have to conclude that the subject of the utterance is the narrator who is in this case also the protagonist. That is, the author tells us *about* the narrator/protagonist. However, the "real" author as subject of the enunciation is hidden from us and unavailable to our reading. The discourse is attributed to the narrator, surrogate for the author. Reading involves us in a fiction to the extent that we experience the text as the utterance of its first person narrator. (One need only check the critical literature to see how persuasive a fiction this can be; look, for example, at A. M. Haberman's citations of passages in the novel as sources for biographical material on the author.)

As if the force of narrative could change the world, *A Guest for the Night* contains indications of an impulse to transform and restore a degraded reality through language. Recurring images and allusions in the novel link the Guest's mission with the notion of *tiqqun* or repair of that which has been broken, a familiar theme, particularly in Jewish mystical thought. Furthermore, the journey back into the past takes on something of the air of a mystical quest, as the narrator meets guide figures such as the old locksmith (*masger*), who fashions him the key with which he can enter the holy House of Study. The narrator notes, indeed, that there are special words that can open doors and grant one access to treasure (words that function as keys, in effect). One impulse motivating his journey may be the wish to recapture just such a magical use of language, or, put somewhat differently, to renounce the particularly abrasive discourse of individuality. (Kurzweil points out in an early essay on the novel that success would mean the novel had transcended itself and entered the world of miracles—the world of Hasidic folk tales, perhaps, but not of a modern novel [1970, 53].)[8]

Within the novel, the Guest alludes obliquely to his regenerative mission when he cites a passage from the Talmud that expresses a central preoccupation of his quest: "If the House of God is not built within a man's lifetime, it is as if it has been destroyed in his lifetime" [Agnon 1968a, 316; 1968, 4:295].[9] The saying suggests the obligation of the individual to continue the existence of the House of God within his own spiritual life, but it implies as well the destructive nature of the failure to adhere to that spiritual structure.

The disrepair of the writer coincides with that of the town: the town used to posssess a bookstore with an array of books of useful function and also those amusements called "novels"; now only the degraded texts that are called novels remain and the Guest observes that "Even now they make books they call novels, just as they still call our town a town" [1968a, 45; 1968, 4:46–47]. Similarly, the narrator admits reluctantly to being a *sofer*, acknowledging the degradation implicit in his use of a term that is used to designate one who wrote out the words his master dictated to him. In this respect, the *tiqqun* or restoration that the Guest undertakes involves the dismantling of his identity as a writer and the undoing of his youthful defiance of his father's wish that he become a rabbi.

Later in the novel, the Guest encounters a childhood friend who presents him indirectly with a view of his mission that is undone by irony. He meets Aaron Schützling, salesman of patent medicines—whose last name means "little protector," an apparent comment on the false cures that are his trade. When asked to picture future generations, Schützling offers the Guest a vision of restoration turned inside out, for he points to the three flawed figures who greeted the narrator on his arrival and says: "In the future to come all creatures will walk on their false legs and gesture with their rubber hands and snort 'Money! Money!'" [1968a, 340; 1968, 4:316–17]. One can see, then, that the narrator must keep from becoming Aaron, the purveyor of false solutions; as the narrator of his own experience, he alternately resists and yields to irony. Hovering between the figures of Moses and Aaron, he is defined more by the tension between them than by an identification with either.

The Guest as narrator becomes the focus for an ongoing process of ironic inflation and deflation of the role of the writer in the world. He attempts to sustain the unsustainable fiction that God's in His heaven and all's right with the world, provided one is willing to see things that way. But at the same time, a fundamental contradiction makes itself felt. All is *not* well in Szybucz. In order to tell the story of a harmonious world, the protagonist must play God and author his own version of the universe. To conceal his narrative presumption and to play down the very artifice with which he has made his tale fit mythical patterns, the narrator fails to tell us, until almost the end of the novel, that he is a writer; he pretends that the fiction we read is not a fiction, particularly not one that he has *composed*. The text is built on a contradiction: We have before us the record of his engagement in that form of creative self-assertion that he ostensibly seeks to renounce. As a result, we can say his journey to reconciliation cannot succeed because the goal of the quest conflicts with the very artifice of its structure.

Hence, his disclaimers of authorship. The narrator's account of his journey is punctuated by denials of what we come to realize is its purpose. Thus, he periodically denies the symbolic significance of his return in a way that serves effectively to make us take note of it. He tells us that he is not one of those who compare the present to "days gone by" [1968a, 12; 1968, 4:14], an observation that makes the implicit comparison of present-day Szybucz to his memory of it all the more prominent. Or he asserts that he is not one of those poets who compare winter to death and snow to its shrouds, an overly flowery image but one that does essentially express the function of winter in the novel. This sort of narrative disclaimer affirms by negation the ritualized structure of the quest, but it does so while maintaining that it is not the protagonist who has arranged things this way.

The illusion of spontaneity is maintained in part by diminishing the role of the retrospective narrator.[10] Commenting on the "digressive" structure of the novel, Gershon Shaked notes the stories of wartime that are told to the protagonist, stories in which a third person, an outsider, plays a decisive role in the life of a family, usually for the worse [1976, 230–36; 1989, 142–43]. We can amend this view to suggest rather that the protagonist attempts to enter into the lives of the people of Szybucz as just such an outsider, but as one who will affect their lives for the better. Tales of war make manifest the opposition in the world to the narrator's mission of repair; they constitute one of the forces to which his restorative efforts are opposed. In addition, however, while the Guest and others refer often to a time when the world had not been torn apart by the "horrors" of war, one suspects that the phrase, "before the war" (also something of a refrain in the novel), refers not just to modern European history but to the history of the protagonist whose rebellion—"warfare" in its own right—tore apart the world of his fathers.

Varieties of Return: Silence and Speech

The wholeness that the Guest seeks belongs to a number of characters in the novel who either have remained within tradition or have returned to it. They belong to the story as narrated subjects, subjects of the utterance who do not attempt to become speaking subjects or producers of their own discourses. On the contrary, each exists in conspicuous silence.

One such figure in the novel, Reb Hayyim, illustrates a return akin to that which the Guest attempts, but one that reaches fulfillment because of its unambiguous nature. Reb Hayyim had been an outstanding student of the Torah whose brilliance as a youth diverted him from Torah study for its own sake and caused a dispute that disrupted the whole town.[11] Reb Hayyim returns to the village after a long exile due to war (a separation analogous to the Guest's years away from Szybucz) and he is completely transformed: he lives the life of a saint, asking nothing for himself, performing the most menial of chores in the House of Study. It becomes quite clear that Reb Hayyim's self-abnegation represents atonement for his former brilliance; indeed his death in the latter part of the novel merely confirms the renunciation of discourse that he has achieved.

In the earlier sections of the novel, the Guest works at establishing an identification with Reb Hayyim by taking on a share in his devotion to the House of Study. As narrator or subject of the enunciation, the Guest is then able to speak of himself and Reb Hayyim as narrated subjects who fulfill, in companionable silence, the obligation to sustain the House of Study. Speaking of them both as structural supports of the House, the Guest tells us: "We would sit as one in our old House of Study like two beams upholding the ceiling and supporting the whole building and neither speaks with the other" [1968a, 160; 1968, 4:152]. The silence that joins them signals the absence of discourse and is as much the indicator of atonement as is the architectural image of integration into the House. Incidentally, the "beams of the house" to which the narrator refers are nominally the same *qorot* that form the title of Agnon's genealogical work, *Qorot bateynu* (*Pillars of Our House*). (See chapter 4 for a discussion of this work.)

Given this heavily laden construction of Reb Hayyim's role, we may be somewhat surprized by the Guest's response to Reb Hayyim's announcement, late in the novel, that he plans to rejoin his real family. In fact, it is the Guest as narrator who sets us up for surprize by telling us what should have been his response and then summarizing his resentment at the burden of "housework" that will now fall on him:

> It would have been proper for me to rejoice that this old student of the wise (*talmid ḥakham*) to whom many sorrows had come was leaving the woodshed and going to his daughter in the country, where all his needs would be filled without difficulty, nevertheless I did not rejoice. For all the time that Reb Hayyim is here, all the bother of the House of Study is on him, and now that he's going I will have to bring water in to clean the floor and so too do the rest of the things that I am not used to doing [1968a, 394–395; 1968, 4:369].

The irony is evident. We are meant to understand that the Guest's use of Reb Hayyim as a surrogate has served to distance him from the very mission he has undertaken. The Guest may attempt to ally himself with Reb Hayyim, but it is Reb Hayyim who does the chores. As narrator, the Guest spins fictions of identification in an attempt to gain a form of spiritual credit for Reb Hayyim's service, but he also provides us with the conflicting data that disclose his duplicity.

For each person, entry into discourse occurs with the assumption of the personal pronoun "I" in relation to a "you" [Benveniste 1971]. In this respect, Reb Hayyim's return suggests an undoing of the discursive practices that testify to subjectivity. Extending the analogy, we can classify narrative as utterance and understand silence and return to be the renunciation of discourse. Indeed, the silence of Reb Hayyim contrasts markedly with the volubility of the Guest, who continues to engage without pause in the construction of the fiction of his existence as he would like it to be. Reb Hayyim, who speaks no more, stokes the fire in the House of Study. The Guest, by contrast, never gives up the narrational effort to order his universe, and so he can never complete the gesture of return that he has initiated. In the drama of speech and utterance that is the novel, insofar as the example of Reb Hayyim can be applied to the narrator, we can see that it is impossible to *narrate* a completely successful *return* (to be both artist and Reb Hayyim) because return implies the cessation of narration.

"Return" is offered a striking formulation in the Guest's expression of the wish to "stretch out" or "prostrate himself on the graves" of his ancestors. (In the Talmud, this gesture expresses remorse and reconciliation. [cf. Hagigah 16b, 22b; Sotah 34b.][12] In the course of carrying out the self-imposed task of restoring the House of Study, the Guest links his efforts to retrieve missing volumes to visiting the town's cemetery: "I did not hope to find there the books that had disappeared from the House of Study, but I went like a man who happened to be in the town of the graves of his ancestors and goes to prostrate himself on them" [1968a, 82; 1968, 4:82]. Prostration on the graves suggests here a wish for reunion with the family members whom the Guest left behind in his departure from the town: in effect, he rejoins them and the books in the House of Study through his acts of devotion.

Shortly after, the Guest recounts a dream that further emphasizes the deathlike features of return. He dreams of entering a bookstore in Jerusalem where an old man tells him, "If it's books you're looking for, come with me" [1968a, 93; 1968, 4:92], an invitation that turns into the offer of "four cubits in the land of Israel" and the opportunity to go to the old man's "house," which turns out to be a crypt filled with dead people. ("Four cubits" is the biblical measure of a man.)

The Guest describes his response to the crypt with a detachment that distances voice from body and speaker from utterance: "My limbs became quiet as if they had separated from my body and even my body seemed to separate from me, and I felt nothing except for a headache in which there was a kind of pleasantness, as if the hand of a loved one caressed my head. Finally my whole existence ceased, except for this pleasantness that did not cease" [1968a, 93; 1968, 4:93]. Insofar as the crypt is in the earth, it carries the suggestion of return to the body of mother/earth, a suggestion that is all the more pronounced since caresses that are maternal in nature form part of a pleasurable loss of self. Encoded into this dream are possibilities that the narrative, focalized through the consciousness of the narrator, does not develop explicitly or articulate fully. The dream scene implies the undoing of individuation as it absorbs the speaker back into a prelinguistic oneness.

This dream prepares us for an even more central encounter with death, an encounter that discloses further the deep ambivalence about "return" that undermines the explicit project of restoration. This encounter situates the narrator in relation to the figure of Hanokh the wagoneer. In order to find wood to keep the fire in the House of Study going, the Guest hires Hanokh, who is the embodiment of humility, poverty, and unself-consciousness. In a comment that underscores the difference between them, the Guest observes that Hanokh cannot grasp what goes on "above his shoulders" and goes on to talk to him about "the strength of imagination" [1968a, 111; 1968, 4:109]. Using "house" imagery that offers bitter comment on his own restorative efforts, the Guest tells Hanokh that house owners come to the "house" that is the theater when they are sick of their own houses; there, they watch people who have never owned houses behave as if they know everything there is to know about houses; this makes the house owners very happy and they laugh and cry bravo [1968a, 112; 1968, 4:109].

This echo of the Platonic indictment of the artist comes from the Guest who, like the actor of his own anecdote, *simulates* house-building, producing the illusion of a restored House of Study for his audience, the townspeople. The Guest communicates this allegorical anecdote to the unreflective Hanokh. In the terms that the analogy uses, however, Hanokh is closer to real tenancy insofar as he engages in the actual labor of sustaining the House of Study.[13] Beyond Hanokh as nominal auditor, we as readers stand to make the connection between the artist in the anecdote who generates persuasive house *fictions* on a stage and the Guest who *declares* his intentions of rebuilding a house, gives the appearance of doing so, and then goes out and hires Hanokh to carry out the work.

Hanokh appears with the onset of winter, keeps the fire going and then, abruptly, disappears in the snow until, in a dreamlike scene, the Guest meets him late on a snowy night. Amid thoughts of

Szybucz which "casts out her sons and then returns and gathers them all" [1968a, 225; 1968, 4:211], the Guest hears a bell and sees a horse and wagon, whose driver turns out to be the missing Hanokh. In response to the Guest's demand that Hanokh return to his wife and children, Hanokh replies that he must go first to the "grave of Israel." While this formulation resembles the Guest's own departure from wife and children to, as he put it, "prostrate himself on the graves" of his ancestors, he rebukes Hanokh as if there were no kinship between them: "I said to him, You've lost your mind Hanokh, you show yourself as living and you speak as if you're dead. Answered Hanokh and said, Dead" [1968a 226; 1968, 4:212]. But while he may scold Hanokh as if they had nothing in common, the Guest gives access to data that subvert that dissociation: "Hanokh sank into sleep and so did his horse. Just then the bell on the neck of the horse was ringing. The sound began to put my limbs to sleep and my eyes began to close" [1968a, 228; 1968, 4:213–14]. As with his response to the old man in the cemetery, who offered him the books he sought, the Guest's experience of physical relaxation expresses the loss of self or renunciation of discourse inherent in the conciliatory aspect of his quest. In both encounters, the Guest extricates himself from something of a deathlike trance by vigorously dissociating himself from the death figure. As narrator or subject of the enunciation, he both records and dismisses his own experiences as subject of the utterance. Despite those efforts at denial, however, his response to each of the two figures discloses a regressive desire whose object is the undoing of subjectivity or loss of discursive capacities.

Both Hanokh and Reb Hayyim achieve an atonement that remains unavailable to the narrator because of the status of "guest" that sustains his detachment. As the title by which we know him, "Guest" contains within it the sense of belonging and not belonging that defines his position. The narrator draws attention to his "observer" status by referring to himself as a "guest who came for the night", in chapters 7, 24, 71 [Halkin, 1964, 92]; as the person who lives "in the house of the hotel" [1968a, 21; 1968, 4:26]; and, at the conclusion of the novel, when he observes that he has left the status of a guest [1968a, 476; 1968, 4:444]. Of course, it is his very status as *guest* that insures his capacity to survive his visit and to render the account of it, fictionally speaking, that we read. (Band notes this positive side of his guesthood [1968, 323].) As subject of the enunciation, the Guest must sustain a distance even from himself as subject of the utterance in order to author his discourse. The contra-diction involved in shaping a discourse that attempts to repudiate discourse belongs to the opposition between the positions of speaker (subject of the enunciation) and spoken (subject of the utterance). Caught in that discursive split, the Guest continues to assert his fidelity to the mission of repair he has undertaken, even as he insures, by virtue of the very structure of his discourse, its failure.

Inherent in the very structure of subjectivity, this discursive split becomes particularly evident in a first person novel in which the narrator attempts a remaking of himself. We have seen, moreover, that this narrator provides us with some of the very material that undermines his project. Disingenuously, he records data that raise questions about his place in the structure he has created. In this respect, the narrator uses a recurring image of the relationship of craftsman to created object that provides an illuminating parallel to his own project of self-renewal. First, in proposing to spend the winter in Szybucz, the Guest commissions a coat and marvels at the creative capacities of Schuster the tailor to give form to cloth: "There is something marvelous about this cloth, which the tailor has cut. Yesterday it was formless; now he has passed his scissors over it, and cut it and given it a form" [1968a, 59; 1968, 4:59]. (This warm coat, by the way, protects not only against a bitter Szybucz winter, but also serves to ward off intimacy with the townspeople, who have no such protection against the cold; thus the Guest's alliance with the people of his hometown is undercut by the artifice of the coat that sustains his difference from them.)

When the Guest has to find a way to replace the key to the House of Study (a key he accepted and promptly misplaced), he turns to the locksmith, another figure whom he endows with the divinity of creation: "The locksmith kept his promise and made me a key. I took the key and said: Yesterday you were a lump of iron; the craftsman cast his eyes upon you and made you into a precious thing" [1968a, 108; 1968, 4:106]. Here, too, the craftsman possesses magical capacities, since the key is the key to the House of Study (made to replace the original that the Guest misplaced), and serves to unlock the treasury of wisdom stored in sacred books.

The third in this series comes closest to home. Following directly on his response to the locksmith, the Guest extends form-giving capacities to his own relationship to the House of Study or *beit midrash*. In this instance, however, it is significant that he reverses the subject-object relation: "Similarly, I said to myself: Yesterday you were a lump of flesh; now the *beit midrash* has been opened to you and you have become a man" [1968a, 108; 1968, 4:106]. As narrator of his own experience, one might have expected him to cast himself in a role analogous to that of the tailor or locksmith whose potencies he so admires. Instead, he likens himself to the inert material that the craftsman shapes. Yielding place, as well he might, to the Creator whose instrument, the House of Study, will mold him, the narrator is no longer subject of the enunciation, but subject of the utterance. The very structure of his statement elides any difficulties associated with uttering statements and thus bypasses the frictions of subjectivity in favor of a fiction of perfect sonship.

Sonship and Utterance

When the Guest first enters Szybucz and is overwhelmed by the decline and ruin of the town since he last saw it, he finds one intangible survival of its former wholeness in the "odor of millet boiled in honey, which never leaves the town from the day after Passover until the end of November" [1968a, 2; 1968, 4:8]. It is Reb Hayyim, once more at home in Szybucz, who offers the Guest a taste of that resonant dish: "Looking like good gold, the millet filled the plate; it was covered with honey refined and pure as gold, and the fragrance rose as on the sunny days in time gone by when everything was in order and the world was joyful" [1968a, 393; 1968, 4:367].[14] Reb Hayyim's capacity to provide the food of wholeness marks a shift in his position from the filial rebellion of his past to an alliance with the father. His is a story that encompasses both filial rebellion and return to the father, both displacement and replacement of the Torah as the center of Jewish life. Leaving the condition of sonhood to join the father, it is ultimately the position of the father that Reb Hayyim occupies in relation to the Guest.

Reb Hayyim's paternal function for the narrator is confirmed for us after his death, when the Guest enters the House of Study to study Mishnah in his memory. In that moment, the Guest is able to identify fully with Reb Hayyim and to shed, at least momentarily, his dissonant selfhood:

> I raised my voice until the voice of Torah conquered the voice of time. . . . A man should always try to pray in public since the prayer of many can be heard, but at that hour that man forgot that there was a public and there were many, but the Holy One blessed be He filled, as it were, the entire world. And that man made himself small until his existence ceased. [1968a, 441; 1968, 4:411–12].

The larger communal utterance of prayer here dissolves the abrasiveness of individual utterance, subsuming the Guest's temporal identity into a larger structure.

Biography offers us a strikingly parallel text to this episode. In 1913, following the death of his father, Agnon wrote to a friend, another writer, describing the huge outpouring of public grief in the town as well as his own inability to break down and mourn openly [1970a, 587]. According to his own account, it was only when he entered the House of Study to read passages of Mishnah in memory of his father that the barriers to his resistance dissolved so that he could rejoin his father through the activity of study. We can speculate that, at the time of the 1913 letter, the youthful letter writer is concerned with establishing his independent existence. By contrast, the fictional world of the novel, written during the thirties, allows a far greater measure of freedom to play with the idea of return and to plumb far more deeply the impulse to go back in a movement that undoes individuation.

The narrative plays with possibilities of return that reverse and ultimately threaten to undo the formation of the individual in time. We find evidence of this undoing of temporality in the uses that the novel makes of the very old legend of the infant in the womb who possesses perfect knowledge of Torah. Thus, for example, the Guest describes his reentry into the House of Study as entry into a timeless sphere and pictures it as a return to the womb: he compares his resumption of study of the Torah to the fulfillment enjoyed by the embryo lodged in its mother's womb "who is taught the entirety of the Torah and as soon as he comes to the air of the world an angel comes and strikes him on the mouth and causes him to forget the entirety of the Torah" [1968a, 108; 1968, 4:106]. In this instance, a deeply traditional image is placed in a context in which it illustrates ambivalence. While the narrative context discloses a backward movement or "regression" that carries negative psychological connotations, the image of the wise infant supplies deep-rooted cultural ideals that valorize some forms of participation in community or Torah over the achievement of individuation. The culturally specific elements of Torah and House of Study offset or at least temper that negative sense of regression by associating it with attainment of an ideal of knowledge that is suffused with mysticism. The compressed narrative of the infant in utero offers an image of an idealized, mythical embryology; it is an image of intrauterine wholeness that has apparently exercised considerable appeal, since it recurs throughout the sources.[15] As a prototype of mystical experience, the infant whose knowledge of Torah is complete exists in perfect union and harmony with the Creator.[16]

The Guest's moment of study in memory of Reb Hayyim and the recurring use of the wise infant image offer two important instances of a conflict in the novel that is central to its importance: they demonstrate the richness of Agnon's engagement in both European novelistic and Jewish mystical traditions. As a text that follows the patterns of human life, the novel registers time. Because of the temporal nature of the activity of reading, the novel lacks completeness at any given moment. Furthermore, the text is defined by a tension between the unfolding time of the events depicted in it and the reader's time of reading. In a strong contrast to these discontinuities, *A Guest for the Night* uses several variations of the wise infant tale to generate glimpses of a mythic Torah, the text of simultaneity; this mystical or mythic Torah is present all at once, with none of the delays and deferrals that characterize post-uterine textuality.

The wise infant supplies the myth of an originary presence to the narrative of development that the novel traces. The completeness of the embryo's participation in Torah knowledge contrasts poignantly with the divisiveness and fragmentation of human life, or, for that matter, human narrative acts. The novel sharpens this contrast by depicting the infant's experience of the moment of birth as the occasion for mourning—emergence out of perfection into a flawed state of being. But of course, birth is also the moment at which individuation begins. As such, it is the first moment in the history of the artist. Thus, the very image of the wise infant condenses one of the novel's central themes and paradoxes. The ideal of timeless possession of Torah in utero introduces a dramatic alternative to the novelistic patterns of development that portray a protagonist's entry into the social world. The wise infant's perfect knowledge and filiality contrast sharply with the formation of subjectivity through the appropriation of discourse, that process of development that the Guest describes in his recollections of his own youth. It is this very process whose outcome he attempts to undo in his return or move to atonement with the tradition he had abandoned.[17]

As the Guest first applies it to his own reentry into the House of Study, the image of the wise infant marks that movement of return as a movement back into lost wholeness. But while the impulse toward return enlists the wise infant image in its service, the text also allows us to reconstruct the actual biography of its narrator (and the implied biography of its author) as a narrative of *departure*. We find that the novel portrays formation of the writer as a process that occurs in relation to the holy tongue, shifting between subordination to and appropriation of language.

The first moment in this implied biography can be found in the Guest's description of childhood study with his father. Under his father's tutelage, he would find one verse of Scripture beginning with the first letter of his name, and then another with the second letter and so on. This is the only place in the novel where we are able to piece together the given name of the protagonist and it turns out to be Samuel, the same as Agnon's [1968a, 398; 1968, 4:372].[18] The text invites the reader to engage in a form of "active reading" or detective work that leads to the extraction of the Guest's name from the Torah passages that he cites. In this bit of emblematic play, the novel highlights the reader's role in the production of the text.

We have here an instance of self-conscious intertextuality, on the model of the anagram, in which one complete text is woven into another [Jenny 1982]. The novel pictures the perfect interweaving of two texts: the Torah passages coexist peacefully alongside the emerging "text" of the Guest's name.[19] In the plot of the novel, it is the prior text of Scripture that shapes the youth, who finds himself *in* the letters of Torah, although there is at least an implicit tension here between the authoritative text of Torah and the name of the writer-to-be as a text potential within it, a reading on the verge of becoming a writing.

This depiction of a harmony of texts carries through to the level of character, as we see in the Guest's recollection of the aura of light that surrounded his father and the men of the community as they prayed in the synagogue. That recollected radiance embraces father, communal structure and sacred text in the aura of the divine.[20]

Suggestions of a portrait of the youthful artist in the making disrupt this radiant circle. The Guest recalls his efforts as a young man to write his own words of poetry in the House of Study at a time when he was supposed to be studying the Torah. In this initial assertion of artistic individuality, the House of Study occupies a space defined by the texts it houses, primary among them the Torah; within this territory, the would-be poet attempts a writing that is a violation of the space it traverses, transgression in effect of the preexisting text.

As part of the Guest's narrative of atonement, these recollections correct his own youthful wish to become a writer in opposition to his father's wish that he become a rabbi. In effect, the Guest as narrator depicts the experience of return in terms that suggest absorption into the preexisting texts of sacred literature. Through his return, the

Guest attempts to undo that youthful departure by reintegrating himself into the fabric of texts that constitute Jewish tradition. Thus, for example, he cites a legend about the spirits of departed scholars who continue the studies they engaged in when they were alive. The citation enables him to formulate his custodianship of the House of Study as a rescue mission that will save the books from oblivion and revivify tradition so that it is not just the dead who study.

Birth and Rebirth

Nevertheless, return to Torah, on the model of the infant's perfect knowledge, is the fiction of the Guest who knows, as narrator, that transgression or departure is essential to utterance. This doubleness or even duplicity in the narrative accounts for multiple plots that coexist uneasily in the text. With self-conscious awkwardness, the Guest indirectly directs our attention to one such subplot involving the birth of an infant who is, in many ways, his spiritual heir and whose birth is figured in light of the wise infant image. It is no accident that the Guest speaks of himself as the son of kings just before he meets Rachel, the innkeeper's daughter, and has a conversation with her in which she rejects his suggestion that she take up the burden of tradition by looking upon herself as the daughter of a king. Despite Rachel's forceful rejection of the Guest's suggestion and the reality of her impregnation by her husband, Yeruham Hofshi, the Guest's narrative compiles hints that point to a fantasy in which it is he who impregnates Rachel, producing an offspring who takes his place in the symbolic scheme we have been tracing.[21]

A confluence of narrative strategies, including the Guest's *sotto voce* expressions of illicit interest in Rachel, provides a subplot that casts the newborn infant as the Guest's production (while leaving no doubt, all the while, that this is fantasy). The child comes into the world through the mediation of the substitute key, an aid to childbirth that the Guest provides; the child bears the name of the Guest and also, in the Guest's eyes, incarnates the legendary wise infant who possesses in utero the entirety of the Torah. Thus, the infant's birth suggests that new life has come to the town through the Guest's mediation. Even further, as his namesake, the infant assumes an equivalence to the Guest that suggests that the Guest has achieved the rebirth he had come back to his birthplace to accomplish.

These multiple significances converge at the circumcision ceremony, at which the Guest is godfather, filling a role his grandfather had played for the town's newborns. While admitting that he lacks the perfect piety of his grandfather, he hints that this will be remedied through his "son," for he perceives in the newborn the living out of the legend of the infant's knowledge of Torah when it is in its mother's belly:

> And as soon as he (the infant) remembered those days when he was settled in goodness and he was taught the entirety of the Torah a smile rose to his lips. He wanted to go over his studies and forgot what he had learned. He opened his mouth and began to seek with his tongue. He felt the mark on his upper lip where the angel had hit him on his mouth and caused him to forget the entirety of the Torah. He stirred and began to cry. [1968a, 460; 1968, 4:429]

The child brings closer to life the legend that the narrator had earlier applied, metaphorically and wishfully, to his own return to the House of Study [1968a, 108; 1968, 4:106]. At this later point, the infant embodies the rebirth he would like to believe he has undergone. (The angel's mark helps along this elevation of the text by recalling the mark and consequent speech defect that the legendary infant Moses acquired when he touched a hot coal to his mouth.) That the Guest views the child as the missing link can be seen as well in the gift he chooses for it: he gives his namesake the key to the House of Study and suggests that he is passing on the unifying power contained in it: "They say in the *Gemara*, 'Houses of Worship and Houses of Study that are outside the Land are destined to establish themselves in the Land of Israel,' happy is he who has the key in his hand and can open and enter" [1968a, 462; 1968, 4:431].

Text as Key

A manuscript with a history of its own plays a significant role in this saga of regeneration, return, and life-giving substitutes. Through a seemingly minor component of the plot involving a question as to the authenticity of a manuscript, the novel engages questions of authorship and the power of writing, particularly the power of a later text or transcription, as opposed to that of an earlier or original text. The use in the plot of this manuscript, titled *Yadav shel Moshe* or *Hands of Moses*, ties together the themes of birth and regeneration with issues of writing and texts. The manuscript *Hands of Moses* had long been used as an amulet to aid in difficult childbirths. Relatively early on in the novel, two old women come to see the Guest to ask him to sell the manuscript, since the dying town, in which births no longer occur, has no need of it. He notes its medicinal odor and stained pages, tangible evidence of its life-giving history, but feels some discomfort with it: it does not strike him as being the authentic manuscript, written by the hand of the sage. Indeed, thumbing through it, he discovers that it is a transcription, carried out by a disciple. How can a manuscript that is not original possess the life-giving powers of the original, he wonders:

> I turned the pages and went back and delved into it a bit here and there. The words were the living words of God. Not for nothing had the book been accepted in all the reaches of Israel. Nevertheless I didn't feel anything more in it than a man would who held an ordinary manuscript in his hand. It occurred to me that this wasn't the handwriting of the author. But if this wasn't the handwriting of the Righteous Man, how had women been saved by it? [1968a, 233; 1968, 4:218].

The Guest forces the question, I would suggest, in order to bring to the fore the question of the potency of texts, originals and copies. The question of whether this manuscript is the original or a copy parallels the motif of the key in the novel: the Guest accepts the key to the *beit midrash* from the town's residents as a signal of acceptance of responsibility for that house of study; however, he promptly loses it and has to have a *substitute* key made. (The manufacture of the substitute key is an enterprise in itself that takes the Guest in search of the locksmith.) The motifs of manuscript and key converge when the women of the town, trying to help Rachel in her labor, come to the Guest in search of the old manuscript. When that cannot be found, they ask for a succession of legendarily potent keys to synagogue and House of Study, which brings them ultimately to the Guest's substitute key. The substitution of key for manuscript makes clear the equivalency between them. It is the last in the series, the substitute key to the *beit midrash*, that enables the birth to take place and implies an answer to the question of the novel: can a later substitute work as well as a lost original?

Ultimately, it is the *substitute* key (or the later text, one might say) that eases the labor of the young woman who gives birth to the child who is the Guest's namesake and spiritual heir. The later substitute—the key—shares in the life-giving capacities of the earlier text—the *Hands of Moses*—which was itself a substitute, that is, a transcription of an even earlier text. As a result, questions of manuscript authenticity and originality blur. Distinctions between earlier and later, original and copy, recede in importance in light of a more generalized fiction of textuality that endows even latter-day copies of lost originals with life-giving potencies. The series of substitutions involving manuscript, copy of manuscript, key, and substitute key supports the view of the novel itself as a restorative first person account of a year's journey of renewal.

In effect, the Guest is not just "father" to the child, he is also the child itself, the product of the "renewal" that was the project of his year's stay in the town. Through this birth, then, the narrative suggests that the Guest has become his own life-giving text and given birth to himself. "He" is his text, the document through which we know him. Rachel's birth pangs, alleviated by the (substitute) key, are the analogues of the stages of the quest that the narrator must pass through in order to give birth to "himself," that is, to his discourse—the novel we read. This is the culmination of the imagery of rebirth and the attempt of the text to go beyond itself, to retrieve a mythic linguistic capacity.

In both *A Guest for the Night* and in the short story "A Whole Loaf," the question of the authenticity of a predecessor text arises. In each, the power of the prior text is unquestioned; that is, both Dr. Ne'eman's book and the manuscript *Hands of Moses* are credited with the capacity to do good in the world. (See chapter 3.) In *A Guest for the Night*, doubts about manuscript authenticity accompany a demonstration of the capacity of the very manuscript in question to relieve suffering; this narrative coincidence creates support for the possibility that a later text can share in the potency of its predecessors. Through the story of the manuscript "Hands of Moses," the novel thematizes its own effort to retrieve a lost linguistic potency.

"Moses" forms the link between "A Whole Loaf" and *A Guest for the Night* in this respect. It is scarcely insignificant that Dr. Ne'eman is a Moses figure and that the holy book with which the Guest is entrusted bears the name of Moses in its title. In both, it is the faithful servant of God who transmits the restorative word. "Moses" constitutes something of a meeting ground for the human and the divine, uniting an ideal of creativity and of tradition in a writing that is no longer just writing. In effect, the narrator of the novel attempts to lift his text into a frame that is not at all secondary or derivative, but capable of generating new life.

Multiple Endings

Is that the final claim of the novel? *A Guest for the Night* provides us with the evidence of this attempt to transform the novel into a life-giving utterance, but that is by no means the whole story. Multiple endings, each the outcome of a strand in the novel, all contribute to the potential number of interpretations of the novel's resolution, so that the reader assumes a particularly active role. Structurally, the narrative moves self-consciously towards a fruition that is the product of natural and religious cycles. The Guest's sojourn in the town falls into a cycle of seasonal renewal, that is also marked by the major dates in the Jewish calendar.

The quest must seem to unfold through the seasons of the year in as natural a manner as the progression of Rachel's pregnancy. Hence, the importance of arriving in Szybucz on the eve of the Day of Atonement that falls in autumn, as the world enters into the period of death that is winter. The passing of winter finds its narrative correlative in the burial of Hanokh the wagoneer. The burial of Hanokh is followed immediately by signs of spring, underscored by the narrator's thoughts about the approaching holiday of Passover, celebration of freedom and the spring harvest. The holiday of Shavuot marks the next stage of his emergence; this festival of the first fruits and of the giving of the Torah brings with it an invitation to visit a group of young people who live at the "village of preparation," a kind of kibbutz in the Diaspora, where youths work the land of a gentile farmer in order to train themselves for emigration to Israel. While the Guest's excursion to this ideal community may point up indirectly the inconsistencies in his own commitments, it also signals his emergence from absorption in the House of Study.[22]

Perhaps the final touch is the Guest's departure from Szybucz on the ninth of Av. In a powerful coalescence of religious, seasonal, and biographical motifs, the Guest leaves the town in the fullness of summer on the date that commemorates the destruction of the Temple, and also anticipates its renewal; it is, additionally, his birthday. The effect of the fiction is deepened if we remind ourselves that the ninth of Av is the date Agnon chose to designate as his birthday. (The novelistic fiction, in this instance, reinforces the autobiographical fiction.) From the eve of the Day of Atonement on which the novel opened with the narrator's return, to the ninth of Av, which marks his departure, nine months trace his rebirth.

Nevertheless, the project of restoration supported by this cyclical structure is undercut in the novel's concluding description of the Guest's return to Palestine and his resumption of family life. When his wife finds the original old key to the House of Study in his baggage, the Guest dismisses its importance and so undermines his yearlong involvement in and narration of his mission to save the House of Study.[23] He settles, as indeed he must, for symbolic solutions, for compromises that point up the incompleteness of his quest. Citing the legend that, one day, all Houses of Study will come to the land of Israel, he allots to himself a passive role as he declares his intention to watch and wait for that to happen. This explicit renunciation of an active role and acceptance of the observer's stance (always implicit in his role as *guest*) is echoed in the manner in which he disposes of the key. It is too heavy for the heart to bear, he tells us, and so he locks it away in a box and carries with him, instead, the key to the box. He settles for a representation of a representation, in effect for the rendition of the story that we read.

Additionally, the "digressive" subplots of the text produce a variety of endings that open and close, parody and fulfill, the questions about word and world, text and context that the novel has raised. Let us briefly consider several of these "endings." Reb Shlomo Bach appears at the start of the novel as a guardian figure when the Guest accepts the key to the House of Study. Through the novel, Reb Shlomo's directedness toward the promised land supplies an ironic counterpoint to the Guest's efforts to turn to Szybucz as the solution to his dilemma.[24] At the end of the novel, both the Guest and Reb Shlomo find themselves in Erets Yisrael, but with a difference. Reb Shlomo takes his dead son's place in a communal settlement, where he discovers that when he cannot understand a passage in the *Mishnah*, he can unravel it by going outdoors and listening to young people converse or by talking to a gardener. He understands why it is said that "There is no Torah like the Torah of the land of Israel," [1968a, 473; 1968, 4:442] where word and world interpenetrate to form one encompassing text. His study bears fruit, literally and figuratively, when he becomes the caretaker of a garden and finds in it tangible evidence of the approaching redemption of Israel.[25] Reb Shlomo continues the idealization of working the land found in the young people at the "village of preparation," but combines that idealization of labor with living a life according to Torah. The effect is a view of the land redeemed as a text come to life.

The wholeness of Reb Shlomo (who is, in this respect, aptly named) is not to be found in a number of splintered characters who populate the novel. The union of text and world that he embodies is inverted in a minor figure in the novel, Lebtche Bodenhaus. This relatively minor character sits in his room, beneath a picture of Moses, aptly enough, translating the Pentateuch into rhymed German verse. His "project" suggests a pathetic model of text production that not only parodies the Guest's ambitions, but brings to mind the *Biur*, the eighteenth-century project to use a translation of the Torah into German, retaining Hebrew lettering, as a way of secularizing German Jews. Are we to read Lebtche Bodenhaus as a parody of Moses Mendelssohn and the hopes of the Enlightenment for an integration of Jews and Judaism into the secular world? If so, the parody makes us feel keenly the discrepancy between those naive hopes of the Enlightenment and the subsequent history of Jews in Europe to which the novel's characters testify in abundance.

It is certainly instructive to note that while Lebtche may appear initially as a caricature of the naive artist, he tells a harrowing tale of confrontation between man's healing powers and the brutality of the real world that demolishes any hope for reconciliation of the two: he tells of a battlefield doctor who put back together, with ingenious bits of prosthesis, a soldier who had been torn apart in battle; forced to release to the world his fragile and dependent patient, the doctor attaches a card with instructions for proper care to the young soldier's neck who, shortly thereafter, is thrust from his seat in a wagon by a German soldier and is left on his own to perish. Thus, Lebtche, whose occupation at the time of the novel expresses a childlike faith in art, offers a tale of the power of art to make things whole again and of the impotence of that art once it ventures forth into a world populated by German soldiers.

While Lebtche appears initially as a gentle parody of the writer, he touches upon a central aspect of the Guest's attempted transformation of reality. The power of the imagination is the healing power that the artist brings to the world; its energies may be directed towards the task of repairing the broken ark in which the Torah resides in our time. If the artist could truly summon it forth, he would be able to restore the flawed figures who greet him on entry into Szybucz. But while art can fashion a rubber hand or a wooden leg, these devices fail to provide their "wearers" with substantial remedies for the "horrors" that necessitate their contrivance.

Indeed, the sickliness of the imagination—its inability to translate its beautiful schemes into life—finds its embodiment in little Rafael Bach, grandson of Reb Shlomo. This child is described in terms that suggest that he is both an incarnation of the infant in the Torah legend, and at the same time, a creature incapable of sustaining normal life: "At first glance he appeared as a child and at second glance like a youth, and at third glance neither like a child nor a youth, but as a container of skin and flesh into which the Creator has stuck two burning eyes" [1968a, 136; 1968, 4:131]. With these eyes, little Rafael sees visions of life and death and spins tales of fantasy that suggest holy visions; he does so, however, from a sickbed which he cannot leave. There is irony in his name, for Rafael means "God heals" and all the protagonist's efforts to "heal the broken instruments of our spirit" cannot bring Rafael out of that bed into life. This child suggests the potency of the imagination or spirit, and yet its inability to move out into the world and cure the ills of the age.[26]

Thus, the project of regeneration is counterposed to the sense of the secondariness of writing, of its lack of life or potency. It is just this latter devaluation of writing that punctuates the novel and undercuts the mythopoeic impulse. The narrator proceeds from the legend of the infant poet to note that he and those of his generation no longer possess the strength of such as this *payyetan* [1968a, 448; 1968, 4:419]. We have strayed from the activity of writing down what our master laid before us, he says. Nothing that was created in the first six days of the world was meant to undergo any change from its original function, a precept, he notes, that certainly applies to writing.

The novel, then, posits repair as it demonstrates its own state of disrepair. It attempts to go beyond itself while acting out the limitations or, one might say, the conditions of its being. Variations on the theme of the infant's knowledge point to timeless perfection; the narrative itself resides in time and so constitutes and deconstitutes itself endlessly. In this, it is very much the novel of the artist, the occasion for the working through, the playing out of the role of the creative figure. The artist has the capacity to glimpse past wholeness, but he cannot yield himself up to it without undoing his very nature as artist and so losing himself.

It is interesting to consider, in this respect, Agnon's contributions to *Sefer Buczacz* (*The Book of Buczacz*), a memorial volume completed after the destruction of the town's Jewish community. As a memoir, it is not the occasion for the expression of conflict and so, at the outset, he very pointedly excludes his personal mythos from the endeavor:

> Out of a love of order, to give each thing in its place, I will tell in another place how I left my town and for what reason I left my town

> and what I found in all those places for whose sake I left my town. Here in this place I will tell of what I found on the day that I returned to my town and what happened to my town between departure and my return. [Cohen 1968, 9]

By virtue of this exclusion, the memoir becomes the occasion for a portrayal of the wholeness of the town and its harmonious relationship with the Creator. Once the competitive artist-creator is out of the way, Eden can, in fact (or at least in fiction), be restored. Indeed Agnon places the town within the context of a very old legend. He describes the worthiness of the citizens of Buczacz to receive the Messiah, who was on his way there and would have arrived had he not been misled en route. This claim for the spiritual completeness of the town must be understood in the context of the Zohar's suggestion that redemption would become possible if only one Jewish town were entirely repentant [Scholem 1954, 250]. Utterly destroyed in reality, the town becomes the myth, the book of its past, the roster of its inhabitants and their achievements. *A Guest for the Night*, by contrast, is the book of the artist, who feeds upon the town as a central source of his creativity, but continues endlessly to play out the terms of his separation from it.

Thus, we see that the journey of return has involved the virtually impossible effort on the narrator's part to abandon his separate identity as a writer, a writer who no longer transcribes what his master laid before him; through devotion to and even immersion in the House of Study, he attempts to break down the terms of his isolation and rejoin the life of Torah, to abandon his use of language in order to recapture the lost or hidden alphabet of creation. The novel that we read, however, testifies to his failure. Consider this medieval variant on the Midrash of the wise infant. Why, asks Eleazar of Worms, a thirteenth-century mystic, does the child forget his knowledge of Torah? "Because if it did not forget, the course of this world would drive it to madness if it thought about it in the light of what it knew" [Scholem 1954, 92]. The figure of the writer stands in the middle between forgetting and remembering, unable to complete either movement and perhaps defining himself through the tension between them; the novel responds to that tension in reflecting both the necessary forgetting that goes into the life of the individual in the world and the longing to remember, to go back and recapture. It is perhaps in this sense that Agnon has forged a particularly modern scripture whose very fraudulence in one sense renders it authentic in another.

Chapter

6

Inclusion and Exclusion: Three Stories

> Not like all other tongues is the holy tongue, for all the other tongues are only conventional, as nation after nation agreed upon its tongue, but in the holy tongue the Torah was given and with it the Holy One Blessed be He created the world.
>
> Agnon "The Sense of Smell"

Invoking Hebrew as the language out of which the world was formed, Agnon draws on a myth of language in which word is deed. This sense of the originary character of sacred language is deeply rooted in mystical and rabbinic sources. Genesis Rabbah 1:2, for example, relates that God looked into the Torah for the blueprint of creation, an approach to language and text that indicates "a belief in the omnisignificance of Torah," to borrow David Stern's phrase [1988, 150].[1] This conception of sacred language stands in diametric opposition to mundane languages whose relation to the world is conventional. "Conventional" can be taken in Saussurean terms, as referring to sign systems in which the relationship of signifier to signified is arbitrary and unmotivated. The tension between these two conceptions of language can help us to understand a certain dynamic in Agnon's short stories, where we find both affirmation and negation of a relation to language.

In three short stories of the 1930s, writing, texts, and relations between texts move into the foreground of attention to become elements of plot, disclosing dramas of what I propose to call "inclusion" and "exclusion." Inclusion implies fit on a number of levels: fit of word and thing, writer and community, text and tradition, whereas exclusion suggests an inevitable disharmony, displacement, or distance from the source.

The epigraph to this chapter, Agnon's statement of the originary chapter of Hebrew, comes from a 1934 story: the story, "*Ḥush hareaḥ*" ("The Sense of Smell") is itself steeped in references to traditional texts and approaches to them, but it also plays with those texts and uses them to position itself in relation to sacred language. This short story discloses and even unravels a mystique of language, which nevertheless continues to function as a source of structure in it.

An unraveler of more recent vintage, Jacques Derrida takes issue with a concept of an originary language in which word and thing are given, when he asserts that "In the beginning was hermeneutics" [1978, 67]. His playfully allusive phrasing works as a provocation, jostling the theological certainty of an originary Word by insisting on the traces of interpretation in it. While Agnon does not simply move in the direction of Derrida's deconstructive play, his writing enacts a double move that allows for an interrogation from within of value-laden structures, while sustaining their importance to the text.

Two stories of the 1930s, "'*Al even aḥat*" ("Upon a Stone") and "*Ḥush hareaḥ*" ("The Sense of Smell"), evoke predecessor texts in order to invoke the world-defining capacities of earlier writings and to position themselves in relation to them. Their seeming achievement of inclusion, however tentative it may be, allows for a slightly broader glimpse of the structure of language, text, God, and nation out of which Agnon's literary efforts take shape. In between the readings of these two stories, I have placed a discussion of a story that is their very different contemporary. "*Hate'udah*" or "The Document" [1932], one of the stories collected in "*Sefer hama'asim*" or "The Book of Deeds," offers a disjointed narrative that takes shape around a central representation of an unidentified text.[2]

"'*Al even aḥat*" ("Upon a Stone") and "*Ḥush hareaḥ*" ("The Sense of Smell") offer tales of the writer that occupy a middle ground between the early stories of Hemdat, the artist as youth (see for example, "*Giv'at haḥol*" or "Hill of Sand"), and "*Sefer hama'asim*," the book of deeds in which nothing happens, but the act of telling itself. With the model of the world-containing language of Torah before him, Agnon enacts the attempt and failure to attain the linguistic level of the sacred. Or, as in "Upon a Stone" and "The Sense of Smell," he enacts brief moments of participation that appear to lift language beyond itself, but are essentially mock-heroic. That is, the text adumbrates a move by which it will try (and fail) to transform itself.

Tale of a Text: "Upon a Stone"

"Upon a Stone," written in 1934, mimics a passage in the *Sefer Shivḥe habesht* ("The Book of Praises of the Baal Shem Tov"). The *Sefer shivḥe habesht* is a compilation of stories of the Besht, acronym for the Baal Shem Tov, the eighteenth-century holy man, around whose life and works Hasidism developed; while the Besht wrote nothing down, his followers recorded his deeds and tales. In the source passage in *Shivḥe habesht* [Horodetzky 1975, 51], the Baal Shem Tov apostrophizes a stone, addressing it directly, so that it opens up and he can place his writings in it. Without ever explicitly referring to the Baal Shem Tov, Agnon's story invokes this act of enclosure in a variety of ways that may make us aware of the story of the Besht as well as of other stories of wonder-working rabbis. This relationship to a predecessor who possesses wonder-working capacities or, for that matter, to a singularly endowed predecessor text, constitutes a recurring narrative impetus and something of a paradigm for Agnon.[3]

The first person narrator of "Upon a Stone" is a writer, but he opens his story by referring to the days in which he devoted himself to study of the deeds of the wonder-working Rabbi Adam Baal Shem, a predecessor of the Baal Shem Tov, who used the holy writings in his possession to bring about the redemption of souls in Israel. As the narrator presents it, his position is more transcriber than it is writer. He identifies himself as a writer by delineating his distance from the kind of linguistic power with which the Rabbi Adam Baal Shem's holy writings endowed him: "Indeed even if I did not attain to reading in them [the rabbi's wonder-working texts], I attained to telling about them" [1968, 2:303]. Those writings do not belong to the roots of his soul, as he puts it, and so he cannot possess their world-creating powers. The Rabbi Adam Baal Shem used his writing to enact miracles; the story that we read can only testify to its distance from that sort of language use.

"Upon a Stone" mounts a genealogy of texts, within which the earlier text has priority over its belated successor: the predecessor can bring about the union of word and deed, but the later text can only tell the story of such miraculous events. Nevertheless, while "Upon a Stone" acknowledges its belatedness as successor text, it also subverts that genealogy. This "subversion" occurs insofar as "Upon a Stone" moves away from merely *telling* and toward *reenactment* of an important segment of the story of Rabbi Adam Baal Shem. The narrator may open "Upon a Stone" with an acknowledgement of the spatial and temporal distance that separates his use of language from that of the wonder-working rabbi, but the narrative shifts emphasis in a way that suggests a move toward substitution.

In a seemingly pious image, our narrator depicts himself as the metal that surrounds or encases precious jewels, but does not mingle in substance with the precious jewels (the earlier texts) that it holds: "I would sit and look at them [every letter, word, column and page of the Rabbi's writings] and my eyes would surround them like a metal that surrounds precious stones and the precious stones do not mingle with it" [1968, 2:303]. The picture of the metal as container appears to indicate the separateness that defines the stance of the narrator. On closer scrutiny, however, the image offers a provocative ambiguity. Picturing the narrator as container for the precious jewels of Rabbi Adam Baal Shem's texts speaks ostensibly of separateness, but it does so through a figure of incorporation. Narration moves into the foreground, consuming plot along the way and drawing attention to telling as a form of action.

In apparent conformity to the conventions of his role, the narrator tells us how the Rabbi Adam Baal Shem went to the forest to give up his writings to a rock, in a pious gesture of renunciation, when the time for his death drew near. At the same time, however, through a series of highly emblematic encounters, the narrator "inadvertently" reenacts a latter-day version of this renunciation; the result is a linguistic play that mimics a mystical moment in which word and world are fused. This reenactment or move toward substitution begins when the narrator takes his own writing to the woods, just as he is approaching the point in his work at which he will describe Rabbi Adam Baal Shem's move to the forest to give up his writing.

The move outdoors brings the narrator into nature, God's book writ large, where he sees a world that is indeed in harmony with its Creator. Not only animals, but every bush as well converses with its Maker, he notes with word plays that are lost in translation, but suggest the mingling of word and thing: "*Kol siyaḥ mesiyaḥ im hamaqom*" ("Every field-shrub converses with the Omnipresent") [1968, 2:303]. The spelling of shrub, *s-y-ḥ*, is the same as the root for "converse," suggesting the sort of playing with homonymous roots that is widely used in midrashic interpretation. In addition, the term for God (*hamaqom*) also indicates place: God is place and place is God, a further suggestion of the unity of God and nature. The language play of the later text, that is, the one we read, establishes the unity of God and nature that constitutes the divine text.

But the narrator as writer finds himself situated ambiguously between the traditionally structured world that is governed by God's law and his devotion to his own labors, specifically, his writing. This split becomes evident as plot complications set up a suggestive opposition between, on the one hand, the Sabbath with its prohibition on transgressing the *teḥum* and on the other, the narrator's attachment to his writings, which have remained in the forest outside the *teḥum*. (The *teḥum* is a communal boundary within which certain actions, otherwise forbidden on the Sabbath, may be carried out.) Writing is an activity that threatens transgression of the *teḥum*, all the more so the narrator's writings that refuse to remain within one structure. In fact, the narrator's dilemma demands choice between devotion to his own texts or to God's. Lest we overlook the parallel, the narrator reminds us that six days of labor have gone into the creation of each: "If I go to the town, I will end up forfeiting everything I accomplished in six days, and if I go to the forest the holy Sabbath will come in and I will not come in with it" [1968, 2:304]. In a manner reminiscent of midrashic hermeneutics, the nouns that indicate his alternatives are anagrams of each other: play with the *y-ʿ-r* of *yaʿar* or forest produces the *ʿ-y-r* of *ʿir* or city. The presence of this kind of anagrammatic play in Agnon's text contextualizes the narrator's dilemma in a tradition of interpretation and suggests that the solution will consist of still further interpretation.

In a passage that begs the question of intentionality, the narrator records the resolution of his dilemma: "As I stood deliberating in my mind my legs picked themselves up and went to the forest" [1968, 2:304]. The narrator returns to the forest to find his writings exactly as he left them on the rock, miraculously undisturbed by wind or beast or bird. But as he stands there gazing at his texts, the stone opens up, takes in his writings and closes again. God's world, God's language, exerts its priority over man in the enclosure of his texts.

The narrator's loss of control over his own texts resembles the voluntary action of his predecessor, the Rabbi Adam Baal Shem, who entrusted his texts to God by acquiescing in their enclosure in a stone. The narrator's texts may not be as wonderful, and his relinquishing of control over them may not come of his own volition, but, in reduced form (appropriate to our time, Agnon might say), the parallel remains.

The outcome of the narrator's instance of yielding is an enchanting moment of conscious participation in the harmony of nature. In effect, the narrator tells the story of his achievement of inclusion: "I surrounded the stones with my eyes, like the dirt of the land that surrounds the stone" [1968, 2:304]. The verb *h-q-f* is used for the movement of his eyes that "encompass" the surroundings; it is used again for the earth that "encompasses" the rocks he sees before him. The verb is central to the action here, which is more the drama of language in Creation than any conventional notion of plot. The narrator first used the verb *h-q-f* for the image of his relationship to Rabbi Adam Baal Shem's texts; "And my eyes encompassed them like the metal that surrounds precious stones . . ." [p. 303]; at that earlier point, he imagines enclosing the texts visually, but acknowledges his inability to read them. By contrast, the later usage affirms his enclosure in God's world/text; the narrator achieves a marvelous "fit" into the world, although his eyes as recording instrument retain the capacity and thus identity of the observer: the eye of the "I" sustains a difference that is crucial to the production of narrative.

Narrative is predicated on the difference between the teller and the tale, or teller and told. This is the difference between the subject of the enunciation and the subject of the utterance, a difference that persists even when speaker and protagonist are nominally the same, as in first person narrative. Accordingly, the narrator of "Upon a Stone" may speak of his enclosure, but it is the very fact of speech that preserves him from absorption into the scene that he describes. The eye of the "I" is the "I" of enunciation.

At the same time, a landscape opens before the narrator in which language forms the world and it no longer matters which rock has enclosed the narrator's particular texts. The model and the context for this unfolding landscape are to be found in mysticism; Gershom Scholem has shown us that it is the particular nature of Jewish mysticism to utilize the very notions of text, writing, even the letters of the alphabet as the vehicle for (rather than the obstacle to) communion with the divine. These features of textuality are not discarded or surpassed, but rather are incorporated and transformed into a more encompassing textuality constituted by the world-forming text of Torah. Thus, Scholem [1971, 293] speaks of the language "which lives in things as their creative principle"; "the secret signatures (*rissumim*) that God had placed upon things are as much concealments of his revelation as revelation of His concealment." The narrative energies of "Upon a Stone" are directed towards just such a moment of revelation in which narrative defies momentarily the condition of its being to mount a fantasy of a move through and beyond language.

The text of "Upon a Stone" appears to bring about a shift in its status: no longer dissociated from the wonder-working capacities of earlier texts, it reconstitutes itself as a survivor text that recounts the story of its own lost predecessor text. This relationship of survivor to predecessor fits the model established by the folk tradition of tales that recount the deeds of wonder-working rabbis. Agnon's text redefines itself to join the Besht story or the story of the Rabbi Adam Baal Shem as one more story of miraculous deeds told, at a narrative distance, by a follower or latecomer. Like the texts of the Rabbi Adam Baal Shem (and, for that matter, the writings of the Besht that were sealed in a stone), Agnon's predecessor text appears to be lost to us; nevertheless, according to the model, enclosure in a rock expresses the surrender that is piety. The predecessor text may be lost as text, but it has been absorbed back into God's text.

But of course Agnon's predecessor text is a *fiction*, a narrative fantasy that is produced by the story we read. By generating the fiction of a predecessor text and telling a story of miraculous enclosure or absorption into God's prior text, the Agnon text defines itself on the basis of contiguity and so enlarges the compass of tradition to include itself. Through these narrative maneuvers, "Upon a Stone" manages the delicate suggestion that it has remained within the *teḥum* itself, has refrained from transgression and has thus achieved the exquisite moment of participation in a linguistic universe with which the story closes.

If we turn to the *Sefer shivḥe habesht*, *The Book of the Besht* or Baal Shem Tov, we find that the holy writings that the Besht possesses go back to the time of Abraham and Joshua [Horodetzky 1975, 51]. Their magical powers stem from their antiquity or closeness to the world-creating language of Torah. "Upon a Stone" deepens its linguistic roots through its use of a tale from *The Book of the Besht*. We might also keep in mind that "Baal Shem," a title that long predates the rise of Hasidism, designates one "who knows the secret of the Tetragrammaton pronounced, as well as other 'holy names' and also knows how to work miraculous deeds with the power of these names" [Scholem 1962]. In telling the story of the Baal Shem Tov's capacity to perform magical deeds with the writings, the narrator of *The Book of the Besht* (*Sefer shivḥe habesht*) tells a story of the collapse of difference, the transformation of word into deed.

Aryeh Wineman [1978] notes a significant difference between the source story in *The Book of the Besht* and "Upon a Stone": in *The Book of the Besht*, the Rabbi Adam Baal Shem designates the Rabbi Israel of Okopy (who was later to become the Baal Shem Tov) as the recipient of his writings, that is, the one who will retrieve them from the rock. Thus, the earlier story sets up a structure that implies transmission of the texts in question to a spiritual heir. In contrast, Agnon's story simply recounts the sealing of the Rabbi Adam Baal Shem's writings in a rock. Wineman concludes that Agnon omits this portion of the Besht story in order to imply that his narrator, unlike the Besht, is not fit to receive the holy writings of the Rabbi Adam Baal Shem. Insofar as Agnon's story mimics an existing narrative pattern, Wineman's comments draw the reader's attention to an omission in the story's structure, a kind of negative space that produces meaning by making us aware of what Agnon has left out. Agnon's text enacts a fiction of inclusion that conceals within it acknowledgment of its marginality.

A Different Writing: "The Document"

The designation of "Upon a Stone" as a text of inclusion comes from the explicit identification in it of writings that sustain a vital link to the Torah through the activities of prayer, study and commentary. In "Upon a Stone" and, as we shall see, in "The Sense of Smell," moments of inclusion are carefully engineered and briefly achieved, indicating a measure of participation in the space defined by a geography of texts. In contrast to "Upon a Stone" and "The Sense of Smell," the stories of "The Book of Deeds" invert the structure of inclusion to picture exclusion; relationships to predecessor texts (which are less explicitly identified as sacred writing) function oppressively. In "*Sefer hama'asim*," texts such as "*Pat shlemah*" ("A Whole Loaf"), "*Hefqer*" ("Renunciation"), "*Hate'udah*" ("The Document") speak their ambivalence to tradition, as they shrug off the burdens of relationship to the texts of the past.

"*Hate'udah*" ("The Document"), written in 1932, centers on the speaker's reluctant efforts to obtain the document that gives the story its title. This first person speaker receives a call for assistance that is presented so as to emphasize that he will be aiding someone other than himself yet somehow related to him: "My relative so-and-so, whom I didn't even know by name, wrote to me from a city of which I didn't even know that there was such a one in the world that I should go to that office and get a document for him on which his whole life depended" [1970, 68; 1968, 6:114]. Syntax here sustains a tortuous link between the protagonist and a text that is identified as both vital to another person and remote from the speaker himself.

This first sentence initiates a "dance" of the document: summoned, by his own account, to the task or even mission of obtaining the document, the speaker records his own reluctance, false moves, and failed initiatives.

But what of this "document" itself? The unspecified document constitutes the sole link between the speaker and his unknown relative who lives in an unknown place, a link moreover that forms the basis for a life-or-death plea. This is, then, no ordinary piece of paper, nor is the choice of noun that designates it an innocent one. In its faceless urgency, this "document" finds a place among the official papers of twentieth-century mass society. At the same time, it also fits a more traditionally rooted conception of the central "document" through which the Jewish people sustains its identity. Intertextual evidence supports an association of the *te'udah*—the "document" that places such a strong moral obligation on the narrator—and the Torah. The association of Torah and *te'udah* is not new; see, for example, Isa. 8:16: "Bind up the testimony (*te'udah*), seal the teaching (*torah*) among my disciples." Agnon's narrative exploits the history of the word from the Biblical equivalence with *torah* or "teaching" to documents of identification in the bureaucratic mazes of the twentieth-century, as in *te'udat zehut* or "identity card."

The word *te'udah* is the stimulus for an intertextual expansion of the narrative. Its various usages are activated by the narrative to produce a particularly biting satire of bureaucracy and writing. There are enough hints in "The Document" of shared characteristics between *te'udah* and Torah to support the elaboration of the intertextual link: the *te'udah* is an official document; a whole organization exists in "The Document" to handle matters pertaining to the word, an organization that can be perceived as a debased and depersonalized form of the priesthood. From the central (but *absent*) text that gives the story its title, a structure can be articulated that both mimics and parodies the hierarchy of Jewish ritual life.

Nevertheless, on the paradigmatic axis of possible nouns, the Torah remains a possible rather than a necessary identification in Agnon's story. The invocation of "Torah" does not cause a substitution that would involve condensation or the collapse of one term into another. Agnon's *te'udah* remains an ambiguously defined document. The story may be dream*like*, but it maintains a difference from dream structure in which condensation does collapse identifications into a single term.[4]

The narrator of "The Document" tells us he spends three days in the "office of the gray bureaucracy" [1970, 68; 1968, 6:114], and during that time he is unable to utter the "official" words of the humble supplicant that his mission necessitates. To whom do the words belong? This drama of the utterance engages a conflict over language use. The physical symptoms that he cites to explain away his immobility center on the speech organs, and thus center the conflict in the use of language: "I was aching in my throat and in my whole body, nevertheless I got up early" [1970, 68; 1968, 6:114]. As a first person narrative, the story contains within it a representation of the act of speech, implicating narration itself in the conflict that the story dramatizes. Through the story of his own ambivalence, the narrator places himself at a distance from the potentially redemptive use of language with which the story opens. Indeed, at one point the speaker sees someone whom he identifies as a fellow "countryman" by the name of "Nahman Horodenker," which happens to be the name of the grandfather of Rabbi Nahman of Bratslav. This very indirect reference to Rabbi Nahman's wondrous narrative capacities may serve here to underscore our own speaker's limitations.

The last section of "The Document" shifts abruptly from the bureaucracy that has occupied it to a scene that can be read almost as an inversion of the linguistic harmony and inclusion with which "Upon a Stone" ends. The speaker of "The Document" engages in a dispute with a grammarian over the derivation of one of the letters in the word *hefqer*, a word, hard to translate, that can mean "chaos" or "lawlessness." They disagree over whether the letter "*f*" or "*v*" is original to the word.[5] The linguistic nature of the question resembles the grammarian's dispute that we will examine in "The Sense of Smell"; in this instance, it goes unresolved. In an abrupt transition of the sort that characterizes "The Book of Deeds," the speaker finds himself suddenly on a porch overlooking an expanse of water.

While this sudden removal from the bureaucratic maze might promise relief, the setting itself fails to convey reassurance, transcendence or a sense of escape. The story's conclusion reads like a much distorted variant of the ending of "Upon a Stone," insofar as the moment lifts the speaker out of the constraints of his egocentric preoccupations. "The Document's" change of scene is more threatening in its vastness than it is affirmative of any higher order. The speaker is "at sea," not so much in the sense of joining in an "oceanic" feeling of oneness with the universe; rather, he is lost in a world without structure.[6] One could argue that a principle of *hefqer* or "lawlessness" enters the narrative universe at large: it can be discerned in the failure of narrative elements to cohere and to close.[7]

In his generic classification of the stories in "The Book of Deeds" as "open parables," Avraham Holtz [1973] describes the disrupted universe of the stories, in which causality, time and place become questionable. At the same time, central situations in the stories can take on metaphorical weight through their association with holy days and rituals of purification. Holtz aptly describes the reader's effort to "complete" the text and the text's frustration of that effort; as a result, the reader moves closer to the narrating "I," in the shared experience of confusion and inability to discern or create order.

If we consider the first person narratives of "The Book of Deeds," such as "The Document," in terms of the distinction between subject of the enunciation and subject of the utterance, we find that the first (the teller) exercises little if any priority or superiority over the second (the told). The reader is brought into an "open text" such as "The Document" to the extent that he or she attempts to remedy the text's disjunctiveness: the more active the reader, the more he or she moves closer to the position of subject of the enunciation and away from identification with the subject of the utterance.

Housed in a Word: "The Sense of Smell"

In contrast to the dependence on the problematic enunciation of a first person narrator that we find in "The Document," stories such as "Upon a Stone" and "The Sense of Smell" summon up "utterances" or uses of language that are prior to the texts themselves. In "Upon a Stone," the speaker describes what could almost be considered a wish: were he able to read the texts of the Rabbi Adam Baal Shem that were hidden in the rock, he would be able to "join together" worlds out of them [p. 303]. "Upon a Stone" implies levels of linguistic activity, in order of descending strength, but on the model of a world-creating use of language. "The Sense of Smell" (*Ḥush hareaḥ*"), written in 1937, enters this mythology of writing by building on the traditional belief that language is prior even to creation.

The holy tongue may be constituted in Scripture: "But the holy tongue is that in which Torah is given and with it the Holy One Blessed be He created His world, and *serafim* and *ofanim* and holy creatures praise Him in the holy tongue and even He, when He comes to praise Israel, in the holy tongue He praises them as it is written Behold, you are beautiful my love, behold you are beautiful" [1968, 2:296]. Agnon incorporates a phrase from Song of Songs, "Behold you are beautiful my love, behold you are beautiful"; in doing so, he draws also upon the rabbinic approach to that text as a figure of the relation of God to Israel. According to the Midrash, God's repetition of the phrase "Behold you are beautiful" in his address to Israel signifies his capacity to choose another nation [Song of Songs Rabbah I.16.1]. Agnon's story offers an extended exploration of language that assumes the support of Scripture and rabbinic commentary for its intertwining of God, nation, writer, and language.

"The Sense of Smell" is a story in which the persona of the author figures as speaker. He refers to himself as *meḥaber*, meaning "author," or more literally, "composer," in the sense of "joiner of words." And it is the very activity of joining words that the story brings up for question, since it is a dispute over linguistic usage that provides the stimulus for the mock-heroic text that we read. Agnon is actually making use here of an annoying incident in which he was censured publicly for incorrect word usage by a member of the National Committee on Language (*va'ad halashon*). [See Bar-Adon 1977, 165–201.] He writes a story of the author in which language assumes a central role.

Stylistically, the story is, as Arnold Band [1968, 229] notes, "deliberately archaic." Each of its seven sections bears a lengthy title that delineates a step in an argument that invokes language, a feminine presence, and draws the relationship between the *meḥaber* and language itself. The first section establishes the priority of language, even to God, and delineates the potency of language through a roster of curative, therapeutic verbs. Because of the particular nature of the Hebrew language, it becomes a moral and spiritual obligation to continue its use: "Therefore all Israel are obliged to take great care with their language that it should be clear and precise, all the more so in the last generation, close to redemption, in order that our true Messiah, may he reveal himself quickly in our time, will hear our language, and we will hear his language" [1968, 2:296]. Language is redemptive: to use the holy tongue well is to hasten the time of communal salvation, an invocation of language that implicates the poet in the fate of his people.

The second section takes its stand "Against the Wise Men of the Age Who Write in any Tongue and do not Write in the Holy Tongue." The *meḥaber* goes on to criticize as well those who do use the holy tongue, but whose usage distorts it [1968, 2:296]. The "wise men" of the time either "twist" the language even when writing simple words or they write in other languages, neglecting the holy tongue. The verb *mishtabeshim* or "distort" derives from that highly resonant verb *sh-b-sh*, to "twist" or "make crooked." The use of *sh-b-sh* here goes to the heart of the matter: the holy tongue can be used either to hasten redemption or it can be used wrongfully, with all the metaphysical weight that *mishtabeshim* carries.[8]

These elaborations of possible relations to the holy tongue provide a preface to the imaginative geography of the third section, "The Secret of Writing Stories."[9] Here the *meḥaber*—the speaker as writer—situates himself at a carefully defined distance from the Torah, via an elaboration of textual space:

> If the Holy Temple were still in existence, I would stand on the rostrum with my brothers the poets and every day I would recite the song that the Levites would recite in the Holy Temple. Now while the Holy Temple is still in its destruction and we have no Priests in their work and no Levites in their songs and their melodies, I occupy myself with Torah and prophets and with the writings of the Mishnah and with the details of Biblical exegesis and the fine points of the Sages. And when I look into their words and see that from all our loveliness of days of old only the memories of words remain to us, I become filled with sorrow. And my heart trembles with that sorrow, and from that trembling I write books of stories, like a man who is exiled from the palace of his father and makes himself a small shelter (*sukah*) and sits there and tells of the glory of the house of his ancestors. [Agnon 1968, 2:297–98].

The last sentence of this geographical passage contains the word that literally houses the *meḥaber*: the little *sukah* or shelter that he makes for hiimself is defined both through its modesty and through its relation to the "palace" of its linguistic predecessors. It is interesting to note that *sukah* has a history of usage not only as "hut" or "booth," but also to indicate "sanctuary" or "temple." N. Wieder [1957] traces the use of *sukah* or "sanctuary" as a metaphor for Scripture, as, for example, in the parallel between the three divisions of the Bible and the three divisions of the sanctuary; he traces a number of sources that demonstrate this concept of text as structure or structure as text, the word that houses. Thus, while the use of *sukah* in this passage functions ostensibly to acknowledge pious distance, a relationship based on contiguity, it contains within it the move to substitution, the move of metaphor.

On the axes of linguistic combination and substitution, we can locate metaphor on the paradigmatic axis, while relations based on contiguity are to be found on the syntagmatic axis. The paradigmatic axis draws upon a storehouse of possible terms out of which one is selected; its operations are not apparent in discourse. The syntagmatic axis is revealed in discourse; combination of words into syntactic units on the syntagmatic axis produces not only sentences, but also the larger units of narrative.[10] Insofar as the word *sukah* becomes "house" in this story of Agnon's, the substitution of one word for another becomes the locus of action. The narrative progress of "Upon a Stone" is interrupted by this drama of word choice that makes manifest the workings of the axis of selection (the paradigmatic axis) in the discourse.

In fact, *sukah* is not only the shelter of the *meḥaber*; it is also the word that forms part of a phrase whose usage brings the *meḥaber* under attack from a grammarian. The phrase is *sukah meriḥah* or "the *sukah* gives off a fragrance." The verb *meriḥah* suggests that the *sukah actively* exudes its scent. Agnon actually used this phrase in a 1934 story that he wrote for *Davar*; his usage of the verb was criticized subsequently in *Davar* by A. Avronin who wrote as the representative for the National Committee on Language [Bar-Adon 1977]. By implication, the text sets up a mock-epic battle in which poet confronts *daqdeqan* (grammarian). What is the nature of the poet's usage? Does it defile language or affirm it? The sonship of the poet is at stake.

In a world of commentary on sacred texts, the expertise of the commentator lies at least partly in familiarity with the history of uses of a word. Agnon is a writer whose first acquaintance with the language came about through reading sacred texts, but who also came to inhabit a social world where Hebrew was once again the language of daily use after an interval of many centuries. In this respect, the appointment of a committee with authority over language, the *Va'ad halashon*, is a sign of the gap that preceded the invention of modern Hebrew. Taken overall, these continuities and ruptures form an important source of narrative energy for the modern writer.

Out of fidelity to language, the *meḥaber* considers erasure; in effect, he proposes to undo the linguistic act that constitutes him as *meḥaber* or word joiner. But, he tells us, when he tried to erase the two words, "the *sukah* came and its fragrance rose before me until I saw that it really gave off fragrance, and I left things (*devarim*) the way they were" [1968, 2:298]. The *sukah* asserts itself to confirm the poet's usage by demonstrating its capacity for fragrant action, prompting the *meḥaber* to leave words (which are things) as they are. *Davar*, of course, can mean "word" or "thing." Gershom Scholem [1972, 167] points out the richness of linguistic texture that manifests itself in "the Hebrew word *dawar* [in which] we find concealed the double meaning of thing, subject, and word, speech." Agnon's text generates a drama of language in which a word asserts its being; the *meḥaber* is placed in a position in which he can only acknowledge the greater glory of sacred language, an acknowledgment that makes a space, along the way, for his own poetic usage.

In a characteristic paradox, it is the writer's expression of willingness to sacrifice his poetic text that inaugurates a transformation of the language of the text itself. As the *meḥaber* speaks of sitting down to read a holy book, his narrative utterance imitates the language of creation:

> Beautiful was that hour of reading psalms. The lamp stood lit on the table and its light adorned each word and each letter and each vowel and each accent. Opposite it the window was open to the south and the breezes did not put out the light of the lamp and did not tangle with the wick, but they whirled around with the trees and bushes in the garden and a good smell of laurel and dews rose like wild honey and sweet oil. [Agnon 1968, 2:301].

The passage presents an image of luminous textuality: the light of the lamp and the winds that blow through the open window unite the letters of the text of Psalms to the elements of the natural world. In distinct contrast to the behavior of the quarrelsome grammarian, the wind does not "tangle" or "cause strife" with the wick; rather all the elements dance together in a figure of linguistic harmony. As in "Upon a Stone," the writer's bow to larger priorities effects a moment of redemption in which word and thing join, and the world is seen as a radiant text.

Acknowledging the priority of language appears to be the condition that makes possible the enactment of a fiction of language in the text. As in "Upon a Stone," "The Sense of Smell" makes a move to present itself to the reader as the history of a predecessor text: in "Upon a Stone," the earlier text became lost in a rock; in this instance, the narrator records his willingness to erase, that is, lose, the earlier text. Through this maneuver, "The Sense of Smell" displaces the burden of poetic autonomy onto the earlier text (which is, along the way, cleared of the imputation of linguistic transgression). "The Sense of Smell" is thus a fiction that pretends that it is not a fiction, although its very self-consciousness about language works as a wink to the reader that engages our complicity in the play of the text.

"Righteous Men (*tsadiqim*) from the Garden of Eden Come to Support the *meḥaber*," declares the heading to section 5 of the story [1968, 2:299]. "The Sense of Smell" provides for something of a family romance as, in a dream, the *meḥaber* recognizes the famous sage R.

Ya'aqov MeLisah. "The great men of Torah do not look like their families," observes the text, thus establishing a new family whose kinship systems are intertextual [1968, 2:300]. The figure of the sage, interchangeable with his book, directs the *meḥaber* to a piece of paper marking a passage in the book that contains the phrase for which the grammarian had faulted him. In effect, the sage adopts the *meḥaber* and authorizes his linguistic innovation, by showing that it is already contained in the already written.

The narrator is able to recognize the sage as Rabbi Ya'aqov MeLisah although he resembles no one in his family, because, as with those who "devote themselves to words of Torah," God has endowed him with a special radiance [p. 300]. There is a suggestion of closure to the circle of this family romance in that the *meḥaber* earlier described himself as one who "devotes himself to words of Torah" [1968, 2:297]. Through language, the faces of the *meḥaber* and the Rabbi Ya'aqov MeLisah are transfigured into the face of the text, a suggestion of dissolution of distance through participation in the radiance of the holy tongue.

The text draws to an end with a one sentence paragraph that opens with the "greatness of the holy tongue", and, by means of the bridge of the Righteous Man, who journeys from the garden of Eden, reaches its conclusion with acknowledgment of the labors of the artist: "Come and see how great the holy tongue is, that for the sake of one word a great *tsadiq* took the trouble to come from the Academy on High from the Garden of Eden and unrolled his book before me and the matter evolved so that I would rise in the night to recite Psalms and would find a word" [1968, 2:302].

The title *meḥaber* can designate both the scribe who insures transmission of holy writings and the one who composes original creations; the root *ḥ-b-r* is also used in words denoting forms of social organization. This story is about being a *meḥaber*, but its exploration of that function moves toward suggestions of community where, ultimately, it is language that joins together sages of the past and the figure of the writer. The concluding paragraph of the story establishes a community of those devoted to the holy tongue when it refers to the *tsadiq* who journeys from Eden, identified as the "Academy on High" or *yeshivah shel ma'alah*, in order to come to the aid of the *meḥaber*. Agnon's reference to the *yeshivah shel ma'alah* not only suggests the timeless community of those who devote themselves to Torah, but it replaces the authority of the *va'ad halashon* or Committee on Language (established in 1900) with that of a higher body.

Agnon owned an 1858 edition of the *Siddur derekh haḥayyim* of the Rabbi Ya'aqov MeLisah. On page 298, in the section on the laws for observance of Shavuot, a passage concerning the custom of gathering flowers in honor of Shavuot refers to flowers that give off a fragrance for the joy of a holy day; the word *meriḥah* ("give off a fragrance") is underlined in pencil. The editor of the *Siddur derekh Haḥayyim* refers to himself as the *meḥaber*. One might suggest that Agnon affiliates himself with his predecessor through the adoption of the title for his narrative persona.[11]

"The Sense of Smell" takes shape around a prior act of linguistic use, but it subsumes that bit of history into a fictional structure that broadens out into a timeless realm; that larger and higher domain includes users of the holy tongue from God to the Rabbi Ya'aqov MeLisah, other members of the Heavenly Academy and, not least of all, the *meḥaber*. Agnon's poetic usage, attacked as a distortion of language, is given place in a geography of language use that stretches back to Torah. Thus, proof of prior use does not diminish the potency of the present use but rather strengthens it by associating it with earlier strata of language, joining it to a myth of origins where language is presence, word is thing, and the *sukah* gives off a fragrance in honor of a holy tongue.

"Upon a Stone" inserts itself into the lineage of the Hasidic tale, while "The Sense of Smell" manages to associate itself with the "Academy on High." Each of these texts is shaped by an attraction to revered figures, sages, and writings of the past, to whom writing in the present gives access. It is that access through the text to higher strata of writing that is crucial here: both of these stories use texts and experiences of language to build in a vertical dimension that lifts language above the mundane.

"The Document," by contrast, flattens the possibility of that vertical dimension, locating itself in a bureaucratic maze in which its speaker carries out ambivalent gestures in relation to a document that is never produced. But is not that flattening to a mundane horizontal itself a necessary part of any move to recover a vertical dimension? "The Document" evokes the presence of an absent text, allows an association of that text with other "documents," both worldly and sacred, but ultimately fails to reach the momentary elevations of the text that we find in "Upon a Stone" and "The Sense of Smell." We may conclude that, despite these differences in experiences of the text, both sorts of movements and directions form part of a double gesture of the writing. Agnon's writing engages a linguistic universe that resists assignment to either the sacred or the mundane, while sharing in aspects of each and indeed suggesting their interdependence. The tension between these two linguistic domains structures the fiction and engages the reader in linguistic dramas of exile and return.

Part III

Anatomies of Culture

We turn now to two novels, each of which engages in a narrative decomposition of some major cultural myths, whose construction is covered over in culture. *Tmol shilshom* (*Only Yesterday*) is shaped by the circumstances and ideologies of Zionism and the Second *Aliyah*, the wave of immigration from eastern Europe in the early years of this century. I consider this novel in the comparative context of the *Bildungsroman*, that subgenre of the European novel that concerns development of a youthful protagonist. Classical issues of youthful rebellion, relationship to the father, entry into society, and assumption of a social role, all make themselves felt in the text, but are set awry through the interaction of the youthful protagonist with a dog on whose back he paints the words "mad dog." That interaction in a moment of writing unleashes a madness that challenges the form of the *Bildungsroman* and discloses the breakdown of an Oedipal narrative.

Shira, in turn, is set in the German-Jewish academic community of Jerusalem in the 1930s, amid signs of the impending destruction of European Jewry. Themes of disease and body combine with the novel's attentiveness to European culture to produce a text that anatomizes culture. *Shira* prompts interrogation of metaphysical oppositions between nature and culture, body and book, female and male. Agnon's posthumously published novel can be compared to Thomas Mann's *Doctor Faustus*, insofar as each explores the catastrophic collapse of twentieth-century Germany, although from quite different angles. *Shira* takes the perspective of the German Jew, transplanted to Jerusalem, formed in a culture that now rejects him: from this vantage point, the novel explores some of the paradoxes that inform cultural definitions of gender, body and book.

Chapter

7

Inscription and Madness in *Only Yesterday*

Comparative *Bildung*

In the wake of Freud's explorations of the decisive impact of the Oedipus complex in the formation of personality, it is not surprising that narrative theorists have turned to the "symbolic triad of the family" [Macksey 1983, 1008] as a fruitful starting point for studying the novel as genre.[1] The importance of the "paternal metaphor" or the "name of the Father" to the formation of the subject has given rise to a current emphasis in literary criticism on the search for the father as motivator in narrative.[2] For our purposes, we might note that the *Bildungsroman* as a literary form derives much of its narrative energies from the struggles of sons with a paternal principle: the struggle to find the father, the struggle of the hero to give birth to himself, or to be his own father.

Bringing structuralism together with linguistics, Jacques Lacan constructs the Oedipal narrative in culture as the formation of the subject through an access to language that imposes the Law of the Father: "The primordial Law is therefore that which in regulating marriage ties superimposes the kingdom of culture on that of a nature abandoned to the law of mating. . . . This law, then, is revealed clearly enough as identical with an order of language" [1977, 66]. "Family" must be understood, then, not only in terms of its specific members, but also as "a set of symbolic relations which always transcend the actual persons defined by them. 'Mother' and 'father' signify cultural positions" [Silverman 1983, 182]. The novel as a genre exploits this intersection of the individual with the cultural: the specifics of plot and character carry broader resonances and tell a story that belongs ultimately to the larger domain of culture. (This patrocentric schema, however, should not lead us to overlook issues of differentiation, fusion, departure and return, that are bound up in preoedipal relations; narrative reflects the gendered dichotomies through which subjectivity takes shape.)

In this context, I propose reading *Tmol shilshom* (*Only Yesterday*) as a *Bildungsroman* and major modernist text, with particular attention to the ironies generated by the failure of the subject to "develop," that is to go through the sort of *Bildung* we might expect. From this perspective, I suggest setting *Only Yesterday* alongside James Joyce's *Portrait of the Artist as a Young Man,* and Thomas Mann's *The Magic Mountain*. (Later portions of the discussion will use some comparisons to Franz Kafka's works.)

First, some points of comparison that have bearing on the discussions of Agnon's novel to follow. In *Portrait of the Artist*, I am struck by the importance of motherland and homeland, both Ireland and Church. The novel plays out an Oedipal drama, focusing on Stephen's efforts to differentiate himself from the maternal, as well as on his search for a father. Despite the opening child's-eye glimpse of the father's hairy monocled godlike face, the novel sets up the father as the site of an inaugural lack from which the narrative takes shape. We follow Stephen as he moves among priests, sinners, nationalists, and ultimately, of course, back to Stephen himself, priest of the imagination, as he declares himself to be his own begetter. But while the novel traces the journey of the hero through Christian and pagan structures, it also sets Stephen up for an Icarian fall, which his name suggests. Doubts about Stephen's development and self-proclaimed formation are also raised by his autoeroticism and his relation to the female. In particular, the motif of the kiss poses a threat of absorption into the maternal, from which Stephen recoils defensively. We see this in his response to his schoolmates' teasing question "Do you kiss your mother?" (a reference to St. Aloysius Gonzaga, Joyce's patron saint, who was too pure to do so [Anderson, 490]), as well as in his ultimate resistance to his mother's demand that he make his Easter devotion. Along the way, Stephen sums up the danger when he refers to Ireland as "an old sow that eats her farrow."

In *The Magic Mountain*, I would draw attention to the novel's wonderfully seductive portrayal of illness—"life on the horizontal"—as narrative manifestation of Mann's growing preoccupation with the death instinct in European culture. In terms of its function and link to the death drive, tuberculosis plays a role in *The Magic Mountain* that can be compared to the role of religious fanaticism in *Only Yesterday*. Disease presents itself seductively in Mann's novel; it carries with it the aura of *Steigerung*, or elevation of the organism to a higher plane, and so deflects the momentum of more outwardly directed ideologies of progress. (Mann was scarcely unaware of this irony and commented in a letter on the parody inherent in the notion of renewing the *Bildungsroman* through the use of tuberculosis [Reed 1974, 226].) The lure of Eros intertwined with the death drive can be seen in Hans Castorp's response to Prbislav Hippe and Clavdia Chauchat in *The Magic Mountain*. A comparable mingling of attraction with the threat of dissolution can be found in Yitzhak Kummer's response to Sonia and Shifra in *Only Yesterday*. Critic Hermann Weigand's designation of *The Magic Mountain* as a *Zeitroman*, "in that it strives to express the psychic temper of a whole age" [1965, 10], can be applied as well to Agnon's *Only Yesterday*. A look at each of the two protagonists, Yitzhak Kummer and Hans Castorp, shows us that each is a child of the times: Hans Castorp is "life's delicate child," while Yitzhak is associated with the "face of the generation."

Each of these three novels assumes decline from the world of the father. Yitzhak Kummer's father is distinguished by his failure to figure significantly in the social world. While Yitzhak looks to his grandfather, Reb Yudel Hasid, for whom miracles occurred, the narrator notes the absence of such miracles for Yitzhak. *The Magic Mountain* introduces Hans Castorp via his family lineage, from the dead father back; Hans Castorp seems to inherit from his grandfather Castorp only the latter's tremor of the neck, and the novel implies a history of decline on the order of that found in *Buddenbrooks*. Simon Dedalus, Stephen's father, cries for the dead hero Parnell and paints a picture of his own father for Stephen as a giant among men; in doing so, he raises a mythical standard that functions simply as a measure of his own impotence and inability to provide guidance for *his* son. In each of these novels, the protagonist's father is missing or can be seen as a failed son himself. Each grandfather is cited as figure of more than human proportions whose evocation serves as a measure of the decline of the present generation and so contributes to the inaugural lack that is the stimulus for the narrative.

Only Yesterday makes its Oedipal drama available to us through a surreal plot of filial usurpation and sacrifice. The impetus for this cataclysmic action is an inscription on a dog; that random writing stimulates a grotesque comedy of inscription. It unleashes a madness in the text of the sort that writing, in its delineation of a stable message, is meant to suppress and contain.

"Mad Dog"

Let us consider now a novel in which a young man, impulsively and for no apparent reason, paints the words "mad dog" on the back of a stray mutt; the dog then wanders around Jerusalem in search of a reader, who can decode for it the mysterious inscription on its back, all the while terrorizing the pious inhabitants of the city's Me'ah She'arim section. Eventually, due to a poetic justice whose logic we shall consider, the dog bites Yitzhak Kummer, the young man who painted the words on his back, with a bite that eventually causes that young man's death. That death, which brings the novel to a close, is linked to the coming of rains that end the drought that has been plaguing Jerusalem.

While this may all seem quite mad, we should also keep in mind that the novel is set in the period of the Second *Aliyah* or wave of immigration, during the years 1905–1914. Yitzhak Kummer, the protagonist of *Only Yesterday*, leaves his father and siblings in eastern Europe in order to journey to the land of Israel to become a pioneer. He arrives in Jaffa, joins up with his peers, most of whom more or less fail to find the work and renewal they seek. This novel captures so well the atmospheres of Jerusalem, Jaffa, and the early agricultural settlements, not to mention the lure of ideology and the promise of Zionism to youth of the period, that it has been heralded for its importance as a "social novel" and is cited as a source for descriptions of the Second *Aliyah*.[3]

Now there is a further problem to be considered here and that is the puzzle or contradiction in Yitzhak Kummer's death from a dog bite given by a dog who may or may not be rabid, but who bears the *inscription* "mad dog" painted by the protagonist himself for no apparent reason. *Is* the dog rabid? Critics have taken the dog's condition for granted[4], but the question of causality cannot be answered in terms of veterinary medicine or animal psychology.[5] Arnold Band [1967] provides a context for the painful disproportion between Yitzhak's negligible "sins" and the severity of his death by noting that while the novel is set in the early years of this century, Agnon wrote most of it during the years 1943–45, when the signs of the destruction of European Jewry were unmistakable. From this perspective, the irrationality of Yitzhak's senseless death (the sacrifice of this latter-day Isaac) is a mere reflection of the larger insanity of the Holocaust. Of course, Band's reference to extraliterary events contemporary with the writing of the novel points up rather than resolves the problem of closure. Reacting to the severity of Yitzhak's end, Dan

Miron [1987, 10] finds the concluding conjunction of Yitzhak's death with the end of the drought to be more in keeping with a pagan notion of sacrifice than it is with Judaic values.

These discomforts with the novel's problematic closure may bear some connection to the difficulties the author appears to have experienced in fitting together the stories of Balak the dog and Yitzhak the would-be pioneer. Sara Hagar's [1978] manuscript research documents the development of the novel out of the initially separate stories of Yitzhak and the dog, Balak; her study shows the varying degrees of emphasis and ascendancy accorded to each at different points in the composition of the text and demonstrates as well the difficulties the author encountered in fitting the two plots together. The development of the manuscript of *Only Yesterday* and the history of the novel's reception draw attention to not only the author's but also the reader's discomforts with the interrelations of the two plots—Yitzhak and Balak—as well as with the problem of closure in the novel. My study of the function of the inscription of "mad dog" in the text of Agnon's novel takes further Kurzweil's investigations [1970, 104–15] into the relationship of the "demonic" dog to Yitzhak and other characters by looking at the role of the dog in the text as a writing cut loose, "demonic" in its randomness.

Rather than looking for ways of normalizing or conventionalizing the novel, I suggest that we look more closely at the relationship of the inscription—"mad dog" or *kelev meshuga'*—to the creature who bears it on his back, and the relationship of that creature—the dog as text—to the various characters, "readers" we might call them, that he encounters in his wanderings through Jerusalem. This will lead us to Yitzhak, who is writer of the inscription, reader of it and, ultimately, its victim.

If we examine the position in the text of the onset of the dog Balak's "symptoms," we find it follows upon an extended discussion of the dissemination of that same Balak as text. Balak becomes a wandering "text" in the sense that the writing on his back is subjected to endless efforts at decoding and interpretation. This dog who bears a Hebrew inscription on his back passes by "readers" in the novel who belong to the constituent communities of Erets Yisrael, the Land of Israel. Take, for example, the Frenchman, principal of the French "Alliance" School, who reads the writing on the dog's back from left to right and calls the "Balak" as a result of that *mis*reading (a name, moreover, which the narrative voice has already adopted).

The critic Bar-Adon [1977] points out the centrality of the Hebrew language to Agnon's conception of the Zionist idea and the life of the nation. He argues as well that Agnon perceived a danger to Hebrew's ideological centrality and to its emergence as a language of daily use, amid the other languages (French, German, English) that were competing for ascendancy at the time of the Second *Aliyah*. Bar-Adon has shown the dog to be the key to a socio-linguistic critique that centers on the disputes over the revival of Hebrew and the relationship of Hebrew to other languages. These disputes over the politics of language choice were most intense in the years before World War I, that is the period in which the novel is set. One could construct a walking tour of Jerusalem out of the dog's wanderings that would cover the territory of this political-cultural struggle.

At one point in his wanderings through the Me'ah She'arim section of Jerusalem, the dog Balak encounters a sermonizing preacher, Rabbi Gronam Yekum Purkan, who mesmerizes the religious quarter of Me'ah She'arim with his apocalyptic streetcorner sermons. Rabbi Gronam is a "reader" who appropriates the dog as "text" for his own ideological needs: he places the dog in a talmudic context in order to make the dog the reading of the generation and the vehicle for his exhortation. "The face of the generation is like the face of a dog" [1968, 5: 585–86], he declares, citing a talmudic source with the passionate conviction that grows out of the speaker's confidence in his control of text and audience.[6] But in the midst of this fire and brimstone sermon in which he uses the dog as *mashal* or example, the *mashal* itself "takes on skin and bones" in a sudden materialization of the text that suggests a writing out of control. In fact, the subject of the interpretation asserts its primacy over the interpreter, as the barks of the dog make themselves heard over and above the shouts of the preacher.[7]

And what of the writer of the inscription himself as a reader? When the attention of our protagonist Yitzhak is finally drawn to the writing on the back of the dog that has been terrorizing the pious inhabitants of Me'ah She'arim, he dismisses it as a writing that he himself produced, a text that he controls: "And are we obligated to believe everything that is written?" he asks. "But I'll tell you, I myself wrote on his hide, and I know that he's a healthy dog, because if he were mad, I wouldn't have had anything to do with him" [1968, 5: 589]. But the "text" is out of control now: Yitzhak's dismissal of any danger coincides precisely with the onset of "madness" in the dog. As the narrator tells us, Balak begins to "doubt his [own] sanity" [1968, 5: 591] just at the moment that people's concerns about him are allayed by Yitzhak's words. In effect the writing asserts its independence of its putative author. The result is something of a comedy of readers, as texts of all sorts—canine, talmudic, homiletic—run amuck.

The dog stimulates activity in the novel that surrounds questions of language, the stability of meaning, the capacity of writing to name a thing. On the one hand, dogs are shown to be the vehicle for a particularly authoritarian writing: the novel cites the practice of tying notes of excommunication onto tails of black dogs, even once writing the actual words of the ban—*"Epiqoros muḥram umenudeh"* ("banned and excommunicated heretic")—on the fur of a bunch of dogs in order to cast out a reformer [1968, 5: 276]. On the other hand, newspapers battle in their reports on the dog Balak and their efforts to interpret the significance of the canine phenomenon, so much so that when the Jaffa papers take up the case, their readers assume that the account of the dog is an "allegory" and wonder how to "learn the hidden (meaning) from the explicit" with the end result that "the number of interpretations was the same as the number of inhabitants of the city" [1968, 5: 459]. Along with the obvious satire of reader/interpreters, the dog's wanderings suggest the instability of any text, the breakdown of the kind of authoritarian writing the pious men of Jerusalem espouse and carry out in their posting of excommunications.

The novel shows how the newspapers pick up on this canine controversy, although, after a time, that journalistic focus gives way to coverage of the war over use of the Hebrew language. One wonders, nevertheless, whether this displacement does not rather substitute one set of signifiers for another in what is really an ongoing war over control of the "text." Ultimately that "text" is the holy tongue and the land with which it is identified:

> Since the war over Hebrew returned and reawakened, the rabbis of Jerusalem came out in a war for Torah, until all the walls were filled with writs of excommunication against breakers of the fence that was established (fenced in and bounded) by the first ones who were like angels, the elder rabbis the learned ones of former years, the strong ones of the land of Israel, in order to pass the stringent prohibition that included all the schools in the cities of the Holy Land that had taken for themselves the essence of the religion the Hebrew language and the holy tongue, for they are desecrators of the sacred.[1968, 5: 461]

The rabbis are representatives of the old *yishuv*, within the walls of the Old City, who take talmudic injunction to "build a fence around the Torah" as the guiding precept in their violent resistance to secularizing movements. The "fence breakers" to which the passage refers are those who take sacred language beyond its paternally authorized usage; in this instance, the reference is to schools that use Hebrew as the language of instruction.[8] The righteous ire of the rabbis is aroused by the efforts of the new *yishuv*, prominent among its members, Eliezer Ben Yehudah (against whom a writ of excommunication was actually issued), to revive Hebrew as a language of daily use. Posted on the streetcorners of Jerusalem, these writs attempt to impose a definitive structure on physical space and on the discourse of its inhabitants. The writs are the fences that delimit land and language in an effort to constitute and sustain a definitive text.

The dog violates authorized usages of writing, acting out an upheaval of the meaning and authority that such paternal writings are meant to exclude and suppress. Specifically, Balak as a mad writing defeats the efforts of two men of Jerusalem, the preacher Rabbi Gronam and the fanatical Reb Faysh, to anchor meaning in a text. The sermonizing of Rabbi Gronam and the excommunicating activities of Reb Faysh are terminated abruptly in encounters with the dog. Rabbi Gronam is silenced when the dog disrupts his speech. Reb Faysh reaches out to retrieve and rescue what he thinks are fragments of a Hebrew text (sacred writing) lying in the garbage, but finds instead the dog with an inscription on his back; the shock of this encounter leaves him prostrate and powerless.[9] The radical loss of speech that both men experience testifies to their loss of power to nominate, denominate, name, and exclude when they are confronted with the signifier cut loose, the "mad" dog roaming the alleys of Jerusalem.

In following the dog's wanderings and encounters, the novel tells a story of a writing gone awry; in effect, we witness the madness in writing given free play. In this context, we can say that the dog is mad because he *is* writing. The dog makes manifest the madness in the text, a possibility that is always there, no matter how stable we may believe the writing to be. Shoshana Felman [1985, 110] argues that representations of madness in literary texts give access to the madness inherent in writing, by showing "the functional possibility of permutation of signifiers between speaker and addressee". The inherence of madness in language consists in a fluidity that destabilizes the social order of language.

Between the Generations

"The face of the generation is like the face of a dog," shouts the preacher, linking the writing on the dog to the generation of youth. Rabbi Gronam's theme assumes new meaning: "*Pnei hador kipnei hakelev*" works as something of a cryptogram to the text. In it we find encoded the structure of the novel's relations and forces, from the opening sentence that gives Yitzhak place amid "the sons of the Second *Aliyah*," to Yitzhak's inscription of the dog with the words "mad dog," and on to the dog's biting of Yitzhak, ending finally with Yitzhak's sacrificial death, scapegoat for the "sons of the generation."

The conjunction of the preacher's indictment of a generation of youth with the random writing produced by one of those young people should prompt an inquiry into the intergenerational world of the novel. The narrative voice in *Only Yesterday* appears to speak out of an alliance with Yitzhak and his youthful peers, the generation of young people who left eastern Europe for Palestine imbued with the romance of Zionism.

This peer sense that the narrator expresses extends into a pervasive discomfort with the older generation. Yitzhak's intergenerational encounters fall into a virtually paradigmatic alignment of Jerusalem with pious elders and the concept of "*Yerushalayim shel ma'alah*" (the "heavenly Jerusalem") as opposed to the young men who have come to work the land in its physical being, as we can see in this passage early in the novel:

> The old man asked Yitzhak, "What are you doing here?" Said Yitzhak to him, "I am travelling to Erets Yisrael." The old man was amazed, "And is it the way of a youth to go to the Land of Israel?" Said Yitzhak to him, "To work her land I am going." The old man became even more amazed. "Is not the land of Israel made up entirely of synagogues and houses of study. Is not the land of Israel exclusively for prayer, so what does working the soil have to do with heavenly requirements?" He had figured out that this young man was from the group of the Zionists who were seeking to tear the land out of its holiness and to make it like all other lands. He began to complain about Yitzhak, in the manner of the elders of Israel of that generation, who looked upon *us* as if *we* had come, heaven forbid, to turn the world to heresy. [Agnon 1968, 5: 32; emphasis added]

Not only does this passage underscore the departure of the youth from the way of the fathers, but as it unfolds, the alliance of the narrator makes clear the Oedipal rebellion that supplies the generation's identification of itself.

The opening of the novel, in its delineation of Yitzhak's youthful activities and aspirations as a Zionist, suggests the definition of character through ideology, at least superficially. Ideology here organizes character and names the subject on a conscious level. At the same time, in its portrayal of Yitzhak as naive and yet inscrutably death-drawn, *Only Yesterday* demonstrates the opacity of the subject in ways that dissolve the certainty of conceptions based on the transparency of consciousness.[10] The narrative voice tells Yitzhak's story without necessarily comprehending the direction it takes in a manner that suggests the generation's noncomprehension of itself.

The historical record supplements and bears out the sense of an unease in the text that raises questions about any simple romantic version of Zionism. We can remind ourselves of some of the relevant statistics: of the approximately 30,000 Jews who left eastern Europe for Palestine as part of the Second *Aliyah* something like 80% returned to their homelands or continued on to America within weeks of their arrival [Sachar, 1982, 72–73].

In the novel, the dilemma of youth in the Second *Aliyah*, takes the shape of a movement of desire and the attempt to secure an identification with Zionism as signified. Yitzhak is the function of a shift—ideological, geographical, political—from Diaspora to Zion. Lacan describes the consequences of such a shift, when he observes that "the slighest alteration in the relation between man and the signifier. . . changes the whole course of history by modifying the moorings that anchor his being" (1977, 174). Yitzhak attempts to affiliate himself—literally, to become the son of—Zionism. But there is an excess here; there is more going on than can be subsumed into the name, the noun, "*Tsioni*". In effect, read from the angle of history, the novel records that effort to stabilize the process of signification and anchor reality in the sign.

Only Yesterday is motivated by a search for identity through the father that produces a series of substitutions; its underlying premise is the failure of the Diaspora father. From one angle, in acceding to his son's schemes, the Diaspora father fails to provide for his son's passage through the Oedipus. This abdication is signaled early on in a sentence that appears to arise from the father's despair over his son: "A curse has descended on the world, a son does not listen to his father and a father doesn't rule over his son" [1968, 5: 9]. Yitzhak's *aliyah* to Erets Yisrael is financed by a father who deprives himself in order to support his son's visionary scheme. One might conclude that the father's failure to exercise paternal authority (the paternal "no") makes possible the son's presumed accession to power through adoption of an ideology and emigration to a new land, except that the novel reads as the story of the son's failure to engage and exercise that power. Or, looked at from a different angle through the biblical text of the *aqedah*, the sacrifice of Isaac, to which Yitzhak's name alludes, we could say that the father sends the son out to an *aqedah* from which he fails to rescue him: there is no last-minute substitute for the filial sacrifice that Yitzhak ultimately provides.[11]

Yitzhak's adoption of Zionism suggests a first effort at paternal substitution. The failure of this substitute "father" can be seen in Yitzhak's gradual disenchantment with the Zionist functionaries, so dazzling to him from the distance of exile, whom he meets first in Europe and then in Jaffa. The cafe scenes in which they take him to eat rich cakes express Agnon's characteristic scorn for bureaucrats. Chief among them is Mr. Asqanowitz, whose name derives from *asqan* or "busybody": he displays a map of Erets Yisrael to a delegation of Zionists from the Diaspora in a manner that suggests the land is his to dispose of; at the same time, he pays scarcely any attention to Yitzhak, the would-be pioneer who cannot find work [1968, 5: 62–63].

The desire to rebuild the land of Israel from its destruction and to rebuild oneself through it produces, within the novel's opening paragraph, a biblical vision of the land, laborers returning at dusk to sit, one man under his grapevine, another beneath his fig tree, gathering his wife and sons and daughters around him. This vision of the promised land offers a radiant alternative to the poverty and impotence of the Diaspora family. What is striking here is the language of "return," derived certainly from the heart of Jewish longings for Zion, but coming from a youth for whom this journey constitutes just as much a departure, a most radical break from the world of his father. Yitzhak imagines a "return" to a world he has never known, or more accurately, the "return" frames an attempt to enter a family romance announced on the first page of the novel.

The imaginary nature of his wishes becomes clear later on in the novel when Yitzhak visits Ein Ganim, a *moshav* or cooperative settlement whose workers bring to life Yitzhak's romantic vision, with some significant modifications: "And every day after returning with evening from their work in Petah Tikvah they would go out with their wives and children and would weed out the thorns and raise dust and make bricks" [1968, 5: 169]. These workers hold fast to their vision and integrate it into the world through labor; but while their success gives pride to onlookers such as Yitzhak, it is also a source of shame. Speaking for Yitzhak and his "brothers," the narrator observes: "This was the guilt of all of us who came to work the land and did not work it" [1968, 5: 171]. Ein Ganim makes an important statement: it testifies to the actual founding of settlements by Jewish workers and so constitutes a success story in the present tense of the novel. (As such, it plays a role like that of the village of preparation in *A Guest for the Night* and the cooperative farm in *Shira;* each asserts its reality in the social world, but remains somewhat apart from the central conflicts that the novels explore.) Nevertheless, as far as Yitzhak is concerned, Ein Ganim is relegated to a separate sphere akin to the mythic realm inhabited by Reb Yudel Hasid:

> [Yitzhak] was reminded of one of those stories that were told of his grandfather Reb Yudel Hasid, that once in the course of his journey for the sake of a dowry (*hakhnasat kalah*) he happened on a village where he passed a Sabbath with one of the 36 righteous men (*lamed-vav tsadiqim*), on whom the world stands. [. . .] And when Yitzhak thought over these matters [the deeds of this righteous man] he smiled and said, And I Yitzhak the grandson of Reb Yudel Hasid passed a weekday not with one righteous man (*nistar*) but with a whole group of the righteous (*nistarim*) on whom the world stands. [Agnon 1968, 5: 173]

Reb Yudel, it should be noted, is the protagonist of Agnon's novel, *Hakhnasat Kalah (The Bridal Canopy).* By associating these workers with Reb Yudel as well as with the legendary "36 *nistarim,*" Yitzhak perceives them as inhabiting a realm separate from the situation in which he finds himself.

Only Yesterday is a large and panoramic novel that takes in the social scene of a period in the development of the State of Israel. At the same time, as the account of the *aliyah* of Yitzhak Kummer, it contains its end in its beginning. Consider the quasi-deceptive opening sentence:

> Like the rest of our brothers, men of our redemption sons of the Second *Aliyah,* Yitzhak Kummer left his land and his birthplace and his city and went up to the land of Israel to build it from its destruction and to build himself from it. [Agnon 1968, 5:1]

Is Yitzhak in fact representative of "our brothers . . . sons of the Second *Aliyah*?" His end might seem to testify to the contrary.[12] One might well ask, then, if Yitzhak functions as a sacrificial creature for his peers, representative of a tendency denied in them through its displacement onto him. Representative of a generation's rebellion, he acts out its ambivalence, bringing to the surface the movement of return that is hidden in the generation's separation from its elders.[13] This sort of displacement onto the other amounts to denial, rather than any kind of a working through on the level of the individual psyche or in narrative structure. In fact, this displacement onto Yitzhak may help to explain the unsatisfying nature of the novel's conclusion: to link Yitzhak's death to the end of the drought is to confirm and underscore the primitive expiatory aspect of the plot. But more of that later.

In Search of the Maternal

Indeed in *Only Yesterday,* one begins to suspect that Yitzhak seeks not so much the missing father as he does absorption into something larger than himself that will relieve him of the challenge of an individuality he has so far resisted. The search for a paternal identification discloses an even deeper drive that threatens to undo the forward motion of the plot. Consider for example the image of Zion that reveals itself in the structure of Yitzhak's expectations. On board ship on the way to the promised land, Yitzhak is asked by an old man: "'You have relatives in Erets Yisrael?' Said Yitzhak to him, 'Who needs them, all Yisrael are friends, all the more so in Erets Yisrael'" [1968, 5:33]. Yitzhak's reply is intelligible in terms of the rhetoric of the day, but we should not overlook the manner in which it shapes a primitive set of expectations. Yitzhak's response sidesteps or ignores actual heterogeneity.

The text notes that Yitzhak feels "orphaned" (*meyutam*) on arrival, when he sees the other immigrants meet their relatives [1968, 5: 39]. Yitzhak had been anticipating absorption in the most concrete sense. Strikingly, moreover, his experience of feeling "orphaned" on arrival is succeeded immediately by denial as Yitzhak comments to himself on the young men who take his bags at the harbor, using language that the text designates as *melitsah* or flowery, highly rhetoricized language: "Our mother Zion sent her sons to welcome their brother who has returned to her" [1968, 5: 39]. *Melitsah* serves here to sustain the level of fantasy. Language buffers Yitzhak, although its ironic discrepancy with the situation at hand is not lost on the reader.

"Yitzhak was a man of imaginings/fantasies (*dimyonot*), from the place where his heart desired, he would imagine his imaginings (fantasize his fantasies)" [1968, 5: 1]. Here in this novel the imaginative capacity functions ostensibly in service of the Zionist vision of a rebuilt homeland; nevertheless, the text discloses a movement back to origins that collapses differences and can be discerned even in action that appears to be forward-directed.[14] Similarly, on a geographical axis, the novel appears to utilize a Jaffa-Jerusalem polarity that sets the youthful community of Jaffa against the ingrown traditionalism of the old *yishuv*. At the same time, however, Yitzhak's journey discloses a psychological mapping that alters that apparent opposition. While Yitzhak's move from Jaffa to Jerusalem appears to reverse the direction in which he has been traveling and so to signal a major change in milieu and ideology, it is possible to discern here again the drive for incorporation, the wish to regain fusion. The unique status of Jerusalem in Judaism easily justifies its place in the psychic structure that the text generates.

As maternal geography in a literary text, Jerusalem bears comparison to Joyce's Ireland. Within their respective texts, Dublin and Jerusalem are a form of homeland, *heimlich* and *unheimlich*, that is, both homelike and uncanny. (Freud [1919] suggests that the source of the feeling of the "uncanny" or *unheimlich* is the recollection of our original "home" or *heim*, that is, the womb.) Like Agnon, Joyce is aware and wary of place as a threat of absorption, a consciousness he pushes to satire in his characterization of Stephen Dedalus in *Portrait of the Artist as a Young Man.* In contrast to Stephen's relationship to Ireland, we can note that the structure of *Bildung* or development in Agnon's novel places the protagonist in a tension between two poles, two homelands—the Diaspora and Zion, in a complication that the fiction exploits fully. While Stephen Dedalus poises himself for flight into an unknown future out of which he will "forge" an identity for himself and his "race" (with all the ironies that "forge" carries), Yitzhak Kummer turns to a "new" homeland that is at the same time the ancient birthplace of his people. In contrast to Yitzhak who lacks a mother and is born into exile, Stephen is born in the motherland and sees exile as the necessary condition to individuation. He must become father to himself, not only to escape the paternal authority of God and priesthood, but also on what is arguably a deeper or more primary level, to avoid the danger of incorporation into a primitive matrix. Hence, Stephen's declaration that Ireland is an old sow that eats her farrow.

Agnon gives us not the Joycean effort at stream-of-consciousness, but a more limpid prose and less stressed syntax where, nevertheless, in a manner not unlike Joyce's, sentence structure and wording generate the structure that is character. Juxtaposition of two passages, one early and one late in the novel, brings out the constancy of drives that is Yitzhak. Consider Yitzhak's experience on arrival in Erets Yisrael:

> That very night Yitzhak learned what he had not learned in all the years, all those years in which he had seen the new Erets Yisrael as *one piece (ḥativah aḥat)*, that same night he learned that even she (Erets Yisrael) had made herself *pieces and pieces (ḥativot ḥativot)*. [1968, 5; 55; emphasis added]

Compare this early expression of Yitzhak's wish for union (to be of "one piece") with his brethren in Israel to the moment, much later in the novel, at which he says *Kaddish* at the Western Wall on the occasion of his mother's *yahrzeit* (a moment that is anticipated midway in the novel when Yitzhak's first Sabbath visit to the Wall leaves him feeling like "an infant without sin" [p. 263]):

> Now that he had said Kaddish he was drawn closer as if in and of itself to the holy stones. His heart began to pound and his legs to shake. And with the shaking of his legs and the pounding of his heart his voice went out with the voice of all those standing next to the Wall. . . . The stones were swallowed up in the darkness, and all the worshippers became of *one piece (ḥativah aḥat)* before the Omnipresent (*hamaqom*, literally 'the place'). [1968, 5; 531; emphasis added]

The moment seems to supply the reunion or reabsorption—into one *piece* or *ḥativah*—that Yitzhak failed to find on first entry into the land of Zion. Indeed Yitzhak is "swallowed up" into corporate unity with other worshippers before God whose appellation here supports further the sense of absorption into place in a concrete sense.[15]

It becomes interesting, in light of this relation to what one might call "maternal presence" (or the lack of it), to look at the sequence of females with whom Yitzhak becomes involved: first Sonia and then Shifra. Semantically, the names underscore the difference between them: the Russian Sonia, of Yaffo's youthful community, suggesting secular studies and Shifra, who is part of Jerusalem's Me'ah She'arim, the clarity of simple piety [Band 1968, 429]. The description of Sonia's education in "general knowledge" (*yedi'ot klaliyot*) suggests a light satire of Enlightenment, as well as a pointed contrast to Yitzhak, who knows only what he has learned in *ḥeder* and in the *beit midrash* [1968, 5: 129]. The relationship of these two young people suggests a comic allegory of secular versus Torah education.

Nevertheless, despite the apparent opposition of "Sonia" to "Shifra," the sound equivalence of their names may serve to remind us that they occupy the same position in relation to Yitzhak—that of the forbidden woman.[16] When he is with Sonia, Yitzhak thinks constantly of her link to his absent friend and age-peer, Rabinowicz. Curiously, however, the narrative undercuts his obsessive guilt feelings by demonstrating that the link between Sonia and Rabinowicz is more the product of Yitzhak's *need* to position her as forbidden object, than it is an accurate reflection of the structure of relations between the young men and women of Jaffa. For example, "Even though matters were already finished between Rabinowicz and Sonia, Yitzhak didn't see himself as clean. . . . [1968, 5: 152]. In a society of peers, the effort to position one of the "brothers" as the forbidding Father lacks persuasiveness.[17]

This aura of the forbidden may well signal a deeper danger than either paternal or fraternal wrath. Two passages suggest the direction in which this danger lies. Before the first kiss with Sonia: "[Yitzhak's] heart answers and says, You are turning her heart from him[Rabinowicz]" [1968, 5: 126]. But then, right after the kiss: "This was the kiss that was preserved in his mouth from the hour of his mother's death" [1968, 5: 127]. No wonder Yitzhak needs to maintain Rabinowicz as a rival. The defense precedes the kiss, which produces all those longings for the lost mother and so threatens Yitzhak with collapse into the other. Maintaining a triangular structure, however shaky and unpersuasive, defends the protagonist against his own longings for absorption into a dyadic relationship. (The dangers of the kiss bring to mind the issue of kissing one's mother in Joyce's *Portrait;* there, too, the kiss is a nodal point for tensions surrounding relations to the female.)

But there is a second, coincident point about Sonia and the mother's kiss with which she is associated. There is no such mother. She is not it. Sonia's desire is metonymic, lighting on Yitzhak, only to pass from him to another, and then on to another, as it had, in fact passed from Rabinowicz to Yitzhak: her kiss is not "a virgin kiss" [1968, 5: 127]. It is only in Yitzhak's Oedipal fantasy that she *belongs* to Rabinowicz.

Readers have been struck by the pictures of dogs in this novel and it is worth noting the canine images that are associated with Sonia. Sonia's bed, for example, is "covered with a colored cover on which a yellow dog with a stick in its mouth was embroidered" [1968, 5: 142]; "And from the cover the dog that was on it looked at [Yitzhak] with an angry face" [1968, 5: 148]. The candy box Yitzhak brings to

Sonia pictures a "young girl [*betulah*] . . . [who] bares her teeth and smiles at him" [1968, 5: 151]. Sonia's kiss is both longed for and feared and can be linked structurally to the dog's bite. Each threatens to take in and absorb, destroying definitions of relationship that maintain separateness.

These emblematic images speak another language than Yitzhak's naive idealism, a language in which, as Baruch Kurzweil notes, dogs are associated with women and function as signs of "desire, transgression, primal forces . . . madness" [1982, 221]. Indeed, the common elements of mouth, bite, and teeth suggest the interchangeability of the canine and the female. These dog images appear to signal the dangers found in society without the father. (In the primitive story of *Totem and Taboo,* the father-tyrant rules and all women are forbidden to the sons; Yitzhak seems to operate under some such stricture, even in the absence of the father, primitive or otherwise.)

Given these dangers, Yitzhak must go elsewhere to find what Jaffa has not supplied—the stern father and the Oedipal situation. As part of his move to Jerusalem, Yitzhak turns to Shifra, daughter of the fanatical Reb Faysh of Me'ah She'arim, in a turn away from the outward-directedness of Zionism as movement and social ideology. There is no doubt that Shifra is the forbidden object: the text makes it abundantly clear that a functioning Reb Faysh would never permit Yitzhak to cross his threshold. Furthermore, the interchangeability of Shifra with her mother, in terms of characterization and domestic role, underscores the placement of the daughter in the forbidden.

Oedipal Inscription Gone Awry

By way of the inscription on the dog, the Oedipal drama is enacted. Remember that the dog has felled Reb Faysh, the most terrifying embodiment of the father imago, and has felled, at least temporarily, Rabbi Gronam Yekum Purkan. Only after the dog's encounter with Reb Faysh, which results in the prostration of that sternly authoritarian figure, is Yitzhak able to move in and assume a relationship to two interchangeable women, mother and daughter; in effect, he takes the place of the father who lies mute, unable to arrest the young man's Oedipal triumph. In this respect, then, the dog is the emissary or vehicle for Yitzhak's aggression against the father.

Shortly after the move to Jerusalem, Yitzhak's specular identification with the father can be seen in his taking on the appearance of the pious men of Jerusalem—"Little by little Yitzhak shed his shape and began to imitate his neighbors" [1968, 5: 536]—and his assumption of the masculine position in the household of Reb Faysh. Is this a version of the story Freud tells in *Totem and Taboo,* with Yitzhak as infiltrator into the father's realm?[18] Anthony Wilden notes that the "specular identification with an ideal, notably with the father, constitutes the subject in the *position* of the real father and thus in an untenable rivalry with him" [1968, 165]. An Oedipal triumph such as Yitzhak's is intolerable; according to the primitive law of retribution, Yitzhak must pay in kind. And, in fact, Yitzhak is bitten by the dog whose "madness" his inscription has produced; he pays for his transgression by assuming the paralysis of the father.

Thus, the dog is also the vehicle for the other side of this Oedipal drama and that is the re-direction of aggression away from the "father" back to the "son," that is to say, Yitzhak. In this respect, the dog, overdetermined creature (or text) that he is, becomes the vehicle for Yitzhak's self-punishment. In effect, one could argue that, by inscribing the dog with the words *kelev meshuga',* Yitzhak has written the *ḥerem* or writ of excommunication casting him out for the worst crime of all—the violation of Oedipal taboos. (Several times, the text compares Yitzhak's writing on the dog to the old practice of tying excommunications onto dogs, as if to prompt our investigation into the Oedipal significance of such writings.) The dog brings about the change in Yitzhak's position from *writer* of the *ḥerem,* a role analogous to that of Reb Faysh and the "men of Jerusalem" (*anshe Yerushalayim*), who produce writs of excommunication, to the *object* of the *ḥerem,* or the one who is cast out. His position changes from grammatical subject of the sentence to its object, or from he who writes to the one who is written, in a manner that parallels the odyssey of the text that is the dog. The dog is initially the "text" on which Yitzhak writes, but in its tireless search for a reader, the "text" takes on a more active role and reaches out to bite Yitzhak.

In a study of the Ashkenazic practice of preserving the cloth used during the circumcision ceremony for later use as a binder for the Torah, Kirshenblatt-Gimblett refers to circumcision as the "cut that binds": "Carrying the child's name and birthdate, and even the blood of circumcision, the binder symbolically binds the child around the law each time it is used to secure the Torah scroll" [1982, 137]. In *Only Yesterday*, a function analogous to the Torah binder can be discerned in the list—the *pinqas* or communal record—that Reb Alter preserves of the names of all those male infants whom he circumcised in Yitzhak's hometown.

As *mohel,* Reb Alter has the responsibility to inscribe Yitzhak in a list, thereby imposing the law that brings him into community. Circumcision signifies the covenant with a heavenly Father and occurs under the authorization of the earthly father, representative of the Law. As the "cut that binds," it names the subject and heralds his entry into an existing network of signifiers. Or, more accurately, since it occurs eight days after birth, it heralds the power and authority of the all-pervasive symbolic order to which the *infans* will gain access through the acquisition of speech and acquiescence to the law of the Father. (In this sense, "family" serves as a "relay point" between subjectivity and culture [Silverman 1983, 130].)

Circumcision, of course, constitutes a *modified* castration; it constitutes the "token" that is exacted as the cost of membership in the social order. Freud comments on the unconscious equation of circumcision with castration and sees this as one of the causes of [western] anti-Semitism" [1910, 95–96]; Lacan shows the movement from castration to the social practice of circumcision, at once a neutralization, an appropriation and an acting out of the aggressivity in castration [1977, 11ff., 199].

From one angle, the dog's bite undoes the ties that circumcision initiates. If circumcision is the inscription of the name of the Father in the flesh of the son, the dog's bite is its opposite, a perverse mirroring that the text does not suppress. It is the consequence of an inscription that occurs in a moment of suspension of the Law in which the utter randomness of writing surfaces. Inscription and bite combine to exclude Yitzhak from community, disqualifying him from the social role to which marriage to Shifra, an event that immediately precedes the dog's bite, has admitted him. (From another angle, one could argue that the dog's bite, as an imitation of circumcision, underscores the aggressivity contained in the ritual.)

After the start of his illness, Yitzhak's condition is brought to the attention of Reb Alter by his wife who dreams that Yitzhak's mother came to her expressing fear that her son had fallen victim to "savage anger" (*ḥaron af*)—a phrase that carries the flavor of paternal wrath, bringing to mind not only its scriptural uses, but also the father-tyrant of *Totem and Taboo.* Reb Alter's wife, Hinda Pu'ah, reports this dream to her husband, thinking that he "will laugh at her" (*yitzḥaq lah*): the verb *yitzḥaq* or "will laugh" is of course the same as Yitzhak's name, echoing parodically the Biblical etymology for the naming of Isaac (Gen. 18:12). Rather than *laugh*, however, Reb Alter confirms his wife's worries by telling her that on his list—his *pinqas*—of those he has circumcised, the letters of Yitzhak's name have begun to fade and become illegible (*nitashtishu*) [1968, 5: 602].

Reb Alter's list of those he circumcised in Yitzhak's eastern European hometown constitutes a writing *into* community, insofar as circumcision, the "cut that binds" in Kirshenblatt-Gimblett's phrase, initiates the inscription of Jewish males into community. This contrasts with the writing *out of* community that we see in the writing on the dog, an inscription that combines with the dog's bite to reverse the rite of circumcision, thus constituting the cut that severs, excluding Yitzhak from the community he entered with circumcision. This writing out of community invokes not only the *aqedah,* as Shaked, Band and others point out, but also the whole of God's promise to Abraham of nationhood. Through Reb Alter's reference to an effaced writing—the fading of Yitzhak's name on his list—the novel comments on itself, in a seemingly hallucinatory moment that epitomizes the structure of its relations. One inscription writes out another in a struggle for legibility for which Yitzhak is literally the locus.

Within the structures that the text generates, Yitzhak has acted out the forbidden; his accession to death is a sacrifice, whose purpose is to "restore" the power of the Father. This can be compared with dramas of filial sacrifice in Kafka's stories: while Gregor Samsa is swept out with the trash, his death takes its place in a sacrificial scheme insofar as it is linked with the sudden burst of spring that brings new life to the family. This concluding note of redemption and renewal in Kafka's "Metamorphosis" parallels the onset of rains in *Only Yesterday* following Yitzhak's death: we can see that Gregor's assumption of guilt, like Yitzhak's, has to do with no sin of his own, beyond entrapment in the web of the Oedipal.[19] These narratives suggest forms of Oedipal guilt for which no atonement is possible. Sons pay tribute with their lives, repaying the debt of a rebellion whose impact is cosmic as much as it is imaginary.

The inherence of this guilt in narrative structure suggests, from a psychoanalytic point of view, something like the refusal of the child to relinquish the primitive desire to be the phallus for the mother, a refusal that makes every encounter with the paternal a struggle to the death.[20] The developmental alternative to these savage dramas comes about through the normalization of the Oedipus complex: the child accepts that he cannot *literally* take the place of the father; through this accession to the law of the Father, the child accepts what amounts to "symbolic castration" and identifies with the *role* or *function* of the father.

In contrast, literature makes available to us a vicarious living out of the Oedipus in its more radical form. Yitzhak's end testifies to a hidden but persistent insistence on the radical nature of his transgression, which in effect resists any modification or integration.[21] It is this insistence, buried in the structure of thc text, that makes necessary the death-as-tribute-to-the-father to which Yitzhak submits. Read back into history, then, the novel traces the dilemma of a generation whose impulse to self-realization, whether on an individual or a national level, carried with it dangerous resonances of early struggles.

In Sophocles' rendition of the myth, Oedipus survives the punishment that we may understand to be castration; he offers himself to the people of Thebes as a horrible example, but in essence a therapeutic one: "Approach and deign to touch me for all my wretchedness, and do not fear. / No man but I can bear my evil doom" (11. 1413–15). In telling the townspeople his story, whether or not they accept it, Oedipus gains access to a dimension of being beyond simple commission of the crime: he has accepted his guilt, but he can make a claim to participation in the social order based on that acceptance and the consequent possibility of integration. In *Only Yesterday*, as in Kafka's "Metamorphosis," the split between the fate of the protagonist and the life of the collective goes unaddressed and unresolved; it remains to the reader to piece together the traces of an expiatory plot structure and to consider the place of that drama in human life.

The severity of Yitzhak's end is offset by the survival of the social world and, unpersuasively perhaps, by the novel's closing reference to a projected sequel that will tell of the "deeds of the rest of our friends" [1968, 5: 607]. Another attempt to offset the grimness of the conclusion can be seen in a discarded final chapter to the novel that contained, by way of "comfort," the meeting of the daughter of Yitzhak and Shifra with the son of Sonia and Yarkoni [Shaked 1971]. (We can keep in mind also the special case of the *moshav* Ein Ganim, a compelling instance of the capacity of workers to integrate their collective vision into the world, but one that is framed and set off from the dilemma of Yitzhak and friends.)

The only significant alternatives that the text offers can be seen in those figures, who have in one way or another, established distance from women as well as social movements. One figure who appears in the novel, but possesses also an identity outside the text, is Y. H. Brenner who is noteworthy in this appearance for his cynicism, clear-sightedness and simplicity. There are several minor but significant characters who posit the alternative of distance as a solution to the madness of unstructured fluctuation between extremes: they include the solitary Leichtfuss, who is marked by his isolation and self-sufficiency, and the artist Blaukopf, who draws a separation (*mataḥ vilon*) in order to practice his art. Kurzweil [1982] notes that dogs tend to be found in the company of the solitary figures in the novel; these figures rule over both dogs and women with a stern hand and so are not threatened by either. In contrast, Yitzhak flees from solitude and has bad luck with dogs and women.

In this roster of minor characters, Arzaf is the extreme of the isolationist tendency: his professional activities as a taxidermist testify to his lack of relationship to other creatures [1968, 5: 200–221, 224]. The deadliness of Arzaf's touch and the deathly seductiveness of his appeal to Balak make clear the sinister nature of the alternative he offers.[22] If it is Yitzhak's fate to succumb to the writing on the dog, to be the sacrifice to his own inscription, then Arzaf stands at the opposite extreme, to the extent of a monstrous detachment signified by the taxidermy he practices. Seducing animals into his studio with the delusory promise of permanence, he practices a craft that can be read as an extreme reification of the other.

A concluding note on writing. As an instrument of communication, writing possesses social function: it is meant to define, delineate, and transmit a message from sender to receiver. That transmission is predicated on the reliable definition of its constituent elements, including the differentiation between self and other that underlies the relationship of sender and receiver. Nevertheless that intersubjective structure is not as stable as one might assume. Jacques Lacan observes that "one can speak of the code only if it is already the code of the Other, and that is something quite different from what is in question in the message, since it is from this code that the subject is constituted, which means that it is from the Other that the subject receives even the message that he emits" [1977, 305]. From this, we may understand that writing itself, as an inter- and intra-subjective medium, contains the madness that is aberrance or the confusion of a "reliable" structure of communication. The madness *in* writing breaks down the distinctions it is meant to maintain. Just as Shoshana Felman takes representations of madness in literature to signal a "radical ambiguity of the inside and the outside, insofar as this ambiguity escapes the speaking subjects" [1985, 13], so my approach has been to take representations of writing in the text as nodal points for study of the interaction of linguistic and psychic structure that is the text. Madness brings forward indeterminacies and instabilities that are inherent in writing as well as in subjectivity, but might be overlooked in the interests of more peaceable readings.

As a novel, *Only Yesterday* contains, reverberates with, and may even be undone by the writings contained within it. Were we to catalogue these writings, we might note the contrast between Yitzhak as *tsabah* or housepainter whose job it is to "make surfaces nice" and the dog who *bites* Yitzhak, penetrating the surface in a biting aimed at getting at the truth. This contrast between superficial embellishment and deeper penetration is supported by the difference in the approaches of Yitzhak and Balak to the central writing that is the inscription of the dog. Yitzhak dismisses the writing on the dog: "And does everything that is written oblige us to believe it" [1968, 5: 589], but Balak expresses a much larger expectation as he searches for Yitzhak in order to decode the writing on his back: "If I bite him, the truth drips and flows from him." Interestingly, the text goes on to note that just as the mythical Great Dog bites the sky to bring blessed rains, so Balak bites Yitzhak to get truth [1968, 5: 593]. This folkloristic analogy expresses a primitive wish for oral incorporation of the desired object; on the level of primitive thought, that expectation parallels the connection between Yitzhak's death and the coming of the rain.

Yitzhak never masters the discourses—Zionism, the piety of *anshe Yerushalayim* (the men of Jerusalem)—to which he attempts to affiliate himself. His writing on the dog, an imitation of the writing of the father, produces a comedy-drama of the instability of the sign that opens up the drama of subjectivity to the text at-large.[23]

Just before writing on the dog, Yitzhak carries out one of the commissions that have earned him a good reputation for colors that do not fade [1968, 5:274]. This is ornamental writing, writing on command for a salary; until this point, Yitzhak has functioned as the instrument of others' intentionality. With the seductive appearance of the dog as potential text, the question of intention disappears into the union of hand and brush. The writing on the dog produces a "text" that is the inversion of the sort of socially acceptable sign painting Yitzhak has been doing: it exchanges the clear and distinct colors of the commissioned writing for the indeterminacy of the dog's coloring—"maybe white maybe brown maybe yellow"—suggesting reversibility of the text and its other.

There is a startling similarity between the moment at which Yitzhak writes on the dog and the moment at which the dog bites Yitzhak. Each involves loss of control, self-consciousness; each is a moment of possession, transport beyond the objective sense of the "I." These moments supply the sense of being of a piece, *ḥativah aḥat* instead of *ḥativot ḥativot, nivlah* or swallowed up in an experience of boundary loss. Each is a moment of writing (as well as a moment *in* the writing) in which the stable distinctions writing is supposed to maintain break down. Such moments of madness or excess collapse distinctions between subject and object, demonstrating the danger of too much closeness, whereas sanity, or the reasonable guarantee of a stable writing, assumes a "correct" distance.[24] In these moments, intersubjective structure collapses, with the consequent undoing of the subjectivity that has been formed through the family. The moments of excess in the novel are atoned for or repressed in the closure of the novel whose rigid Oedipal scheme of filial sacrifice attempts to contain the madness in the writing.

Chapter

8

The Wound and the Book: Gender, Writing and Culture in *Shira*

The Body of the Text

Nazism carried to an extreme a pernicious myth in its designation of the Jew as the diseased other, counterpart to the racially pure Aryan. In service of a fiction of national identity, Nazism attempted a construction of the world according to its own vision. This construction rests on a relation to the Jew as the dark underside of the myth, the other from which the mythic image presumably dissociates itself, but on which in fact it relies. The Jew is the denigrated lower term that makes possible the elevation of its opposite.

Shira, Agnon's posthumously published novel, takes the perspective of that other, the underside of the myth, but does so without dissociating the Jew from German culture. *Shira* explores the contradictory history of German Jews, demonstrating their high level of attainment through identification with German cultural ideals, together with their participation in a culture that designates the Jew as other. Set in the German emigré community of Jerusalem amid signs of the impending destruction of European Jewry, *Shira* raises questions about the relation of the Jew to European culture and the attachment of Jews to a culture which now repudiates them.

While concerned with ambivalences rooted in culture, *Shira* also shows a functioning Zionism, that is removed from the novel's dissection of ideological conflicts. As in other Agnon novels, we visit a collective farm in which young people realize the ideal of a new society. (See the village of preparation in *A Guest for the Night* and the cooperative settlement, Ein Ganim, in *Only Yesterday.*) It is possible to argue, in *Shira,* that the cooperative settlement embodies a positive assertion of nationhood, in the sense that Zionism took the anti-Semitic assertion of the indelibility of national character and transformed it into an affirmation of collective identity [Caron 1989,

508–09]. As in *A Guest for the Night* and *Only Yesterday,* the reality of such cooperative settlements and their contribution to a nation's identity is acknowledged; nevertheless, these social groups exist at something of a distance from the cultural conflicts that the text explores.

In its anatomizing of cultural myths, *Shira* can be compared to *Doctor Faustus,* Thomas Mann's novel of 20th-century Germany. Both novels share a concern, from different vantage points, with modern German history and culture. The density of cultural reference in each testifies to the richness of Germany's humanistic traditions, while the graphic horror of the images that each employs registers the impact of Germany's catastrophic collapse in the middle years of this century. *Doctor Faustus* moves back and forth from the Middle Ages to the Reformation, to modernity, intertwining the development of Adrian Leverkühn's genius with all the currents of German culture. *Shira* threads references to German-Jewish culture through its themes of bibliophilic excess, as it explores the consequences of Enlightenment and Emancipation, as well as the conflict between assimilation and the expression of national identity in Zionism.

In each novel, the metaphysical posture comes into conflict with an attraction to body and disease. Through explorations of tensions between humanistic scholarship and experience of the body, both novels evoke and undo some of the binary oppositions that inform culture. Mann's novel sets up a continuum of relations from its pedantic narrator, Serenus Zeitblom, who inhabits the "high-minded realms of the *humaniora*" [1948, 20], to the demonic Leverkühn, and considers, in turn, Leverkühn's fascination with disease. Not unlike that set of relationships, *Shira* follows the attraction of its scholar protagonist to the nurse Shira, whose name means poetry, along with his attraction to manifestations of the physical—from the female body to wound and leper. Via Herbst and the Jerusalem academy, *Shira* takes note of a spectrum of writings that range from the epitome of German scholarship in the form of the monograph to Herbst's abortive efforts to write a tragedy in which the sole character of his own invention is a leper. Situated in a social world that can be defined in terms of a spectrum of academic and scholarly writings, the novel evidences a crumbling from within, a tendency in the text that works against the authority of such writings.

Through representations of body and of book, *Shira* raises questions as to their relationship in culture. The "book" that figures here is not the Torah but the book in western culture, specifically, the

German-Jewish book as the object of culture. Agnon evokes the panoply of western tradition as his protagonist consults sources from Aristotle through Schiller to theorize on tragedy. (This surfacing of references is unusual in Agnon, whose texts are marked more by the effacement of secular European sources, whatever affinities we may sense in the texts themselves.) *Shira* weaves an abundance of anecdotes about books into its narrative, restoring to the book its derivation as an object from more primitive objects, for which it is a substitute. The effect is a re-instinctualizing of the book as object, demystifying without debunking its place in culture.

As an unfinished work-in-progress, *Shira* is a novel that Agnon chose not to complete. He began working on it in 1945, after finishing *Only Yesterday,* and wrote the bulk of it before he was 60.[1] While permitting, as he neared death, the compilation of the novel into its present form, Agnon had rejected earlier an ending that would have supplied a resolution to the novel's story of the search of its protagonist, Herbst, for the nurse Shira. Current editions of the novel contain that discarded last chapter in an appendix. (In effect, Agnon let his own death provide its ending, inasmuch as he passed on to his daughter instructions for assembly and publication of the text shortly before his death.) The status of the text as unfinished, subject to deletions and insertions over the decades of its composition, suggests that Agnon maintained the novel as process.[2] It was not for want of time that it remained unfinished. *Shira* is a novel that resists closure; that resistance forms part of a more general challenge to metaphysical certainties in the text.[3]

Through a thematics of the book, the novel jostles the status of the book as high cultural artifact. The status of the novel itself as incomplete and somewhat fragmentary combines with this internally subversive process to produce a text that is characterized more by permeability than by boundedness. The permeability that marks *Shira* can be understood in terms of a continuum of possible relations to the body, from the extremes of a metaphysics of transcendence, on the one hand, to, on the other, immersion in or fusion with the body.

Culture is marked by the move to transcendence, a move that contains within it the act of dissociation from an archaic maternal body. That body is "archaic" in that it belongs to strata of experience that are superseded in culture through the Oedipus complex, which positions the subject in the symbolic order. That cultural order provides support for the myth of an inviolable self or, for that matter, of a bounded text. Agnon's text enacts the move away from a logocentric schema in the direction of the rediscovery of a matrix that is devalued and suppressed in culture, but that resurfaces here in a fragmented narrative of fascination with the body and disease. Images of fragmented text and wounded body intersect in the question of culture, a question that is underscored by the novel's setting in the early years of World War II amid growing signs of the destruction of German Jewry.

Gendered Objects

Thematically, the novel's first scene introduces the play of concerns with gender, body and sexuality that characterizes the text. In these opening pages, we find the register of Herbst's responses to a spectrum of femaleness: the weary Henrietta joins the women in the hospital waiting room to give birth, as her husband remarks inwardly on the inappropriateness of the impending birth at this point in their lives; the nurse Shira enters and Herbst is struck by her freckles, "like nailheads in an old wall," as he recalls her impious behavior on a day when all of Jerusalem gathered to mourn a young man murdered by a gentile; he thinks of young Lisbet Neu, whose orthodox German-Jewish piety serves him as a *meḥitzah* [1989, 4; 1979, 8] or religiously imposed separation from his own turbulent thoughts.

The scene continues: "As Herbst *shut his eyes* in order not to look at [Shira], a beggar *blind in both eyes* came in and began to stroll among the women" [1989, 4; 1979, 8; emphasis added]. Syntactic juxtaposition of Herbst's shut eyes and the beggar's blind eyes seems momentarily to put the beggar in Herbst's place.[4] With the accomplishment of this substitution, Herbst is taken over by an apparent fantasy which suggests the gratification combined with terror of what the child both fears and desires to see. First, Shira's body widens to surround the beggar; next, both Shira and the beggar are swallowed up in her left sandal. The beggar's eyes, sightless and bad-smelling, offer a classical suggestion of the penalty for looking, that is, castration. At the same time, Shira's enveloping sandal pictures engulfment in the female, whose body encloses or takes in the castrated male.

The female body is an over-determined text in this novel, fraught with contradictions. The equivocal combination of attraction and threat experienced in response to the female body will surface again in the novel in images of severed legs, a worm-infested wound, and confusions of gender identification. We shall see later how the novel deploys a thematics of the body to disclose contradictions in constructs of gender, art, nationality, and to register the impact of anti-Semitic discourses whose roots reach back to medieval Europe.

At the same time, this thematics of the body takes on a more positive valorization: it offers an alternative direction to a sense of cultural belatedness and scholarly self-hatred. In the midst of the novel's self-conscious concern with western culture, Herbst's own writerly efforts are presented as fragmented and incomplete. His scholarly notes (*pitka'ot*), for example, do not add up to a composition [(*ḥibbur*) (1989, 199; 1979, 204–05], while his more literary efforts do not cohere and demonstrate rather a failure to synthesize new life out of the leavings of culture. (Compare Herbst's dilemma to that of Adrian Leverkühn, who cannot break out of the constraints of parody imposed on him by his position in culture.) The historical researches of Herbst, light parody of the archaeological investigations of scholarship, show a persistent inclination to get into certain subjects—passion, disease, suffering, the body. A late cultural product, the novel moves toward an interrogation of itself through these internal depictions of restless dissatisfaction and parodies of scholarship. Herbst, the autumnal man, can be read as the representation of the man within the (man's) writing. Self-consciously, this novel thematizes and even parodies its own constraints in the fumbling efforts of its protagonist to get past his own limitations.

The unfinished *Shira*, worked on over years, takes up questions of male and female, the nature of desire. The reader becomes aware of a process at work that is not wholly articulated or understood, a process that calls boundaries and gender definitions into question. This effect in the writing recalls stages in development of subjectivity when borders between self and other are not yet fixed and entry into the symbolic order has not been accomplished. *Shira* moves into difficult territory: while maintaining narrative constructs of plot and character, it also engages dimensions of subjectivity that are pre-verbal and pre-Oedipal. Consider, by comparison, the difficulty that Freud articulates in his efforts to describe and delineate "the sphere of this first attachment to the mother," a domain "so grey with age and shadowy and almost impossible to revivify—that it was as if it had succumbed to an especially inexorable repression." This is an area so remote that the discovery of the pre-Oedipal period seemed to Freud, in his own words, "a surprise, like the discovery in another field, of the Minoan-Mycenean civilization of Greece" (Freud 1931, 226). Working of necessity within a patrocentric system, Freud's archaeological metaphor acknowledges the existence of that which is prior, unexplored, mysterious and influential; he identifies those qualities with femininity and the shadowy realm of the pre-Oedipal.

Certain French poststructuralist feminists turn to this domain and privilege a pre-Oedipal stage that is characterized as diffuse, fluid and undifferentiated. The current notion of *écriture féminine* suggests a conception of writing as textplay, rather than as a mastery associated with masculinity.[5] Hélène Cixous and Luce Irigaray, among others, attempt a subversion from within of what they perceive to be a culturally instituted and oppressive writing. In their self-consciously disruptive writing, the play of desire in the text works against monolithic and socially sanctioned distinctions. Nevertheless, others have criticized this sort of privileging of the pre-Oedipal, charging it with continuing the categories of a patriarchal schema, while simply reversing the valorizations of male and female.[6]

Reading back from current theoretical debates, we can situate *Shira* within a horizon defined by the work of Freud and subsequent feminist theorists. While *Shira* carries no explicit ideological agenda, the novel lends itself to a reading attuned to process and joins in the interrogation of a system of power that rests on a system of metaphysical oppositions. A self-consciously playful blurring of gender distinctions signals a more pervasive move within the text to interrogate cultural assumptions about body and gender. The very incompleteness of the text suggests a sifting through narrative or discursive layers that calls into question the boundaries of the text.

In *Shira,* we find, paradoxically perhaps, that this self-questioning is prompted by aspects of the text that appear to be among the most deeply entrenched in conventional attitudes. The novel rehearses conventional gender alignments, but in doing so heightens our consciousness of them and contributes to their undoing. Manfred Herbst is caught in a web of relationships to women, among them two young German-Jewish women, Lisbet Neu and Anita Brik, and his three daughters. His fantasies reflect a rueful wish for return to the primitive law of the Father, that is, "Thou shalt love none other than me" [Cixous 1986, 45]. For example: "[Herbst] lowered his eyes and thought: She is with young men who have rejected the authority of their fathers" [1989, 118; 1979, 120]. And again: "Father Manfred eyes the young man intently. What does Zahara see in him? How could she leave her father for him?" [1989, 273; 1979, 272]. In the context of domestic comedies of family life, such comments reflect the benevolent despotics of a patriarchy which appropriates desire to itself.

A self-consciously masculine narrative voice complements this patrocentrism. For example, in response to the embrace of mother and daughter, the narrator observes, "If there was not here a demonstration of the will to return to one body I do not know what there was" [1989, 330; 1979, 328], a remark that implies distance from a fluidity that is identified as a female.[7] "My novel thickens and goes on. A woman and another woman and another woman. A parable like the parable of the preacher," the narrator exclaims impatiently, referring to an anecdote told of a preacher who is unable to go beyond the level of the specific or concrete example. His observation expresses impatience with woman as subject, resistant to abstraction, rooted in the literal. With the disappearance of Shira early on in the novel, the narrator proclaims her centrality: "I . . . will return to Shira, who is the essence . . . ," while noting persistent difficulty in locating her even within a sentence, as when Herbst cannot say her name: " . . . that same Shira weighed down his tongue" [1989, 297; 1979, 295]. "Enough of this *Weiblichkeit,*" says Herbst in a discarded fragment of the novel [Yaron 1978, 246], a remark that captures a certain tone in the text. While the tone of the narrative may border on misogyny, its insistent repetition of masculinist attitudes turns back against itself producing the subversive effect of parody.[8]

Naomi Sokoloff [1988, 153] argues for the importance of assessing the function of images of women in order to determine whether such images constitute an exploitation of female as other, or whether they are used as a means to self-examination (what Kristeva calls an "autocritique"). The question of authorial intent may be irrelevant to such an assessment, however, and in fact, the answer may lie as much in the reading as in the writing. In giving readers the domestic drama of *l'homme moyen sensuel, Shira* carries to an extreme a narrative posture that is stereotypically conventional, but it also tells, in effect, of its undoing.

This effect of undoing conventions by overdoing them can be found in Herbst's sadomasochistic fantasies of Shira and an engineer, fantasies which dwell on the passive posture of woman as victim and the sadistic activity of the male. These fantasies are fueled by the stories Shira has told Herbst of a past relationship [1989, 110–14; 1979, 112–16]. By mirroring or repeating sexual stereotypes, however, Shira's stories do not so much give substance to, as they disclose the constructedness of these configurations of gender and sexuality. As teller of the tales, Shira gives back to Herbst an account of the man's appropriation of the female body, in stories that reflect woman's role as prop for man's fantasies.[9] That Herbst's relationship with

Shira goes no further than its inaugural episodes serves to highlight and underscore the nature of fantasy as such. Her disappearance (underscored by Herbst's obsession with her) constitutes a nonconsummation, narratively and otherwise, that points up the fictive nature of that construction of female sexuality.

Shira both repeats and reverses stereotypical notions of gender in its persistent play with distinctions between male and female. Herbst, for example, thinks repeatedly of the legend in *Sefer ha'agadah* of the widower who grew breasts in order to nurse his child and wonders if such a child would grow up free of dependency on women [1989, 494, 537; 1979, 482, 520].[10] His young daughter Sara introduces a child's grammar in which "I love papa" takes the masculine form of the verb and "I love mama" the feminine: gender of the subject is defined by that of the object [1989, 529; 1979, 513–14]. Shira puts on man's pants and becomes more womanly [1989, 22, 163; 1979, 26, 164].

An even more suggestively self-conscious variant of this gender confusion can be found in the imagery of birth that shapes Herbst's scholarly and literary activities. Early on, his projected new book is likened to an "embryo in the womb of scholarship" [1989, 41; 1979, 45]. As his scholarly concerns give way to more literary ambitions, the desire to write a tragedy finds expression in language that extends the imagery of birth and reproduction. Herbst makes notes for a historical tragedy, in which the only character that is totally his own invention is Basileus the leper, "this Basileus to whom Herbst gave birth in his imagination" [1989, 381; 1979, 374]. But the leprosy with which Herbst endows his creation works also as a means for Herbst the fastidious to distance himself from the tragedy, to the explicit detriment of his creative efforts: "for a matter in which there is no immersion of the mind is weak [*rofef*], all the more so matters of poetry [*shira*] and vision that require impregnation of the soul, and there is no impregnation without one soul sinking into another out of which a new soul is created . . . " [1989, 287; 1979, 286]. A self-conscious Platonism here uses sublimation to appropriate and elevate to the spiritual a model of physical reproduction. It may well be, however, just this model of sublimation with its metaphysical thrust that the novel calls into question, as it parodies academic scholarship and valorizes the body or the wound.

The birth imagery that shapes Herbst's creation of Basileus the leper is deflected by the repugnance that the fastidious Herbst experiences at the vividness of his own imagination: "Despite the fact that he had been knee-deep in blood and pus when he fought for

Germany in the last war, now that he was in Jerusalem, in peace-time, he avoided the whiff of a whiff of blood, the trace of a trace of pus—even so leprosy, whose very name arouses metaphysical terror" [1989, 288; 1979, 286]. In this terror at the prospect of undoing the metaphysical, we can read Herbst's attraction to and withdrawal from the body. He is caught in culture between body and book.

Rose of Jericho

> I have a wound in the jaw, a wound that . . . demands a lot of care . . . the doctor is not worried about the possibility of *shoshanat yeriḥo* [Rose of Jericho] [1989, 181; 1979, 182].

In the company of Shira, Herbst visits a young woman who has fallen ill of a disease that may or may not be the disease called *shoshanat yeriḥo* or "Rose of Jericho."[11] Herbst approaches with Shira, unaware as yet that the person Shira is taking him to visit is the young German emigree and would-be poet whom he met first in a Jerusalem cafe on the day his daughter Sara was born and whom he saw next working as a waitress in a Dead Sea hotel where she referred to a wound (*makah*) in her jaw which the doctor assured her was "probably not" *shoshanat yeriḥo*, but which needed attention and might necessitate a hospital stay. This definition by negation or denial can be read as a feeble effort at effacing or masking the wound. This ulceration or wound, visible or not, seems to make manifest the failure of the young woman's attempt to make the transition from the gentility of Berlin Jewish life to emigre life in Jerusalem, let alone any further foray into the new land; she mentions its possible identification as *shoshanat yeriḥo* in a conversation in which she refers as well to her unfitness for kibbutz life. (As such, she may be read as a comment on the difficulties experienced by numbers of young women of her generation and cultural background that the novel refers to. See, for example, 1989, 178; 1979, 179–80.)

Herbst's anticipation of the visit to the young woman who is recovering from surgery on her jaw serves as the occasion for two fantasies. In each, the integrity of the body is startlingly disrupted. In the first of his visions, he sees old men, in a desert scene, truncated, buried alive to their waists. While the image of these truncated bodies may suggest castration, that suggestion is even more graphically developed in Herbst's second fantasy. He sees next a scene in which a holy man "indulges" or "enjoys himself" (*mit'aden*) with the worms in the wound in his flesh:

> And again Herbst was removed [in fantasy] and found himself in the emperor's palace, at a feast the emperor had made for a holy man of God whose fame had reached the emperor's palace and he had been forcibly brought to the emperor's palace so that the emperor could intoxicate himself with his holiness. The emperor sat at his sumptuous repast that he had made in honor of the holy man and all his ministers were with him. And the holy man sat at the head of the table and did not eat or drink but indulged himself in his wounds which were giving off worms and maggots, and the emperor and all his ministers saw. Opposite them crept a new worm that was born in the flesh of the holy man and paid no attention to the status of the emperor and of the food of his table and of the seated ministers, and perhaps did not know that it was living in the body of a holy man and that it was holy flesh that it was eating [1989, 246–47; 1979, 246].

These images infiltrate Herbst's consciousness. He is the vehicle through which the text mingles fantasies of holy man and wound with the actual disease of the person he is about to visit. The effect is to direct the reader's attention to the wound as the site of the opening of the body and to the capacity of the wound to take on a life of its own.

The vision of the worm-infested wound of the holy man is rife with cultural/sexual associations. Herbst's anticipatory horror and the thrill of his imagining suggest the sort of terror and fascination Freud attributes to the sight of the female genitals [1922, 273–74]. According to psychoanalytic theory, the female genital evokes castration fear in the male observer. Thus, femininity is defined through negation, as a lack: the female is already castrated. The association of Anita Brik's skin ulceration with the holy man foregrounds the "wound" of femininity and suggests the feminization of the holy man. Herbst's vision of the worm-infested wound that takes on a life of its own can be linked to the psychoanalytic interpretation of the riveting fascination of the Medusa's head.

Furthermore, in the larger cultural domain, Freud [1910] speculates that the Jewish practice of circumcision may have been a contributing factor to anti-Semitism through the castration fear the practice evoked. Herbst's fantasies approach the body, raising issues of gender, bodily integrity, and castration. Within European history, these issues find a place in the formation of anti-Semitic discourses that associate the Jew with imageries of bodily desecration. (See Gilman, 1986, on the association of Jews with disease and Hsia, 1988, on the history of the charges of ritual murder and desecration of the Host in early modern Germany.) Through graphic disruptions of bodily integrity, the images of truncated bodies and of the holy man absorbed in his wound condense some deep-rooted cultural paradoxes surrounding relationship to the other.

Ulcer and wound are suggestive images, grounded inescapably in the body. The fascination that surrounds such images in Agnon's novel raises the general question of the relationship of observer to victim and wound. The holy man who "feasts himself" in absorption in his wound and the waitress Anita whose flesh is being consumed by the organism that invaded her body can be linked to the Jerusalem doctor, mentioned much later in the novel, who injects himself with an organism in order to study the course of the disease it causes [1989, 553; 1979, 535]. In each of these situations, a parasitic organism consumes flesh while observer and/or victim looks on: 1. Anita Brik *is victim* of the organism consuming her body; 2. The holy man *submits to and values* the worms in his flesh; 3. The Jerusalem doctor *of his own volition* injects himself and studies disease in his body. Beyond them all, the novel cites the Nazi doctors who inject Jews with pathogens and watch the course of disease, in what we can understand to be the most extreme split between observer and victim.

In its attention to history, the novel depicts this century's most recent and extreme designation of otherness: the Nazis inflict the wound of otherness by splitting humankind into Aryan and subhuman, dissociating themselves from the disease of humanness by projecting it onto the Jews. The text counters the racist ideology of Nazism, insofar as the holy man of Herbst's fantasy and the Jerusalem doctor appropriate the wound that is the stigma of difference. The fantasy of the holy man initiates the subversion in its exaltation of suffering and the body. The Jerusalem doctor assumes the suffering of the other in the interests of science, producing a sharp contrast to the racism of Nazi pseudo-science. While Nazism as ideology reifies the Jew as "other," the Jerusalem doctor injects himself with "otherness" in a move that internalizes that relationship and transforms it from denial or denigration to assertion.

The ulcerated jaw of Anita Brik, named with the name of a flower, signals an attraction to disease as the body made manifest.[12] One could say that *shoshanat yeriḥo*, the ulcer that bears the name of a bloom, becomes the wound of the doctor who inflicts illness on himself in order to study it. Late in the novel, when Herbst meets this doctor, he kisses his hand, in deep admiration for this noble spirit.[13] Herbst's gesture expresses a valuation of the body in disease that subverts culture's move to dissociation from the body.

These configurations of variables reflect a prevailing system of cultural values, a system based on relationship to the body that is coded as feminine. In this system, sympathy suggests an over-closeness to the body that raises the possibility of contagion. (See Mary Ann Doane 1986, 172–73.) The novel provides graphic evidence of a range of cultural positions in Herbst's oscillation between attraction to and repugnance from the opening of the body that is the wound.[14] The ambivalent valorization of disease or the wound works towards a textuality that engages the problematics of culture experienced in the body.

We find an emblematic presentation of this relationship to the body when Herbst visits a bookshop and finds himself riveted before the reproduction of a picture of a leper. In this picture, the leper's hand, eaten away by the disease, grasps a bell that he rings to warn the townspeople to keep away from him:

> [Herbst's] eyes were pulled in several directions. He stood trembling and astonished. What is this? A leper. A painting of a leper standing at the city gate, ringing a bell to warn the people to keep their distance. Herbst picked up the picture and stood it up so he could see it better. The eyes were awesome and sad. Their sockets had, for the most part, been consumed by leprosy, yet they were alive and wished to live. Sadder and more awesome was the hand holding the bell, a hand consumed by disease that could not be reversed. Even sadder and more awesome was the bell, warning people to keep their distance [1989, 449; 1979, 438].

The leper's eye sockets repeat the sightless eyes of the beggar in the novel's opening scene, while the fascination exerted by his hand seems to anticipate Herbst's kiss to the hand of the Jerusalem doctor. As disease in the body, leprosy can be read as the body made manifest. The picture of Herbst regarding the picture of the leper that is itself the reproduction of a painting underscores this question of relation to the body by framing it in the text and placing it *en abyme.* In this powerfully emblematic image, the leper's hand, consumed by disease, draws Herbst in, transgressing the boundaries that the frame defines and defying also the message of the bell which, despite its ostensible warning, offers an invitation to the onlooker.

Distanced from the social world by the bell, the leper is situated in a sacred space that combines inclusion and exclusion [Foucault 1965, ch. 1]. This liminal space suggests also the position of the Jews in European culture. It is interesting, in this connection, to note the persistence of the belief that leprosy was the disease of the Jews.[15] But this is the space of the woman too insofar as culture marginalizes her, splitting her into images that express both transcendence and degradation, a menacing ambiguity that finds itself situated on the border neither quite inside or outside [Ortner 1974; Gilman 1985; 1986, 244–45].

Research on the evolution of the novel *Shira* [Yaron 1979, 542] has shown that the manuscript originally contained the short story "*'Ad 'olam*" ("Forevermore"), a story that offers an even more striking embrace of disease that is intertwined with a story of involvement with and eventual immersion in a text: Dr. Amzeh (*'am zeh* means "this people"), who has worked for years to complete a history of Gumlidata, finds the information he is missing, as well as a surviving copy of the manuscript of the city, in a leprosarium where the manuscript has been kept. "Forevermore" pictures final fusion with a leprous text. At the expense of recognition in the public eye, Dr. Amzeh decides to remain in the leprosarium in order to devote himself to study of the manuscript that is disintegrating and permeated with pus from sores of the lepers who have read it lovingly over the years.

The account of Herbst's meeting with the Jerusalem doctor is the site in the manuscript of *Shira* at which the short story "Forevermore" had originally been placed. If we read the account of that meeting with this elision in mind, we can say that Herbst's meeting with the doctor covers over the traces of a narrative that underscores and deepens its theme; that theme concerns the question of distance from and closeness to the body. We can extend this thematic reading of the novel's omissions even further, once we realize that Agnon considered ending the novel by having Herbst join the infected Shira in a leprosarium. Had he not discarded that last chapter, the novel's conclusion would have underscored the paradoxical return to or affirmation of the body through disease [Schocken 1978, 238–40].[16] We should not forget, however, that Agnon chose to omit the conclusion; its excision expresses preference for an ambivalent tension over definitive closure. The restoration of that last chapter in an appendix should not lead readers to attach it too firmly to the body of the text.

German-Jewish *Bildung*

Drawn as Herbst is to Anita Brik, to the picture of the leper, to the Jerusalem doctor, to visions of the holy men who cherish and display their wounds, he remains protected by his wife Henrietta: her maternity sustains a definition of gender that isolates Herbst in his study to carry out the business of scholarship. That scholarship, however, is blocked: Herbst's obsessive preoccupation with his *pitqa'ot* or notes—shuffling and reordering, adding to and taking away from them—carries with it more than a hint of an onanistic quality that underscores its nonproductivity. In the realm of language, scholarship offers an important defense against fusion, but brings with it the danger of fragmentation or isolation. Witness the self-hatred in Herbst's citation of his colleague Julian Weltfremd's phrase for scholars who make little notes and practice a "coffee-and-cake scholarship" [1989, 553; 1979, 536].[17]

Collectively, Herbst and his colleagues offer a portrait of German-Jewish scholars who were devoted to and integrated into German culture. These scholars identified themselves through the process of German *Bildung* or classical education: "Manfred Herbst was born and educated in Germany, in German schools, in German scholarship and poetics, like his contemporaries, Jews and non-Jews" [1989, 211; 1979, 212]. George Mosse [1985, 1–16] provides a history of the concept of *Bildung* in the Jewish movement for Emancipation and in the German-Jewish intellectual's self-concept.

Indeed, we can fit Herbst's studies of Byzantium into the context of Jewish scholars who work on aspects of classical civilization and Christianity. In Herbst's biography, we find something of a representative sequence that includes the suppressed or assimilated Jewishness of his father, the history of the young Manfred's studies, the impact of Jewish texts on him, all of which points to the preparation of a space for cultural synthesis [1989, 218ff.; 1979, 219ff.]. His family background in Germany points to the intersection of cultures.[18]

This question of a German-Jewish synthesis brings in an important segment of the novel and that is the family history of Herbst's mentor, Alfred Neu, who figures in the novel as the preeminent example of German-Jewish intellectual life [1989, 224ff.; 1979, 224ff.]. To give one indication of Neu's intellectual eminence, Herbst imagines Neu's latest book, along with the *Siddur* (prayerbook) and *Humash* (Pentateuch), on the table of Lisbet Neu and her mother, awaiting his interpretation of it [1989, 236; 1979, 233]. Alter [1971, 77] surveys the academic types that populate this novel and voices a critical consensus when he characterizes Neu as "a superbly perceptive mind unswervingly devoted to the discovery of truth"; similarly, Barzel acclaims Neu "as so elevated an ideal that the author only lets us observe him from a distance" [1975, 167]. With the difference that he belongs to a secular context, Neu can be linked to other luminous, paternal figures in Agnon's work, such as the grandfather in many of the short stories, the locksmith in *A Guest for the Night*, and the bookbinder in "Knots upon Knots" (one of the stories in "*Sefer hama'asim*"). These are transcendent figures whose names or occupations resonate with peace and completeness and offer the reader relief from the dissonances that otherwise characterize the world of the fiction.

Nevertheless, Neu's *non*-appearance in the novel and the ominous nature of events unfolding in Germany where he remains may raise questions about the absolute veneration in which he is held by characters and critics alike. I would venture to suggest that the image of Neu of the radiant scholarship, hovering just at the horizon of the novel, may be construed in at least two mutually opposing ways, in a contradiction that illuminates the novel. That is, Neu emanates an aura of intellectual purity, dedication to scholarly ideals and moral probity of the sort associated with Moses Mendelssohn and the *Haskalah* or Enlightenment in German-Jewish history; but he can be read also as a critique of those ideals that discloses their dependence on a cultural tradition whose internal contradictions history now makes apparent. In this light, Neu's very purity states its opposite: the effort to overcome by reversal the stereotype of the dirty Jew.

The participation of German-Jewish intellectuals in German culture boxed them into a predicament insofar as the rise of Nazism expressed that very culture's rejection and attempt to degrade and eventually destroy this group of adherents.[19] What is the relationship of the German-Jewish intellectual to his language and his work in a culture that simultaneously forms him and questions his rights to full membership? Any attempt to respond to this question should go back in time at least to Moses Mendelssohn whose qualities of mind and spirit made him the exemplar of enlightenment. (See Altmann 1985, 17–31.) This status brought him the veneration of Jew and Gentile alike and produced, on the one hand, a public challenge to convert to Christianity as logical fulfillment of his virtue, and, on the other, Gotthold Lessing's choice of Mendelssohn as model for his representation of Jewish virtue in *Nathan the Wise.* While Mendelssohn himself managed to sustain the tension between Enlightenment rationalism and an adherence to Mosaic law, this sort of solution did not however outlive him [Meyer 1967, 56].[20]

The effort to synthesize and sustain a multivalent identity is perhaps the distinguishing mark of the German-Jewish intelligentsia, caught over time in the ambivalence of their participation and high achievement in a culture which nevertheless preserves the deep strain of a racist myth and denies such attainments to Jews. This deeply embedded paradox can be felt throughout twentieth-century German-Jewish culture and persists in present-day historiography, where one feels the pain, conflict and divided loyalties in historians' treatments of their culture. Consider the deep outcry contained in this passage in which Alexander Altmann describes the relationship of Moses Mendelssohn to the German language:

> [Moses Mendelssohn] was . . . the spiritual ancestor of all those numberless Jews who cherished in the German language "the sweet sound of the mother tongue." The intimacy with German, for which Mendelssohn had to struggle hard, came naturally to generations of Jews after him. What a travesty of the truth it was when, on April 12, 1933, one of the "Twelve Statements of the German Student Body" said: "When a Jew writes German, he lies." Robert Schumann would hardly have set poems by Heine to music had he felt them to be anything but German and authentically human. The authority of Mendelssohn's German prose remained the hallmark of the best of German-Jewish writers down to Karl Wolfskehl and Franz Kafka. [Altmann 1985, 19]

This sort of pride in language, taken in the historical context that Altmann sketches, is a measure of Jewish participation in and contribution to German culture.[21] See also Gay, 1978, and Grunfeld, 1979, for histories of German Jewry of this period that are informed by the historian's complex relationship to his own cultural formation.

At the same time, it is also in the area of language that we find long-standing stereotypy attributing to the Jews a hidden language of corruption, whose historical development Sander Gilman has traced for us. According to Gilman [1986, 20], it is the "strong tradition of the myth of a homogeneous language that defines the Other as possessing a different tongue." From the late medieval period, when the burning of the Talmud expressed people's fear of the books possessed by the "people of the Book," to the use of medical jargon which made twentieth-century concentration camps parodies of medical structures, Gilman traces the accretion of images of contamination around the figure of the Jew, attributing to him leprosy, a particular smell, womanliness, qualities of an otherness in which language remained a central feature.

In the European psyche, the Jew figures as that other, split off and marginalized, through whom the dominant group is able to consolidate its fiction of itself. Gilman examines the evidence of the process by which the Jewish psyche internalized the hatred directed against Jews by the non-Jewish world and then attempted to rid itself of a negative self-image by splitting the negative image off from itself and using it to define the "bad" eastern European Jews, a stereotype focused particularly on the question of language. (See also Steven E. Aschheim 1982.)

Thinking about questions of representation in *Shira* in light of Gilman's study leads to a curious paradox: the nonappearance of eastern European Jews in the novel might be taken to reflect German Jewry's dissociation of itself from the negative image of eastern Jews. But those same non-represented bad eastern European Jews number among them the author of the novel. Indeed, Agnon's own peregrinations from eastern Europe (1888–1906) to Palestine (1907–13) to Germany (1913–24) and to Jerusalem (1924–70) constitute a text that encompasses some of the moves and directions of twentieth-century Jewish life, including an engagement with European culture that persisted despite gestures at effacement in service of biographical myth.[22]

The German Jewish Book: Histories of the Object

My discussion of the varieties of engagement of Jews with German culture comes under the heading "the German-Jewish book." The German-Jewish book is the product of and high testimony to the culture that ultimately rejects it; as such it is the self-contradictory manifestation of hatred, self-hatred, and love of the book. Self-hatred is the disease of turning inward the aggression and accompanying negative characterizations that are directed toward one. In the context of *Shira's* concerns with Germany, Jews, culture and the body, I would argue that the German-Jewish book emerges as a problematic object, a wound in and of itself. It is a text that takes shape at the site of the meeting of a number of vectors: the valuation of language and formation of the self through language (*Bildung*), and the hatred experienced from the external world and internalized. The wound is the site for the meeting of these forces that produce a cultivated and pain-filled text.

I shall select only a few of the "book anecdotes" that can be found in *Shira* to suggest some of the ways in which accounts of the book as an object with a history of ownership serve to register the contradictions of European Jewish life. The book enters in as encrusted artifact, trailed by its history, object of desire to bibliophiles. In characteristic Agnon style, the forward movement of the novel's plot is deflected through the "intrusion," as it were, of these digressive histories of books, their owners and the wanderings of each. But of course, as readers of Agnon know, what appear to be "digressions" are very much to the point. In this instance, the cumulative impact of stories about books and bibliophiles manifests a concentration in the text that may lead us to explore the complex and conflict of experiences among language, text, and body that constitute culture.

"From the day that the Nazis came to power Jerusalem has become a metropolis for German books" [1989, 135; 1979, 136]. With the descent of the German emigrants and their inability to support themselves, "every street corner in Jerusalem is full of rare books" [1989, 135; 1979, 136]. The narrator observes that Ernst Weltfremd's book has just been published, at the very time that Jewish books in Germany are being burned [1989, 441; 1979, 431]. Herbst boasts to Tagelicht of a first edition of *The Birth of Tragedy* that he bought for a shilling, while Tagelicht attempts to decipher the names of the previous owners from the ornate German-Greek script [1989, 135; 1979, 136]. Herbst displays another book in which his bibliophilic pleasure is tempered by the knowledge of the double suicide of the book's previous owners [1989, 135; 1979, 136]. Herbst remembers, with a blush of shame, his failure as a youth in Germany to return a book out of a set of Nietzsche to a doctor who committed suicide; he feels responsible for the flaw in the set [1989, 445; 1979, 435]. Herbst encounters a library, at the booksellers, that belonged to a rich Jew who collected books and wrote on idols (*'avodah zarah*) in Eretz Yisrael and was killed in violence with the complicity of his Arab driver [1989, 446–47; 1979, 436–37].

The book is an object the history of whose ownership portrays the history of Jewish participation in the culture. The example of the volume of Nietzsche from the set of the doctor who suicided compresses a narrative or at least invites the reader to place those elements in a syntactic structure that tells a story; that story suggests attainment and loss, and a problematic definition of self through identification with culture. Recurring references to Nietzsche that run through these compressed anecdotes may evoke not only Nietzsche's challenge to humanistic values, but the contradictory uses to which his thought has been put in the twentieth century. Whatever one might want to say about the use of Nietzsche in the discourse of anti-Semitism, *Shira's* book anecdotes mark the importance of Nietzsche to the generation of Jews in Germany in the early part of this century, whose world was so soon to fall apart.[23]

In a particularly striking image of the superimposed contradictions contained within an object, we find the description of a reliquary that is offered for sale in a bookstore. It goes unnoticed by Herbst, but is brought to our attention by the narrator and observed from a distance by its owner who has left it to be sold in an effort to offset her poverty as a German emigree in Jerusalem [1989, 442–43; 1979, 432–33]. This reliquary is a container that has been put to different uses over the centuries since the onset of modernity. It concretizes the layered history of books and their owners that I have been tracing. The narrator describes the reliquary's present contents, musical notations written by the composer Mendelssohn, contained in a handmade wooden box, finished in silver, that once housed the bone of a holy man, which was said to have worked miracles until the time of the Reformation. From that time on, the bone lay idle, "since the generation was not worthy" and in time it disappeared. Perfumes and baubles then occupied the case (*aron*); after eight generations the box came to the hands of a singer who placed in it musical notations that had come to her from her teacher, Felix Bartholdy Mendelssohn, "in addition to letters of Schleiermacher through whose means she had entered the Christian faith." This singer's grandson was attracted to Zionists and to a Jewish woman whom he married, thus finding his way back to the faith not of his fathers, but of "his father's fathers" [1989, 443; 1979, 433]. The daughter of this man who found his way back to Judaism now stands in the same bookshop as Herbst waiting to see if her Mendelssohn manuscript has been sold. From saint's reliquary to repository for the manuscript of the composer whose grandfather initiated the *Haskalah* and finally to an elderly emigree's last treasure, the history of the ownership and contents of the box can be read as a palimpsest, condensing European history of the relationship of Jew to Christian.

The reference to the composer Mendelssohn evokes his grandfather, Moses of Dessau, credited with initiating the *Haskalah,* a figure whose importance to European culture we have already cited. The novel invokes the Mendelssohn family history. In citing the full name of the composer, Felix Bartholdy Mendelssohn, Agnon alludes to the efforts of Abraham Mendelssohn, son of Moses and father of Felix, to Christianize the family. Abraham converted, baptized his children and adopted the surname Bartholdy. About the name change, he is supposed to have said, "A Christian Mendelssohn is impossible." His son Felix resisted the name change, but was apparently able to summon up more genuine feeling for Christianity than was his father [Meyer 1967, 88–89]. In the novel, the owner of the box is said to have converted under the influence of letters of Schleiermacher, persuaded perhaps by his view of Judaism as a dead religion, although one must keep in mind his advocacy of civil rights for Jews and his opposition to the use of conversion to Christianity as a means to gaining those rights [Meyer 1967, 77–78].

This history of the box and its contents registers traces of Jewish experience in Europe, involving variously efforts to achieve integration, to efface origins and to obtain rights while retaining national identity. The return to Zionism of the last owner takes its place as the most recent historical phase prior to the move to Jerusalem. It is the last owner who stands unnoticed, conscious of the evidence of the misery of the time in the relegation of a Mendelssohn manuscript to the corner of a bookshop where a customer unwittingly rests hat and coat on them.

The novel provides several structural analogues to the presentation of the reliquary as container for cultural artifacts. Compare, for example, the description of Herbst's bookcase [1989, 170–71; 1979, 171–72] and the history of the collection of a wealthy German Jew who settled in Petah Tikvah [1989, 433–34; 1979, 424]. The register of the contents of each of these containers—reliquary, bookcase, book collection—concretizes a temporal sequence and makes history visible.

As a novel, *Shira* is rich in its amalgam of book anecdotes, histories, and erotics. While one segments the text arbitrarily in order to discuss it, it is impossible to overlook the permutations of desire that surround the book as object. In one compelling sequence that places books in a context that links them to bodily processes and instinctual demands, Herbst enters the "inner rooms" of the booksellers: "The smell of old books came to his mouth, the smell of dust of old paper, of leather, of cloth with an addition of the smell of all the generations who had handled the books"; with an intensity that is provoked by but not limited to books, Herbst is seized by a desire that "resembled the spirit of longing, and changed to the spirit of a desire such that all the books in the world could not fill" [1989, 443; 1979, 433].[24] Desire is abated only by the action of lighting a cigarette, a substitution of cigarette for book that suggests the role of the object in supplying a primitive gratification.

The text expands on the structural analogy between book and cigarette, as Herbst and the clerk discuss examples of strategies for dealing with wartime constraints, such as cigarettes made of newspaper with grass in them. This leads them to consider a further "improvisation"—the clerk's recollection of the sight of a soldier using pages of a book to serve his "personal needs," a book which turns out to be a first edition of Friedrich Schiller's *Das Sendung Moses (The Mission of Moses).* According to the clerk, he rebuked the soldier for his scornful treatment of "our great poet Schiller," to which the soldier responded, "I thought it was one of those Jew books, written by one of their little rabbis" [1989, 444; 1979, 434]. Schiller's book offers a recycling of anti-Semitic propaganda in its account of Moses' theft of monotheism from Egyptian priests; according to Schiller, leprosy was the national illness of the Jews in Egypt and continued to persist among them [Schocken 1978, 235].

Thus, while Herbst and the clerk share an account of putting a book to uses which desecrate it as an object, we must note as well that the book's contents picture the Jew in terms of contamination and disease. The reference to the title *Das Sendung Moses* localizes in the figure of Moses the ambivalence that surrounds the Jews and depicts a fear of contamination with an otherness that is defined in physical terms.

In this cumulative series of book anecdotes, the novel brings together within two pages the "reliquary" with its history, Herbst's tactile and erotic experience of bibliophilia, the examples of cigarette as container made out of printed material and the use of pages of a rare first edition of an anti-Semitic text for "personal needs." These last two examples suggest the simultaneous defilement and erotization of the book in service of oral and anal function. The text accounts for an erotics of the object in transformations of object and body part that are reminiscent of the shifting zones of infantile sexuality. In a partial reversal of sublimation that retains the cultural value assigned to the book, these examples register the significance of the book in terms of what are understood to be the "highest" and the "lowest" of human functions. The book as an object of desire resists stable definition and is shown to form part of a chain of substitutions that derives from infantile attachment to body parts and products.

This series of anecdotes is followed immediately by an affectionate parody of Herbst's bibliophilic excesses that constitutes simply the most recent layer in the novel's history of books and owners.

Herbst experiences the recurring and very provoking memory of how he missed out on a first edition of a book bibliographers had said did not exist—a book he had held in his hand, but had not recognized because it was bound inside another book. He faults himself for not recognizing that the book he held in his hand was thicker than it should have been [1989, 444; 1979, 434]. His attunement to the book as physical object enables him to identify it by touch and feel.[25] Herbst is pictured as the type of the bibliophile, innocently unaware of the autoerotic nature of his experience of desire, as well as its link to primitive experiences of the body.

We find a hint of the instinctual paths that lead to Herbst's bibliophilic intensity, as we examine his response to some art books he comes across at the booksellers: "To a man like him, every art object is close to his heart and he must keep close watch on himself that he won't be dragged after everything that his eyes see, in order that he may be free for his work in order that he may be free for investigations, in order that he may be free for the things he has to do" [1989, 448; 1979, 438]. The object that stimulates this defensive expostulation is one I cited earlier: the picture of the leper, whose disease-wasted hand holds a bell to warn passersby of the danger of contagion. The picture, in its visual presentation, transgresses its own frame in an invitation to the onlooker. For Herbst, absorption in a book is a substitute for the picture; it offers him a defense against looking. But the context suggests that the picture too takes its place in a chain of substitutions that extends from book to picture and back into body.[26]

Herbst remains hovering, poised in the combined moves of attraction and repulsion. His response to the painting demonstrates the never-to-be-completed move to recuperate the body in culture. Moreover, Herbst's bibliophilia provides the occasion for text-play with images of the book that undo its delineation as pristine object, the high attainment of culture. The book, itself a body, takes its place in larger "bodies," among them the libraries, bookcases and store windows that the novel pictures for us. (The reliquary as object, as well container for other objects, reminds us of the variables of focus, perspective and frame that determine our perception.) These books or "bodies" can be opened and closed, read with reverence, or invaded, their boundaries transgressed by violent actions.

In the abundance of its book stories, bibliophilic and otherwise, *Shira* is exquisitely sensitive to the inscription of objects in history and history in objects. The dynamics of inscription situate the book in culture, while showing us the roots of culture in a relation to the body.

This reinstinctualizing of the book constitutes the novel's "shameful secret," its feminine subtext; through it, culture's dissociation of book from body is undone.[27]

Eros, Gender, Violence

The first two parts of the novel end with dream scenes that mingle violence, sexuality and gender confusion. In the dream that concludes Book One, Herbst meets a childhood friend, a classicist who had corrected Wilamowitz's translations of Greek tragedy; the two discuss words that are feminine in one language and masculine in another, and the dream ends with Herbst remembering to buy a sterling silver knife as a wedding present for Shira and Lisbet Neu [1989, 164; 1979, 163–64].[28] The seeming innocence of such language play becomes sinister with the intrusion of knife and homosexual union that poses, implicitly but no less severely, the threat of castration.

Similarly, Book Two ends with Herbst's fitful sleep after the memory of a disturbing incident in Leipzig at the time of his betrothal to Henrietta, an incident involving the discovery of a pair of severed legs, mistakenly identified as those of a boy, but eventually identified as belonging to a young woman, who had been raped and murdered. Herbst's recollection of the desire he had felt, the day before the rape/murder, on seeing that young woman dressed in man's clothes, implicates him in her end. The severed legs, found in *'emeq hashoshanim* or Rose Valley, initiate an associative series in Herbst's mind that includes Shira's account of a jackal that dismembered a baby, and her story of the engineer and his whip [1989, 349–50; 1979, 345–47]. Herbst sleeps finally, only to dream that he is arrested and accused of the rape/murder; he sees Shira and understands that *she* is the murderer/rapist, but that she will make no move to help him [1989, 350–51; 1979, 347].

Knife and homosexual union in Book One, together with the sequence of severed legs, dismembered baby, and Shira as rapist in Book Two, are linked in turn to a series of events in Book Three that further mingle Eros, violence and gender confusion. Herbst spots his daughter Tamara during an anti-British demonstration in Jerusalem and yet fails to recognize her, as she is disguised as a man and, unknown to him, is involved in anti-British terrorist activity [1989, 392; 1979, 385–86]. This confusion and near-recognition of his daughter remind him of the series of notices in the Leipzig train station, picturing the severed legs, first as male, then female. Herbst recalls "how it was" on his first night with Shira when she put on men's pants and he desired her, a memory that completes an associative series linking his daughter, the rape victim, severed legs and his own erotic impulses [1989, 394; 1979, 387–88].

What do these images of dismemberment, cross-dressing, Eros, and violence communicate? Seductive gender confusions surround the object, confusions furthermore that undo the association of masculine with active and female with passive. In this confusion, Herbst's own position, defined by relationship to the feminine, is no longer clear. Recurring images of truncation, dismemberment, and transvestism disrupt a narrative order that has identified itself as masculine. Insofar as Herbst is the man in the novel, or more accurately perhaps, the parody of an archetypal masculine that has exhausted itself, this gender confusion reflects the exhaustion of a particular kind of narrative. Thus, we have in this novel both the placid inactivity of a weary academic, who is unable to alter significantly the patterns of his life, but at the same, that placid surface is repeatedly disrupted by confusions of gender and boundary.

While Herbst is the center of consciousness through which we are given access to this play of images, the text speaks a language constituted by its images that both contains and supersedes the plot of *l'homme moyen sensuel*. Not only are the severed legs linked to the sadistic engineer and the dismembered baby, they also bring to mind the first of Herbst's hallucinatory visions of old men in the desert, truncated and buried to their waists. Through the rose that names both the illness that disfigures Anita Brik's jaw and the valley where the severed legs are found, the novel links Leipzig and Jerusalem, ulcerated jaw and severed legs. Cumulatively, these clusters of images suggest the fascination of the forbidden, the aura of the otherness that permeates the marginalized, the woman, the Jew.

In the combination of horror and fascination that surrounds them, these images of dismemberment carry the weight of anti-Semitic discourses that took shape around charges of ritual murder and desecration of the host [Hsia 1988]. Given the crisis of European culture in the Holocaust, we can conclude that the recurring image of the severed legs collects and registers the violence of a rupture in psyche, culture and history. Herbst's dreams and fantasies register the effects of a cultural dislocation that exceeds the compass of his particular consciousness and discloses the anarchy of the instinctual within culture.

Desire and the Literary: The Question of Shira

In her presence and then absence, Shira is the stimulus for a process in the text that dislocates the narrative frame. Herbst's response to Shira in the opening pages of the novel initiates a play of images of body parts, birth, death and dismemberment, that engages instincts of sexuality and aggression. The language of images raises particularly contradictory possibilities concerning the female body. A double image consisting of Shira in pants and the severed legs of ambiguous gender suggests something like the dynamics of fetishism: the severed legs offer a reinscription of castration, while the eroticism of Shira in pants can be seen in terms of the denial of female castration that characterizes fetishistic arousal. In Freud's account, fetishism sustains two contradictory assumptions simultaneously—acceptance of the lack of the female phallus and affirmation of its presence [Freud 1927, 149–57]. In the text of *Shira*, it is through comparable play with presence and absence, along with confusions of the binary oppositions that rest on gender distinctions, that the text turns back upon itself.

The 1979 edition of the novel makes the discarded last chapter available to the reader in an appendix, as does the English translation. There, Manfred Herbst asks Shira, who is afflicted with leprosy, to give him her hand. The tableau resembles the picture that so engages Herbst at the bookseller's, of the beggar extending his diseased hand, which holds a bell, in a gesture that combines warning and invitation. In this alternate (and ultimately rejected) ending, Herbst can be said in effect to accept the leper's invitation: he elects to stay with Shira, joining her in her illness. Agnon considered ending the novel with a clasp of hands in which sweat covers his and her hands, a kiss, and Herbst's cry, "Shira, Shira" [1989, 559; 1979, 553]. In effect, this ending would have rounded out the novel's opening scene in which Shira joins the women in labor "as if she were sick or giving birth" [1989,4; 1979, 8]. In this discarded ending, suggestions of recovery of a relation to the body would have found definitive confirmation in Herbst's embrace of Shira, an embrace that acknowledges her disease and seals the compact with the other that is empathy.

What a striking alternative that rejected ending supplies to the trace of absence with which the manuscript, as Agnon left it, ends:

> And because I am absorbed in the matter of Manfred Herbst and the nurse Shira [. . .]I will return to Manfred Herbst and to the nurse

> Shira. Manfred Herbst I will show you, Shira I will not show you for her traces are not known and no one knows where she is. [1989, 555; 1979, 537]

The novel ends, or more accurately does not end, in a suspended state. Neither narrator nor character can locate or tell the story of Shira. The text sustains a tension between, on the one hand, the masculine subjectivity of narrator and protagonist, and, on the other hand, the elusive female object. This oscillation produces a fragmented narrative that evades and exceeds its narrator's and perhaps its author's efforts at mastery.[29] Shira the character disappears, amid glimpses of body and suggestions of disease; *Shira* the novel moves towards retrieval of an archaic body that remains, nevertheless, beyond its grasp.[30]

A comparable tension can be found in Freud's "Fragment of an Analysis of a Case of Hysteria" (1905). Steven Marcus (1985) reads the famous "Dora" case as a modernist text with an unreliable narrator: Freud likens the hysterical person's inability to tell *her* story to a river that is blocked. Disturbances in the sphere of sexuality have produced somatic symptoms in the patient that can be unlocked or decoded to tell a story. Despite that theoretical premise, however, Dora's flight from treatment—from Freud's interpretive intrusions—defeats the analyst's efforts as would-be narrator of her story. As a result, the text that Freud produces not only recounts Dora's flight from treatment, but also demonstrates the frustration of his own narrative efforts at mastery. The text that we have is thus both more and less than a case history: its fragmented state, to which Freud's title attests, opens it up to a fuller portrayal of the analyst as a narrator whose material resists and exceeds his grasp.

Charles Bernheimer observes that the *Dora* case can be read as "a symptomatic narrative that invites us to read Dora as [. . .] the name for those gaps in [Freud's] self-knowledge whose intriguing hermeneutic, rhetorical, and psychosexual functions are teaching us to read anew" [1985, 18]. Similarly, the status of *Shira* as unfinished text, teasing us with the disappearance of its eponymous heroine, its gaps and fragments, offers access to an experience of the text that exceeds and evades our grasp, as it appears to have evaded its author's.

Resisting capture in a narrative frame, "Shira" leaves instead her absence as presence, I will cite only one wonderfully cryptic passage whose complexity suggests the problem of representation in the novel. Herbst thinks of Shira:

> and especially he did *not* skip over matters that did *not* occur between them and the more he felt what had been between them, he felt what had *not* been between them, as what had *not* been between them was the essence and it was just that that was missing and forever he would feel its absence. [1989, 527; 1979, 512; emphasis added]

Herbst misses an absence, which is identified as the "essence." Circling around absence (the "consecrated space of the beloved absence" [Schlossman, 905]), this passage delineates the predicament of desire, of desires for which Herbst is the locus.[31] Desire is created by absence and elaborated metonymically through a series of substitutions. The novel cannot name what it does not have, but it moves among images of bodies and books, wounds and fetishes, signifiers that point to a chain of unending substitutions. Those shifting substitutions number among them the bibliophilia whose ramifications and derivations we have traced.

In *Shira,* histories of books and the uses to which they are put discloses the permeability, rather than the boundedness of the book in the diachronic record of its ownership and in the synchronic accounts of its subjection to the desires of would-be owners. These desires manifest themselves in behaviors that range from Nazi book burnings to Herbst's nervous excitation in the presence of books.

The name for desire in this book is *shira*, not simply as the name of the missing woman but *shira* as the noun that means "poetry" or "literariness" and suggests, in this respect, the role of desire in constituting the literary text.[32] That the noun is not only feminine but names a female character, who is first present and then absent, points up the elusiveness of the object of desire to its seekers.

I opened this book on Agnon with a discussion of the early story, "Tale of the Scribe." In looking back, I find that my reading has traced a movement from the Scribe's plunge into the text in that early story to the writing in the body that is *Shira*. In this respect, I return to the focus on representations of texts with which this study began. But with a difference, a difference signaled in the book references in each. "Tale of the Scribe" offers the reader the innocent horror of the Book: centeredness in the Torah scroll that binds Scribe to community and gives a people its identity. *Shira* pictures the book as cultural repository, the complex text of secular modernity, and shows us the German Jew who is both its adherent and its despised object.

In effect, both the early story and the posthumously published novel trace the undoing of a relationship to writing: climactically in the Gothic denouement of "Tale of the Scribe"; slowly and subversively in *Shira*. Considered together, these two texts show also the range of writings that Agnon engages, from the Torah scroll of the short story to the monuments of German culture that populate the novel. Both "Tale of the Scribe" and *Shira* disclose an erotic relation to text or writing in their protagonists, and more importantly, in the field of the text at large. The effect is a reinstinctualizing of text and writing that disrupts the seeming autonomy of the represented text. The text that we read retains the narrative structures that sustain its intelligibility, while demonstrating the ambiguities and tensions that destabilize those structures.

In "Tale of the Scribe," the female body is associated with a contamination from which the Scribe must purify himself in order to carry out his writing. This opposition collapses as the zeal of the Scribe discloses its erotic components. The final fusion of Torah scroll and wedding gown reinscribes writing into the body. The association of women with an archaic relation to the body, becomes, I have argued, the subject of *Shira*. *Shira* is a text traversed by the trajectories of desire. In effect, the novel links what I have called "the German-Jewish book," that is, the "text" constituted by the complex relationship of German Jews to their culture, and the body of the woman. The book as the object of culture becomes the erotized object, analogue to the body.

Shira demonstrates a turn into the negative characterizations of the Jew as womanly, castrated, diseased, leprous. Foregrounding images of body and text and staging defeats of frame and distancing devices, the text reverses the trend of culture to repress writing and the body in a pretense at transcendence. *Shira* works towards recognition of the complicity of culture in the racist myth of the other, yet stops short of repudiating culture in favor of an equally perverse mythologizing or essentializing of the body. The text offers a development of anti-ideological writing, a writing that opens itself up as an alternative to fictions of closure, impermeability and fixed boundaries; the effect is to valorize the permeable or undecidable without repudiating structure. *Shira* chronicles an indeterminacy in the text to which the name of woman is attached.

Chapter
9

"A Sanctioned Babel": Toward a Conclusion

On the way to a conclusion, I invoke complementary texts of S. Y. Agnon and Gershom Scholem, contained in a gift-text, *Die Gabe* as it was called, that was organized by Martin Buber and presented to the seriously ill Franz Rosenzweig on his fortieth birthday in 1926. This collection is a rich compilation of offerings that testify to the political and intellectual currents of the time, as well as to the life of language, the life in language and language's capacity to surprise us.

Agnon's contribution to this collection consists of a passage from "In the Heart of the Seas" ("*Belevav hayamim*"), written out in his inimitable and barely decipherable hand. Unlike virtually every other gift offering in the collection, Agnon's is enclosed within itself: the simple presence of its Hebrew script appears to lack external reference beyond its opening dedication and its closing signature with place and date of writing: "The holy city of Jerusalem, may it be built and established, *Vayechi*, 5687 S. Y. Agnon" [Goldner 1987, 9]. This signature is a small text of its own that invokes the temporal scheme of redemption. It sums up the identity of the writer by joining his name to the restoration of a Jerusalem that is as much the heavenly *Yerushalayim shel ma'alah*, as it is the writer's earthly dwelling place. Dating the letter with the title of the Torah portion of that week, *Vayechi*, inserts the communication into the cycle of Torah reading that is carried out annually, while, of course, the year that is cited refers to a chronology initiated by Creation.

Agnon titles his Rosenzweig-gift, "On the Journey to the Land of Israel" and sends it across the seas in the opposite direction, from Jerusalem to Rosenzweig in Germany. At the same time, the passage itself suggests that a "journey" consists not so much in the geographical voyage across the sea on which he sends his letter, or that which the story's characters undertake, as it does of the entry and passage through the text that is reading:

> The ship set out to sea and sailed along calmly. Our comrades sat on their belongings and sang in good voice "Praise the Lord, You, the Redeemed of the Lord" until they finished the entire psalm. At the end of the psalm, they took hold of their books and read verses from the Pentateuch, the Prophets, and the Writings. A man is driven from home, and wanders to distant places; he opens his sack and removes a vessel that he had used at home with his wife and children—How he rejoices in this vessel! All the more so with a book, which he would read, study, and pore over. There is not one word in it that he has not uttered a hundred times or more, each time finding new meanings, new connotations. Instantly, his face lights up, his eyes well up with tears, and his voice quivers within his throat. This may be likened to a man exiled, who on his journey encounters dear friends who greet him with embraces, hugging and kissing him; he rejoices in them as they rejoice in him; and when he speaks his speech emerges choked from the tears and the joy of finding his friends who now accompany him. So they would sit with their books in hand reading in the Pentateuch, the Prophets, and the Writings. [Goldner 1987, 9]

In selecting a passage from one of his own stories, Agnon creates a new text, a text-gift, that begins and ends with a picture of devout pilgrims en route to the Holy Land. But while references to "our comrades" who are en route to the land of Israel frame the passage, that frame is displaced by the metaphors of reading embedded in it. For Agnon, the direction through the text remains the primary journey and it is always there. His embedded metaphors of the book make that clear. Reading the holy writings is like coming upon a familiar household vessel when one has been driven from home; reading a book one has read many times is like the meeting with dear friends of a man who has been exiled. This unnamed book is itself a metaphor for Scripture, the Book which retains its priority over all others. Any place outside the text of Scripture is, in effect, an exile, from which one returns through the act of reading. This is the movement ceaselessly acted out in Agnon's writing, as it sustains an attachment to its sources, however remote and distorted.

Agnon's gift forms part of a larger collection that is itself a text, composed of offerings from writers, Jewish and gentile, Europeans either living in Germany or transplanted to Palestine, writing in German or Hebrew or both, with even a bit of French and Greek thrown in. While none of the contributors knew what the other was writing, their offerings come together to form a rich cultural weave, in effect, a dialogue with multiple participants. One reads here the intermingled themes of a particular moment in European history. Contributions included S. D. Goitein on the negative attitude to rabbinic Judaism and the exclusion of the Talmud from the new curriculum in Palestine; Gertrud Hallo's memories of Hermann Cohen, lecturing on Greek philosophy in Berlin in 1916–17; Eugen Mayer's affirmation of the flourishing *Wissenschaft des Judentums*; Julius Blau's program for resolving the "feud between the views and factions in German Judaism, as with the Judaism of other countries" [p.11]; Rudolf Hallo's stirring acclaim for the "triad: Homeland—Art—Jerusalem!" [p.26]

This collectively constituted text traveled to Franz Rosenzweig. Its addressee, despite his grave illness, was well situated to appreciate the range and depth of its contributions. From an early move towards conversion, to his subsequent and far-reaching efforts to involve himself more deeply in Judaism, Rosenzweig's life reflected an engagement with significant currents in European philosophical and religious thought. The subsequent travels of the collection add further layers to its historical sedimentation. After Rosenzweig's death, it was sent, along with the rest of his library, on a ship to Palestine, but ended up in Tunis, where it remained until retrieved and brought to the Leo Baeck Institute in New York by Nahum Glatzer [Goldner 1987]. Sixty years later, the Leo Baeck Institute published a facsimile of the collection.

Among the contributors, Scholem writes to Rosenzweig in German about the Hebrew language, expressing concern over the possibility of dire consequences to the effort to secularize sacred language:

> This country is a volcano! It harbors the language! . . . The secularization of the language is only a *façon de parler*, a phrase! It is impossible to empty out words which are filled to the breaking point with specific meanings—lest it be done at the sacrifice of the language itself! . . . Is it not true that almost all of us live with this language over a volcano with the false security of the blind. Must not we or those who come after us stumble into the abyss when we fail to see again? . . . Those who initiated the rejuvenation of the language believed blindly and almost obstinately in its miraculous power. . . . They walked and still walk above this abyss, which remained hidden, and have transmitted this language to our youth together with all the ancient names and seals. . . . May it not come to pass that the imprudence which has led us on this apocalyptic road ends in ruin. [Goldner 1987, 48–49]

Scholem's mix of metaphors indicates a turbulent and highly self-conscious relationship to language. The combination of volcano and abyss suggests the inexpressibility of the linguistic dilemma that is his subject. In the wake of the revival of Hebrew as an instrument of daily use, "secularization" strikes Scholem as an impossibility, a delusory mastery of language. Do his words (written in German) express nostalgia for a language "bursting with meaning," that will one day overwhelm its users? Scholem's letter is a commentary on language; it assembles its own geography, in which "volcano" and "abyss" constitute untenable points in a linguistic territory impossible to negotiate.

I first encountered Scholem's letter (in an English rendition of a French translation) in a lecture given by Jacques Derrida in September, 1987. What drew Derrida to this text of Scholem's? Not so much the complexities of cultural circumstance that inform it, as the evidence in it of a movement toward the critique of a rationalism that presumes mastery of language, and attempts to treat the "abyssal mystery" of language as a "techno-linguistic" problem [Derrida 1987]. In Derrida's view, Scholem attempts in this letter to move between two languages, sacred and profane, fashioning a third that translates one into the other.

Scholem's writing combines scholarly precision and tenacity with the fierce effort to convey the dynamics of the unspeakable in language. Derrida brings to his discussion of Scholem's text the self-consciously disruptive methods of deconstruction, taking further Scholem's queries by turning them back against themselves, reading in them the contradictory positions that inform the letter-writer's relationship to language.

Where does Agnon fit into this constellation of texts? For Agnon, language becomes literature, thus solving the dilemma of a blind secularism that so concerns Scholem. I use the verb "solving" disingenuously to suggest that the activity of telling stories offers Agnon a way of giving form to these conflicts in language, exploring them without necessarily bringing them to a resolution. The "literary" consists in the capacity of language to evoke a variety of meanings simultaneously, summoning up sources and subjecting them to a playfulness that both negates and affirms their prior references. Agnon's writing makes a space for itself both at the margins of tradition and among the texts of a more general and secular modernity whose value proceeds from their duplicity [Barthes 1975, 7]. The literary works themselves transgress their own boundaries, insofar as they may invoke certain cultural horizons, but do not remain defined by them.

"Between Exile and Return": The title of my study is meant to suggest a tension in Agnon's writing, writing that moves in a universe defined by exile and return, playing out the double gesture of transgression and restoration, signaling conventions and disrupting them. The necessary context for my study has been the Jewishness of Agnon's writing, that is, examination of some of the ways in which the writing evokes Jewish texts via citation, distortion, and imitation, and at the same time, responds to the issues and crises of post-Enlightenment Jewry, in particular developments and events of the last hundred years. With that context, constantly alive in Agnon's writing, it has been possible to explore the dramas of writing that begin from a landscape of sacred writing, but do not remain within it.

In one way or another, Agnon's art reflects virtually all of the cultural currents exemplified in the selections of the Rosenzweig collection. From the centeredness in Scripture of "Tale of the Scribe" to the ideological conflicts that inform the larger novels, Agnon's writing encompasses a geographical-cultural sweep that moves through eastern and western Europe, positioning the Diaspora in relation to a Jerusalem that is both mundane and spiritual.

"A man is driven from home, and wanders to distant places; he opens his sack and removes a vessel that he had used at home with his wife and children—How he rejoices in this vessel! All the more so with a book, which he would read, study, and pore over. There is not one word in it that he has not uttered a hundred times or more, each time finding new meanings, new connotations" [Goldner 1987, 9]. In Agnon's image, the vessel that is a text surrounds its owner or reader in a wealth of familiar detail. That "reader" is less the "owner" of the text than he or she is participant in the linguistic world to which it gives access.

The vessel to which Agnon refers is the Torah, mythical point of origin for the intertextual activity that defines a tradition. At the same time, we would not be going far astray, if we were to borrow Agnon's metaphor of the book as vessel and turn it back against itself, applying it to his own writing without losing sight of its original reference. I would argue first that the literary text is itself a vessel, constructed out of fragments, assembled into a new text that bears traces of its predecessors. Each reading is, in effect, a new writing that reconfigures "connotations" and "meanings." Themes of interpretation and writing, dramas of authority and subversion in Agnon's art heighten our awareness of the continuity of reading and writing as related processes in the production of meaning.

In *Qorot bateynu* (*Pillars of the House*), Agnon likens the activity of compiling that collection of ancestral tales to the labor of "a son to whom broken vessels come as a part of his inheritance and he fixes them" [1979a, 64]. That image of fixing or repairing broken vessels pictures the writer's activity as a restoration of the past; the Kabbalistic associations of the verb summon up a primordial shattering to which the activity of *tiqqun* or restoration is a response. Whatever the verb, however, the act of repair remains partial, never quite concealing the fissures and fragments that give the vessel its shape. We read in the text the inscription of previous texts. Erasures and elisions, adaptations and transformations testify to the intensity of those intertextual connections.

In the amplified reading that is literary criticism, we may attempt to supply the citations and references to which the literary text alludes, but each such reading is a new act of "assemblage." Remember, if you will, Rabbi Nahman's parable of the menorah (chapter 1). That menorah is a text in that it allows readers to construe it in ways that reflect them, while continuing to assert its own identity as an object. It is not wholly open to the reader's construction, but neither is it closed or invariable.

Roland Barthes identifies the text of pleasure as a "sanctioned Babel" [1975, 4]. The phrase is suggestive for a reading of Agnon that attends to the irreconcilable dialogue of voices in the text, irreconcilable in that no one voice sustains its ascendance and all contribute to the richness of a reading that can never be completed.

In Agnon's writing, the borders of the text disappear, as we become aware of the relationship of the text to its predecessors, of the writer to his ancestors, personal and communal. Citations are undone and overturned, but retain their voices, making of the text a dialogue with multiple participants. *A Guest for the Night* brings its readers into complicity with a first person narrator whose narrative of restoration discloses deeply contradictory impulses, among them an ambivalent relationship to language and knowledge. A fantasy of text production in which the Guest becomes his own life-giving manuscript constitutes a profound narrative impulse in *A Guest for the Night*, but one that is subjected to irony, undermining the closure of the novel. The oppressiveness of a paternal writing is invoked in *Only Yesterday*, a novel that both unleashes and contains the demonic confusion that the authority of that paternal order is meant to suppress. In *Shira*, we witness the undoing of the text as a bounded entity, in a novel that never really reaches completion; a novel, furthermore, that allows for a play of images of disease and body in a complex anatomy of the place of the book in culture.

Agnon's writing offers itself to the reader with an invitation to explore the discontinuities, contradictions, as well as the glimpses of a lost wholeness, that constitute its richness. The text discloses its writing: the writing is the locus of the particular drama, however various its manifestations, that I have traced. In giving us access to dramas of appropriation, subversion, restoration, and repair in the writing, Agnon's texts enlarge the domain of literature to include the dynamics of textuality as a realm of significant action.

Notes

Chapter 1.

1. This is along the lines of the "deterritorialization" of which Gilles Deleuze and Felix Guattari [1986] speak: there is no firm ground for definitive interpretation of the text; the text resists the claim of any ideology.

2. "*Ḥush hareaḥ*," or "The Sense of Smell," is discussed in chapter 6. For a discussion of the pervasive influence of this image of the son's exile in the formation of the identities of Hebrew writers at the turn of this century, see Alan Mintz, 1989.

3. Jacques Lacan notes that "the paternal function concentrates in itself both imaginary and real relations, always more or less inadequate to the symbolic relationship that essentially constitutes it" [1977, 67].

4. "Not only does language provide the agency of self-loss, but cultural representations supply the standard by which that loss is perceived," observes Kaja Silverman [1983].

5. M. M. Bakhtin examines this quality of polyphony and values texts in which the play of voices is particularly rich and unconstrained. Julia Kristeva develops the concept of intertextuality out of this play of voices or fragments of utterances in any text.

6. Hillel Barzel describes Agnon's familiarity with tales of the Baal Shem Tov and the shared affinity of Kafka and Agnon to Rabbi Nahman of Bratslav [1972, 168–70, 177]. Arnold Band notes that Agnon read *Shivḥe Haran*, tales of Rabbi Nahman, as an adolescent; he emphasizes the impact of Rabbi Nahman's style on Agnon. Y. H. Brenner was the first to notice the influence of Rabbi Nahman on Agnon's "'Agunot" [Band 1968, 9, 60, 92]. Franz Kafka knew Rabbi Nahman's tales through Martin Buber's work.

7. I compared Hebrew editions by Yisrael Har [1981] and Yehudit Kuk [1973] and translations by Martin Mantel [1977] and Howard Schwartz [1983]. "The Tale of the Menorah," also titled as "The Tale of the Menorah of Defects," is not among the original thirteen collected by Rabbi Nahman's

disciple Rabbi Nathan. See editions prepared by S. A. Horodetzky [1922] and Band [1978].

8. One further note: In the tradition of the Bratslaver Hasidim, the prayer that is recited before one of R. Nahman's tales is told breaks down distinctions between teller, listener, and text [Schwartz, 223]. Through the telling of the tale, teller and listeners participate in and transmit traditional tales of the deeds of holy men. The act of telling brings the teller closer to those deeds, imparting to teller and audience a measure of the holiness of the deeds themselves. The teller participates actively in the realization of the tale and draws his audience into the narrative fabric that he weaves. The Bratslaver prayer is an invocation of the power of narrative to transform the experience of its participants.

Chapter 2.

1. Critics began to compare Franz Kafka and S. Y. Agnon early on in Agnon's literary career. The first full-length sustained comparison was Hillel Barzel's [1972]. Gershon Shaked has demonstrated the complex intertextuality that Agnon's relationship to Judaism makes possible. With specific attention to Kafka's "need to stand outside of history," Shaked contrasts Kafka's delineation of an "abstract *universal world* in a detailed and concrete manner" to Agnon's transformation of "a concrete, historical world" in his surrealist works [1987, 15].

2. *"In der Strafkolonie"* was originally published in 1919. Page numbers refer first to the 1971 edition of *The Complete Stories,* edited by Nahum Glatzer and then to the 1946 German edition. In some instances, translations may have been modified.

3. "Now some time ago there came upon the market, under the name of the 'Mystic Writing-Pad,' a small contrivance that promises to perform more than the sheet of paper or the slate. It claims to be nothing more than a writing tablet from which notes can be erased by an easy movement of the hand. But if it is examined more closely it will be found that its construction shows a remarkable agreement with my hypothetical structure of our perceptual apparatus and that it can in fact provide both an ever-ready receptive surface and permanent traces of the notes that have been made upon it" [Freud, v. 19, [1925], p. 228].

4. Clayton Koelb [1989, 69] has written suggestively on the parallel between Freud's metaphor of the mystic writing pad, as Derrida discusses it, and Kafka's more brutal and overtly sexual representation of the writing machine.

5. The Bratslaver Hasidim recite a prayer before the telling of one of Rabbi Nahman's stories that asks for an effect of narrative, enlisting teller and listeners in the shared experience of the tale. Do we have a grotesque version of this in the Officer's description of the religious ceremonial gathering to witness the "inscription"?

6. The first version of the story that was eventually to become "*Agadat hasofer*" ("Tale of the Scribe") formed part of the Yiddish story "*Toitentants,*" written in 1906–07 and published in 1911 in Galicia. "*Be'erah shel Miryam*" ("Miriam's Well") appeared in 1909 in *Hapo'el hatsair*; parts of that story eventually showed up in "Tale of the Scribe" [1919], "*Ḥemdat*" [1947], opening chapters of *Tmol shilshom (Only Yesterday)* [1945], parts of "*Shevuat emunim*" ("Betrothed") [1943] [Band 1968, 110–11].

7. In citing passages from "Tale of the Scribe," reference is made first to the English translation [1970] and then to the Hebrew [1968, 2:]. Translations have been modified.

8. The ingredients of the story have their origin in a Yiddish version and the 1909 "Miriam's Well" of *Hapo'el hatsair* [Band 1968, 110–11].

9. Agnon cannot have been familiar with the phrase Kafka used in a letter of 1904 to Oskar Pollak: "A book must be the axe for the frozen sea inside us" (as cited in Koelb 1989, 72), but certainly the depiction in each of a relationship to a text in terms of penetration and breaking the ice is suggestive!

10. The holiday of Simhat Torah, "rejoicing in the Torah," celebrates the completion of the annual cycle of reading the Torah in the synagogue.

11. In effect, this amounts to an "irruption of drives within the realm of the signifier" that marks a turn "back towards the auto-erotic body" [Kristeva 1986, 102–03].

12. Gershom Scholem [1972, part 2, 167] on mysticism of letters: "For the Kabbalists, [. . .] linguistic mysticism is at the same time a mysticism of writing. Every act of speaking is, in the world of the spirit, at once an act of writing, and every writing is potential speech, which is destined to become audible." Moshe Idel [1988] makes even stronger claims for the importance of ecstatic states to Jewish mystical experience.

13. Ernst Pawel's [1984] biography offers a thorough account of Kafka's Jewishness. Raised in a western European environment that was largely Jewish but ambivalently so, Kafka's perceptions of Judaism derived initially from his father and his experiences of Prague synagogues on the High Holy Days, as well as his perfunctory performance of his bar-mitzvah ritual. As he grew older, however, a more persistent thread emerges: contact with the Yiddish theater troupe in 1911, the impact of the influx of eastern European refugees during World War I, his contact with Jiri Langer, fellow inhabitant

of Prague, who became a follower of the Belzer rebbe, his contact with Martin Buber and Buber's work on Hasidic tales, and his own ongoing attraction to Zionism and desire to learn the Hebrew language. Gershon Shaked's recent study offers a thoughtful assessment both of the evidence of Kafka's interest in currents of Jewish life, and of the ways in which the "collective consciousness of assimilated Diaspora Jewry" finds expression in his works [1987, 10].

Chapter 3.

1. Page references for Edmond Jabès refer to the English translation and then to the French. If only one reference is given, it is to the French and the translation is my own. In some instances, translations have been modified.

2. The effect is akin to the quality of polyphony in the novel, as M. M. Bakhtin [1987] defines it. This quality can be felt in the strength or autonomy of the voices in the Jabès text.

3. Susan Handelman [1982] argues for a "heretic hermeneutic," a complex of displacement and identification, in such twentieth-century thinkers as Sigmund Freud, Jacques Lacan, Harold Bloom, and raises suggestive comparisons to models of interpretation in rabbinic thought. See Stern, 1984 and 1985, for critiques of Handelman's position, and Handelman, 1985, for a rebuttal.

4. Robert Goldenberg points out that as the historical identity of the rabbis subsided in importance, their names came to signify the opinions attributed to them; at the same time, however, "this withering away of earlier rabbis' historical reality served to liberate historical imagination about them" [1984, 157]. José Faur asserts that "the most important feature of Jewish literature is that the frame of reference that is to give meaning to the text is not in the text itself," thus making interpretation necessary; the aim of classical Hebrew literature, he argues, is to bring about a change in perspective in the student from third person to second, so that the "student may eventually view the Tora from the perspective of the first person" [1977, 34–35].

5. David Stern differentiates precisely between rabbinic polysemy and the contemporary notion of indeterminacy: "What differentiates midrash from indeterminacy is not its style, but rather the latter's formal resistance to closure, its final revelation of a perspective that, as Hartman writes, 'may be, precisely, the absence of one and only one context from which to view the flux of time or the empirical world, of one and only one method that would destabilize all but itself, of one and only one language to rule understanding

and prevent misunderstanding.' In contrast, midrashic polysemy is predicated precisely on the existence of such a perspective, the divine presence from which all the contradictory interpretations derive" [1988, 141].

6. At the same time, any account of Edmond Jabès' literary forebears must consider the question of his relationship to French literary tradition, paying particular attention to Stéphane Mallarmé, as well as to the French surrealists, whose literary experiments undoubtedly contribute to the loosening of textual boundaries and norms in Jabès. (Mary Ann Caws 1981, for one, argues that Jewish sources constitute a negligible influence, if any, on Jabès, next to the impact of French writing; see also Zoila 1978.)

7. Originally published in *Moznayim* in 1933, "A Whole Loaf" underwent considerable revision, and was eventually collected in "The Book of Deeds," in volume 6 of the *Collected Stories*. See Avraham Holtz 1971, for a comparison of earlier and later versions of the story. Citations are given for the English translation, then for the Hebrew. In some instances, translations have been modified to restore a more literal adherence to the original.

8. See Jacques Lacan's discussion of the "letter" as "pure signifier" in his seminar on "The Purloined Letter" in John P. Muller and William J. Richardson 1988.

9. Michael Riffaterre defines intertextuality as the "dual action of the sign . . . the perception that our reading of a text or textual component . . . is complete or satisfactory only if it constrains us to refer to or to cancel out its homologue in the intertext" [1987, 373–74]. My students on reading "A Whole Loaf" intertextually: "I felt something more was going on." "The citations supply those added dimensions." Two students noted the ways in which the cited texts disrupt the narrative frame; with further discussion, we agreed that the citations reinforce the narrative isotopically, insofar as they add into or intensify the central drama of the story. (A note of thanks to the members of CO29100, "Intro. to Comp. Lit.," Fall 1988, for their astuteness and enthusiasm.

10. Intertextuality is then a dialogue in the text and can be analyzed using M. M. Bakhtin's differentiation between monologic and dialogic discourse. The more polyphonic the discourse, the more one hears the multiplicity of voices that comprise the text. Bakhtin: "In such discourse, the author's thought no longer oppressively dominates the other's thought, discourse loses its composure and confidence, become agitated, internally undecided and two-faced" [1984, 198].

11. Consider the following sampling of uses of *hungern* and its variants: "During these last decades the interest in professional fasting has markedly diminished" [1971, 268]/"*In den letzten Jahrzehnten ist das Interesse an Hungerkünstlern sehr zurückgegangen*" [1946, 127]; "from day to day of his fast" [1971, 268]; "*von Hungertag zu Hungertag*" [1946, 127]; "during his

fast" [1971, 268]/" . . . *Hungerzeit*" [1946, 128]; " . . . he was fasting as not one of them could fast" [1971, 269]/" . . . *er hungerte, wie keiner von ihnen es könnte*" [1946, 128]; "how easy it was to fast" [1971,270]/"*wie leicht das Hungern war*" " . . . he was in his best fasting form" [1971, 271]/" . . . *im besten Hungern*" [1946, 130]. Other key terms are *Kunst,* translated variously as "profession" [1971, 269, 274] and as "art" when it occurs in the compound noun, for example, "Just try to explain to anyone the art of fasting!" [1971, 276]/"*Versuche, jemandem die Hungerkunst zu erklären!*" [1946, 135].

12. See my study [1981] of key words and their variants in *Das Schloss*. Edna Aphek's study [1979] of recurring word roots and their transformations in Agnon demonstrates a comparable vocabulary of key terms that constitute a linguistic map of the Agnon narrative structure.

13. "An enunciation that denounces itself, a statement that renounces itself, ignorance that dissipates itself, an opportunity that loses itself, what remains here if not the trace of what *must* be in order to fall from being?" [Lacan 1977, 300].

14. Writing of Stéphane Mallarmé, Gérard Genette [1982, 92] takes note of "a daydream of linguistic motivation marked with a sort of semi-nostalgia for some hypothetical 'primitive' state of language, when speech is supposed to have *been* what it said."

Chapter 4.

1. Thus, in *El*, we find the comment of Yukel (one of the "voices" of the writer in the text): "'In the word *amour,* 'love' there is the *mur,* 'wall.' Has no one else noticed this?'/'For a moment, we will have rebuilt the Temple'" ("'*Dans le mot amour, il y a—avons nous été seuls à le découvrir?—le mot mur. 'Nous aurons, un instant, reconstruit le Temple', avait-il écrit*") [1984, 47; 1973, 56]. The dialogue of the lovers or, for that matter, the figure of the writer in the text functions to draw the reader into a process that can be read as building and unbuilding the Temple and, within that, the process of the writing itself. Rather than read this linkage as a reduction of the significance of the Temple, we might see in it a response to a post-Holocaust universe in which the possibility of community has shattered. In Jabès, then, the orthographic coalescence of the lovers into the Temple (*amour* into *mur*) may herald the achievement of structure, although it can do so only by marking its inherently subversive and tenuous nature.

2. Woven into Agnon's *Oreaḥ natah lalun* (*A Guest for the Night*), for example, is the adage: "If the House of God is not built within a man's lifetime, it is as if it has been destroyed in his lifetime" [1968a, 316; 1968,

4:295]. This recurring theme puts forward the responsibility for restoration as a model of action for the Jew, and assesses action in the context of that larger responsibility.

3. In citing Agnon, reference is made first to the English translation and then to the Hebrew original; where no translation exists, the reference is to the Hebrew and the English is my own translation. In some instances, translations have been modified.

4. In citing passages in Edmond Jabès, reference is made first to the English and second to the French original. For texts, not yet published in translation, the reference is to the French and the English is my own translation. In some instances, translations have been modified.

5. Each may think he "inhabits" the words ("*Tu crois les habiter*"), but is rather, as Jabès puts it, the "accidental host of their reflections" ("*l'hôte accidentel de leurs reflets*") [1976, 89]. The "*rassembleur des mots*" does not control the assemblage of words that is the text, but emerges rather as the product of their activity.

6. Roland Barthes [1975, 27]: "As institution, the author is dead: his civil status, his biographical person have disappeared; dispossessed, they no longer exercise over his work the formidable paternity whose account literary history, teaching, and public opinion had the responsibility of establishing and renewing; but in the text, in a way, *I desire* the author: I need his figure (which is neither his representation nor his projection), as he needs mine."

7. "To speak is first of all to depend upon a metaphor of the desert, to occupy a whiteness, a space of dust or ashes, where the victorious word offers itself in its freed nudity" ("*Parler, c'est d'abord s'appuyer sur une métaphore du désert, c'est occuper une blancheur, un espace de poussière ou de cendre, où la parole victorieuse s'offre dans sa nudité affranchie*" [Jabès 1980a, 105].

8. Of a mystical approach to the infinitude of the text of Torah, Gershom Scholem [1972, 180] writes: "In these millions of worlds [of the spheres, the angels, the earthly, and so on] in which created beings hear the manifestation (revelation) and language of God, the Torah can be interpreted in an infinite fullness of meaning. In other words, the word of God, which extends into all worlds, is in fact infinitely pregnant with meaning, but has no fixed interpretation."

9. Edmond Jabès (*Le Livre des ressemblances,* 1976a, 137]: "You said that every man is a Jew on the threshhold of the book"/"*Tu as dit que tout homme est juif au seuil du livre.*" In an observation that illuminates the particularity of the modern Jewish writer, José Faur observes that the canonization of Scripture signaled the end of making books; the Hebrews became the people of the Book by abstaining from writing books: "Because

semantic reading of the Book is inexhaustible, every book is a mere variant of the original Book" [1986, 16].

10. Gershon Shaked [1989, 3–6] refers to "biography and symbolic biography."

11. See, for example, H. N. Bialik's autobiographical "*Safiaḥ*" ("Aftergrowth"), Feierberg's "*Ba'erev*" ("In the Evening"), Y. H. Brenner's "*Bahoref*" ("In the Winter"). See Alan Mintz, 1989.

12. The posthumously published *Me'astsmi le'atsmi (To Myself from Myself)* 1976 contains several autobiographical letters, as well as talks and excerpts from texts containing autobiographical material. Alan Mintz provides an interesting study of Agnon's revisions, during the 1920s and 1930s, of some of his earlier stories. Mintz concludes that Agnon carried out a process of "suppression, conservation, and revision," in order to highlight the figure of the artist (and to contribute to the growing myth of the artist), as well as to shift from the romantic sentimentality of his earlier work to a more ironic stance [1980, 36–64].

13. Paul De Man: "The specular moment that is part of all understanding reveals the tropological structure that underlies all cognitions, including knowledge of self" [1984, 71].

14. "*Gibor Qatan*" was published in *Hamitspe* (Cracow) in 1904 (Beit-Aryeh 1967, 13). The thirty-third day of the Omer (the period between Passover and Shavuot), Lag B'Omer is celebrated as a scholars' holiday, for the lifting of the plague that afflicted the disciples of Rabbi Akiva. It became known, in the Middle Ages, as the "Scholars' Festival." Kabbalists regard it as the anniversary of the death of Rabbi Shimon bar Yohai. According to exegetical sources, *manna* began to fall on Lag B'Omer.

15. In an inquiry into the relationship of critic to text, or interpretation to cited passage, J. H. Miller [1977] asks whether a citation is "an alien parasite within the body of its host, the main text," or whether "the interpretative host [is] the parasite which surrounds and strangles the citation which is its host" [p. 439]. Demonstrating etymologically that "para" is an "uncannily double antithetical prefix, signifying at once proximity and distance, similarity and difference, interiority and exteriority" [p. 441], Miller argues that the ambiguous relationship of guest to host dissolves any seemingly clear distinction between critic and text, outside and inside.

16. Agnon left Israel only once after that 1924 return, to accept the Nobel Prize for literature in Stockholm, where he made his acceptance speech in Hebrew.

17. My thanks to Emuna Agnon Yaron for letting me read this correspondence. See the published portion of this correspondence, edited by Gershon Shaked and Rafael Veiser (1978, 87–117).

18. His study in Talpiyot, which can be seen today, is lined with shelves of traditional Jewish texts, many rare editions among them. As Agnon liked to point out, only one small shelf of European literature could be found off to the side.

19. Portions of this collection were published in *Ha'esh veha'etzim (The Fire and the Trees)*. Volume 8 in *Kol sipurav (The Collected Stories)*. In an afterword to the 1979 volume, Emuna Yaron tells us that the tales were probably written during the 1940s, 1950s and even 1960s (in Agnon, 1979).

Chapter 5.

1. Postcard to Eliezer Maier Lipschitz from Zamosc, 9/3/30, from the Archives of Agnon's papers in the Jewish National and University Library, Jerusalem, Israel. (See Beit-Aryé 1967, 29.)

2. *Esterlayn yeqirati,* ed. E. Yaron (Tel-Aviv, 1983), p. 260.

3. Parenthetical citations are given first for the English translation [1968a] and then for the Hebrew [1968, 4:]. In some instances, the English translation has been modified to restore a closer reading of the Hebrew.

4. Critics have commented at length on the significance of house imagery in Agnon's writings. (See, for example, Band 1968, 217; Levinger 1966, 182.)

5. Early on these ironies are signaled as, for example, in the initial encounter between the narrator or Guest and the townspeople. They give him the key to the *beit midrash* or House of Study, as they prepare to leave the town in search of better lives. The equation of geographical location with God is supported by the double meaning of *maqom* as both "place" and "God." The townspeople explain to the narrator that "We are leaving our place [our *maqom*] because God [the *maqom*] left us and does not provide us with peace." In return, the Guest spells out the double meaning when he stretches his hands towards the walls of the House of Study and says, "A place [a *maqom*] in which your fathers prayed you are going to leave" [1968a, 13; 1968, 4: 18].

6. The narrator/protagonist of the novel convinces Arnold Band, for one, that he has "come to grips with Shibush and its predicament" and has left it behind him "for a new and wholeheartedly accepted home in Erets Yisrael" [1968, 313; see also 308].

7. As Umberto Eco notes, the "exactness of the textual project makes for the freedom of its Model Reader" [1979, 23]. This is the sort of complexity that characterizes *Ulysses,* where the controlled richness of the text supports a reading of the novel as a project for the renewal of the English language.

8. To Baruch Kurzweil's observation of the difference between the novel and the naive folk genre of the Hasidic tale, we can add Cassirer's reflections on the magical qualities that language possesses to the primitive mind: "Whenever we find man we find him in possession of the faculty of speech and under the influence of the myth-making function. . . . To the primitive mind the social power of the word, experienced in innumerable cases, becomes a natural and even supernatural force" [1944, 109–110]. The novel retains elements of this linguistic primitivism, but places them in tension with a more mundane sense of the split between word and thing. Interestingly, in a later essay, Kurzweil shifts his stance to argue that the narrator does achieve a degree of integration through his period of atonement and his return to Israel. This interpretive shift is supported by a rather selective reading of the text that overlooks the contradictory notes that are to be found in the narrator's concluding summations [1970, 273]; nevertheless it does illustrate the variety of interpretive pathways that the text allows.

9. In typical Agnon fashion, there appear to be no precise equivalents to this "citation" in printed editions of either the Jerusalem or the Babylonian Talmud. Two passages that share elements of Agnon's wording can be found in Sanhedrin 22a and 92a (*BT*). The first compares a man's loss of his wife to the destruction of the Temple; the second compares the possession of knowledge to the rebuilding of the Temple. (My thanks to Burton L. Visotzky for help with this search.)

10. Gershon Shaked notes that while Agnon uses direct address to the reader in order to create intimacy between narrator and reader, he does not otherwise emphasize the presence of the retrospective narrator so that we do not have the feeling that the protagonist knows how events will turn out [1976, 256].

11. Here, too, the fiction intersects with biography in the eyes of its readers: A. M. Haberman draws attention to the occasion when Agnon's father gently but persistently pointed out to a Torah scholar that he had created the occasion for argument where none existed in order to display his own brilliance [1969, 85].

12. Two examples of talmudic usage: Hagigah 22b: (1) "Forthwith, R. Joshua went and prostrated himself upon the graves of Beth Shammai. He said: 'I crave your pardon (literally, humble myself to you), O bones of Beth Shammai. If your unexplained teachings are so (excellent), how much more so the explained teachings.'" (2) Hagigah 16b: As a consequence of a question of having sentenced an innocent man to death: "Forthwith Judah b. Tabbai undertook never to give a decision except in the presence of Shimon b. Shetah. All his days Judah b. Tabbai prostrated himself on the grave of the executed man, and his voice used to be heard."

13. It should be noted that the narrative regards Hanokh's menial work as the expression of a kind of mystical piety. Such a view of humble work is

not uncommon in Jewish lore. Agnon makes it part of several characterizations in *Hakhnasat Kala* (*The Bridal Canopy*).

14. I will simply point out here that food plays a significant role in the novel, one that this evocative porridge only suggests. This culinary comedy includes the Guest's claim to vegetarianism, a presumed modesty on his part that is undercut by the impoverished diet of the townspeople and the more genuine modesty of the town's vegetarian doctor.

15. Niddah 30b offers the closest source for Argon's usage. Interestingly, one of the legend's manifestations is to be found in midrashic material attached to the giving of Torah at Sinai: whatever the readiness of the people to receive the divine text, it cannot compare with that of the infant in utero who already has it. Louis Ginzberg [1968, v. 3, 90], notes that in preparation for the revelation at Sinai, "the Israelites brought their wives with their babes at their breasts, and their pregnant wives, and God made the bodies of the pregnant women transparent as glass, and He addressed the children in the womb with these words: 'Behold, I will give your fathers the Torah. Will you be surety for them that they will observe it' They answered: 'Yea.' He furthermore said: 'I am your God.' They answered: 'Yea.' 'Ye shall have no other gods.' They said: 'Yea.' In this wise the children in the womb answered every commandment with 'Yea' and every prohibition with 'Nay.'" See also, v. 3: 34 on Moses and the Israelites and the song by the red sea: "But not alone the adults took part in this song, even the sucklings dropped their mothers' breasts to join in singing ; yea, even the embryos in the womb joined the melody, and the angels' voices swelled the song." Ginzberg gives the following sources: Mekilta Shirah 1, 35a; Sotah, Tosefta 6.4; Yerusahlmi 6, 29c; Babli 30b; Tehillim 8, 77; Zohar II, 60a. As an additional source for Agnon's usage, we should note that the wise infant or *yenuqa* plays a large part in the *Zohar* [Tishby 1948, 19, 66f].

16. Moshe Idel [1988, 245–47] demonstrates the varieties of mystical experience of fusion with Torah. In experiences of an encompassing textuality, the Torah becomes the path to an encounter with the divine and study of the Torah is "regarded as a restoration of the original state of the human body through its purification, culminating in a mystical union with the Torah."

17. There is one variation on the wise infant legend that appears to offer something of a synthesis of the wholeness of the infant's knowledge with the artist's vision. The Guest tells of Rabbi Eleazar Kalir, the *payyetan* (medieval term for a religious poet) who, as a child in his cradle, was shown things from heaven that no eye had ever seen. When he wanted to give voice to them in song, bees came and filled his mouth with honey: "When he grew up and learned Torah, he remembered all the songs and praises that he had wanted to utter in his infancy and he wrote them and Israel established them in their prayers. And from whence did he write lamentations? The bees, who

gave him their honey, stung him and from that sorrow he wrote lamentations for the ninth of Av" [1968a, 448; 1968, 4:419]. The uniqueness of the child's vision ("things no eye had seen") suggests a synthesis of the child's knowledge with the artist's abilities, a synthesis on which the medieval religious poet could draw.

18. In Philippe Lejeune's model [1982], the autobiographical contract requires not only the identity of narrator and protagonist, but also that the name of the narrator/protagonist be the same as that of the historically verifiable author. The author's name is both external and internal to the text. Agnon's use of his own given name offers a partial exception to the model, in its incomplete or partial identification of narrator and protagonist with author.

19. This interweaving brings to mind the medieval poet's acrostic insertion of the letters of his own name into the verses of his religious song; that balance of piety and art is, however, unavailable to the modern artist.

20. This biography in the text can be amplified through correspondences to the life of the author: the memorial volume for the town of Buczacz, to which Agnon contributed, contains a portrait of the twelve-year old bibliophile, Shmuel Yosef Czaczkes, as would-be librarian, cataloguing the books in the town's renowned *beit midrash* or House of Study [*Sefer Buczacz*, 90–91; cited in Barshai, p. 16]; the role of cataloguer offers a portrait of the writer as reader, subordinate to the books and their contents.

21. While not mentioning the narrator's relationship to Rachel, Gershon Shaked helps to find an ironic parallel to it. He cites the following example of a seemingly unconnected subplot ("hidden text") that actually serves to parody the ostensible plot ("open text") and thereby to diminish the stature of the narrator: just after the narrator loses the original key to the House of Study and feels that life has lost meaning, he records the apparently unrelated arrival at the inn of a traveling salesman, a young married man who eats and drinks heartily and carries on a rather coarse flirtation with the innkeeper's daughter, Babtshi. As Shaked observes, the obvious parallel between the two men makes the narrator into a kind of traveling salesman, since both he and his counterpart have left behind their families and live in the inn where they support the innkeeper and flirt with his daughters [1973, 237]. This irony acquires greater force once we consider the place of the Guest's "flirtation" with Rachel in the symbolic scheme of his quest, a connection critics seem to have overlooked.

22. The "village of preparation" finds its counterpart in the novel *Tmol shilshom (Only Yesterday)* in the collective farm "Ein Ganim." In a structural parallel to the relationship of narrator to village, *Only Yesterday's* protagonist Yitzhak Kummer visits (but remains at a distance from) the collective farm, whose inhabitants are seen as active participants in the fulfillment of

the Zionist dream (see chapter 7). In *Shira,* also, the protagonist's daughter and family live in a collective settlement that suggests fulfillment of a social ideal.

23. As Yael Feldman has noted, his key serves more to close than to open doors. Her study of puns that engage Hebrew and Yiddish or German demonstrates the ambivalence in the very language of return that the Guest uses. (See Y. Feldman 1985, 1987.)

24. Reb Shlomo's son, Yeruham Bach, went to Israel and was killed, probably in the same outbreak of violence that destroyed the narrator's house [Band 1968, 309]. The parallel nudges itself upon our notice when the narrator remarks that the date of his departure is also the anniversary of Yeruham Bach's death; although he does not comment on it, his departure from the town one year after the destruction of his house can be said to round out the structure of renewal to his journey. These symmetries and coincidences enable us to compare the fruits of destruction in both Reb Shlomo's family and in the narrator's life, a comparison that acquires emphasis through the narrator's encounter with Reb Shlomo in Israel.

25. He tells the narrator: "We found in the Midrash, for fifty-two years a bird had not been seen to fly in Israel, now that birds have returned here it's a sign that Israel will return to their nests," [1968a, 474; 1968, 4:442–43]. Reb Shlomo suggests an ideal on the order of a Hasidic saint.

26. Possibly relevant here to the characterization of Rafael Bach are the images of womb, birth, and infancy in Job; for example, Job 3:9–19.

Chapter 6.

1. Genesis Rabbah is the collection of homiletical and ethical interpretations of the first book of the Torah. Louis Ginzberg [1968, v. 1; v. 5; 5] notes that the "mystic passages in the earliest rabbinic sources already discuss the idea that God created the world by means of 'letters'." (He suggests comparison with Yerushalmi Hagigah 2 77c; Menahot 29b; Berakhot 55a, and other sources.)

2. Neither "*'Al even aḥat*" nor "*Ḥush haraeaḥ*" has been translated. References to the *Collected Stories* [1968] appear in the text. A translation of "*Hate'udah*" that omits part of the story can be found in *Twenty-One Stories* [1970]; references are given first for the translation [1970], and then for the story as it appears in the *Collected Stories* [1968: 6]. Translations have been modified.

3. See the discussion of Agnon's ancestral text, *The Pillars of our House (Qorot Bateynu)*, chapter 4, and the discussion of the manuscript "Hands of

Moses" in *A Guest for the Night,* chapter 5, for other instances of this model of intertextual relationship.

4. In a comparison of psychoanalytic and linguistic models of signification, Kaja Silverman [1983] contrasts the paradigmatic and syntagmatic axes of language to primary and secondary process in psychic operations. In her view, the literary functions of metaphor and metonymy combine linguistic and dream operations of signification: "Whereas condensation and displacement treat similarity and contiguity as the basis for absolute identification, and paradigm and syntagm establish an irreducible difference among similar and contiguous elements, metaphor and metonymy respond to similarity and contiguity as the basis for the *temporary replacement* of one signifying element by another. In other words, metaphor and metonymy mediate between the extremes represented by the other two sets; they assert neither the complete identity nor the irreducible difference of similar and contiguous terms" [p. 109]. This sort of mediated relationship, hovering between identity and difference, characterizes the suggestive nouns of Agnon's story.

5. Traditional sources list *v* as a variant of *f* in the word. The English translation omits this section of the story.

6. In *Civilization and its Discontents,* Sigmund Freud [1929] cites a friend's experience of an "oceanic" feeling of oneness with the cosmos as a possible source of religious feeling.

7. *"Hefqer"* is also the title of another dreamlike story in "The Book of Deeds": This story concludes with a scene in which the first person narrator confronts a group of Jews whom he assumes have been arrested along with him. Rather than acknowledge kinship, however, the group of people sing obscene words to a prayer melody, a striking image of a sanctified textuality gone awry.

8. We know also that Agnon uses the root *sh-b-sh* to form the name Szybucz by which he designates his hometown of Buczacz. For further work on significant word roots in Agnon's writing, see Edna Aphek's [1979] study.

9. See discussions of this passage with reference to Agnon's relation to sacred language in Alter [1969, 137ff] and Shaked [1986, 285ff].

10. Roman Jakobson observes that narrative is associated with the syntagm, while lyric poetry, for example, draws upon and makes manifest the operations of the paradigmatic axis [1960, 375; 1956, 76–82].

11. Emuna Agnon Yaron notes that it was natural for her father to refer to himself as the *meḥaber* when he was writing about matters of language, in that he saw himself as continuing the ways of his ancestors (personal communication, 5/31/84). My thanks to Emuna and Hayyim Yaron for the information concerning the *Siddur derekh haḥayyim.*

Chapter 7.

1. See for example, Sigmund Freud, *The Ego and the Id* [1923a]: "The broad general outcome of the sexual phase dominated by the Oedipus complex may, therefore, be taken to be the forming of a precipitate in the ego, consisting of these two identifications [with parental imagos] in some way united with each other. This modification of the ego retains its special position; it confronts the other contents of the ego as an ego ideal or superego" [p. 34].

2. R. C. Davis uses *The Odyssey* to offer a model of narrative based on the son's search for a missing father; this lack sets up the condition for narrative by provoking the desire of the son for the father and prompting the inauguration of discourse [1981, 7, 13, 25].

3. Baruch Kurzweil considers *Only Yesterday* to be "the most important and successful effort in the area of the social novel in our new literature" [1982, 216]. See also Gershon Shaked, [1983, v. 2: 206; and 1989, 147]. Most recently, the research of Avraham Holtz demonstrates Agnon's use of documentary materials in the composition of the novel, so much so that characters often quote directly from "contemporary journals, memoirs, and other primary historical materials" [1989, 630]. *Tmol Shilshom* remains as yet untranslated. Translations are my own and refer to Volume 5 in *Kol Sipurav* [*The Collected Stories*].

4. Hillel Barzel, for example, notes that a mad dog will bite and kill; he observes that "the dog in the tradition of Israel is an animal connected to prey and impurity . . . the dog, as Agnon understood from his childhood, in contrast to the cat or the rooster, for example, was known to be an outdoors creature, not a domestic animal" [1972, 223].

5. While Avraham Holtz cites the sources for Agnon's description of Yitzhak's symptoms, he acknowledges that the dog is never actually identified as rabid [1989, 633–34].

6. Rabbi Gronam's source text: Sanhedrin 97a: "It has been taught, R. Judah said: In the generation when the son of David comes, the house of assembly will be for harlots, Galilee in ruins, Gablan lie desolate, the border inhabitants wander about from city to city, receiving no hospitality, the wisdom of scribes in disfavour, God-fearing men despised, people [the face of the generation] be dog-faced, and truth entirely lacking, [. . .] It has been taught: R. Nehorai said: In the generation when Messiah comes, young men will insult the old, and old men will stand before the young [to give them honour]; daughters will rise up against their mothers, and daughters-in-law against their mothers-in-law. The people shall be dog-faced, and a son will not be abashed in his father's presence."

7. There is further satire in Rabbi Gronam's name: "*Yekum purkan*" is an Aramaic phrase from the liturgy, meaning "May salvation arise . . . "

8. My thanks to Professor Avraham Holtz for sharing with me a copy of the actual writ of excommunication that is the source for this passage.

9. Reb Faysh's affliction is termed *shittuq*, a clinical label for paralysis [Holtz, 1989], but also a noun from the root *sh-t-q*, "to silence."

10. In "Subversion of the Subject and Dialectic of Desire," Jacques Lacan writes: "The promotion of consciousness as being essential to the subject in the historical after-effects of the Cartesian *cogito* is for me the deceptive accentuation of the transparency of the I in action at the expense of the opacity of the signifier that determines the I" [1977, 307]. Edward S. Casey and J. Melvin Woody gloss Lacan to suggest the "essential opacity of the 'I' in contrast with the putative clarity of consciousness" [1983, 97].

11. See Gershon Shaked's discussion of the *aqedah* in this context; [1983, 207].

12. Baruch Kurzweil notes Yitzhak's *difference* from his peers insofar as he inhabits the world of his fathers, Reb Yudel Hasid and his townsman Reb Alter, while also engaging in the "liberated" new lifestyle of his peers [1982, 22].

13. Compare with Shaked's analysis of "*Shevu'at emunim*" ("Betrothed"): he remarks the sensitivity with which Agnon "homed in on a neurosis typical of an entire society: the Zionist society of young immigrants who both sought rebirth and thirsted for death. Commanded to set out for new world, they still yearned to return to the bosom of the great mother" [1987a, 51].

14. This regressive tendency within the forward movement of plot suggests to me something of a basis for a psychoanalytic conception of plot, along the lines of that developed by Peter Brooks. Brooks notes that narrative structure is such that "the end is a time before the beginning," that is to say, the end presupposes the beginning. Drawing on Freud's speculation in *Beyond the Pleasure Principle* that "an instinct is an urge inherent in organic life to restore an earlier state of things" and further that "the aim of all life is death," Brooks conceptualizes plot, the action in the narrative, as a "kind of divergence or deviance, a postponement in the discharge which leads back to the inanimate" [1982, 291]. From this perspective, "ends (death, quiescence, non-narratibility)" are set against "beginnings (Eros, stimulation into tension, the desire of narrative) in a manner that necessitates the middle as *detour*, as struggle toward the end under the compulsion of imposed delay, as arabesque in the dilatory space of the text" [pp. 291, 295]. The story of Yitzhak Kummer fits into this abstract formulation. Ostensibly seeking to build and be rebuilt through work on the land, Yitzhak's efforts can be read at the same time as a drive to return to origins.

15. The moment supplies the oceanic feeling Freud's friend cites as a mainspring of religious feeling, but places it under the auspices of the Father, so satisfying what Freud saw to be the human need—infantile and Oedipal—which gives rise to religion. See chapter one of *Civilization and its Discontents.* This moment in *Only Yesterday* can be compared with the passage in *A Guest for the Night* in which the Guest enters the *beit midrash* to study in memory of his father and experiences boundary loss and the feeling of absorption into something larger than himself. (See chapter 5.)

16. Gershon Shaked [1989, 147] observes that Yitzhak is caught between Sonya and Shifra, or between betrayal of his mother and return to the mother.

17. For a discussion of triangles in Agnon, see David Aberbach, 1984, chapter 2.

18. *Totem and Taboo* figures for Jacques Lacan as "the Freudian myth . . . the sole example of a full-fledged myth to have emerged in our historical age" [1982, 42].

19. The Officer of "In the Penal Colony," makes a gift of himself to the machine that is the instrument of law, the "Old Law" according to which guilt is never to be doubted. The machine, of course, is a writing machine (see chapter 2) that can be said to inscribe the name of the Father in a punishment which the "son" does not survive. And of course, we should not forget Josef K's comment on his own death: "'Like a dog!' he said; it was as if the shame of it must outlive him" [1964, 286]. Max Brod cites the point in *Letter to his Father* at which Franz Kafka connects his use of the phrase to the infinite sense of guilt created in him by his father [Brod 1960, 24]. *Letter to his Father*: "Here, it is enough to remind you of early days. I had lost my self-confidence where you were concerned, and in its place had developed a boundless sense of guilt. (In recollection of the boundlessness I once wrote of someone, accurately,: 'He is afraid the shame will outlive him, even.')" [Kafka 1966, 73].

20. "We will take *Verwerfung*, then to be *foreclosure* of the signifier. To the point at which the Name-of-the-Father is called—we shall see how—may correspond in the Other, then, a mere hole, which by the inadequacy of the metaphoric effect will provoke a corresponding hole at the place of the phallic signification" [Lacan 1977, 201]. The concept of foreclosure or *Verwerfung* is one that Jacques Lacan takes from Sigmund Freud (Cf. Lacan 1977, 201, 217]. John P. Muller offers this explanation of the concept: "In psychotic development castration is foreclosed: the child remains in a dual, symbiotic union with the mother in which the child identifies with being the all-fulfilling object of the mother's desire. . . . In attempting to *be* the imaginary phallus or completion of the mother the child rejects the limits implied by castration" [1983, 23].

21. For example, a well-meaning friend of Yitzhak's takes a *minyan* or quorum to the Western Wall to recite psalms and a particular verse mentioning a dog ten times, in what can be seen as an effort to weave Yitzhak back into the fabric of Jerusalem, but his effort does not offset the savage text of madness [1968, 5: 604].

22. David Aberbach views Arzaf's total dedication to his "art" as evidence of a "schizoid detachment" that separates him from people while preserving his sanity; he notes that Arzaf's name means "hellebore," the name of a plant used in antiquity to cure insanity [1984, 135].

23. "Madness is not the *origin* of (the) writing, the *cause* of meaning, but an *effect of discourse*—as is the subject himself" [Felman 1985, 98].

24. See Jacques Lacan, 1977, pp. 246–47 on "correct distance."

Chapter 8.

1. The first three books, approximately 160 pages, are more or less complete, while part 4 is a fragment of fifty pages. Agnon began to publish portions of *Shira* from 1948 on in the yearbook of the newspaper *Ha'arets* [Schocken 1978, 227]. In the present discussion, reference is made first to the 1989 translation of *Shira,* then to the 1979 Schocken edition of the original. In some instances, translations have been modified.

2. The manuscript in the archive of the Jewish National and University Library is a text that incorporates segments of the early *Ha'arets* version of *Shira,* showing the writer's handwritten revisions, deletions and emendations as a kind of embroidery that shows the text in process.

3. Derrida [1981, 3] remarks the tension between writing and the book: "the book form alone can no longer settle . . . the case of those writing processes which, in *practically* questioning that form, must also dismantle it."

4. The 1948 publication of this section of the novel in *Ha'arets* uses a sequence of sentences to present Shira's empathic relationship to the birthing women ("as if she were sick or giving birth"), Herbst's wish to avoid looking at her, and the subsequent appearance of the beggar. Agnon's handwritten revisions show the development of the final version whose syntactic economy brings about the suggestive condensation I have noted. This entire scene with the beggar in the waiting room is subjected to a revision that simplifies syntax, while rendering intersubjective boundaries more ambiguous. In addition, verbs are simplified to become more concrete and powerful; for example, Herbst "sat and was silent" is revised to Herbst "muzzled

his mouth" [*balam et piv*] and said nothing. This sort of change locates action more concretely and graphically in body parts.

5. Hélène Cixous [1986, 85–86] asserts that "writing is woman's. That is not a provocation, it means that woman admits there is an other. In her becoming-woman, she has not erased the bisexuality latent in the girl as in the boy. . . . It is much harder for man to let the other come through him. Writing is the passageway, the entrance, the exit, the dwelling place of the other in me—the other that I am and am not, that I don't know how to be, but that I feel passing, that makes me live—that tears me apart, disturbs me, changes me, . . . " See Hélène Cixous and Catherine Clement, 1986; Luce Irigaray, 1985; Alice Jardine, 1985; Jerry Anne Flieger, 1983; also Sigmund Freud, "The Infantile Genital Organization" An Interpolation into the Theory of Sexuality," [1923b], p. 145.

6. Thus while some feminist theorists argue for a new epistemology or for a change in the relation of the individual to knowledge, others have responded by pointing out that the arguments for such change employ the same assumptions and methods that they would repudiate. (See Ellen Messer-Davidow and David Shumway, 1989.) A further danger consists of replacing patrocentric habits of thought with an alternative that amounts to hypostasizing the maternal. See Domna C. Stanton [1986, 157–82] for an excellent critique of the French feminists' tendency to overuse the maternal metaphor.

7. Similarly, the narrator speaks at an analytical remove in observing mother and daughter in a twilit room: "The two of them, mother and daughter, were unaware of each other and unaware of their own being as well. If I had a tendency to coin phrases, I would call this a state of 'annihilated being'" [1989, 277; 1979, 276].

8. Further instances of this theme of womanhood in all its variations can be found in the feud between two women, Henrietta and Dr. Kreutmeier, that runs through the novel: Henrietta spends her days trying to get visas for German Jews and resents Dr. Kreutmeier's willingness to perform abortions for Jews at a time when the future of the people is in question. Eventually, two late-in-life births of her own redirect Henrietta away from her rescue mission to the nurturing of Jewish life within the family (which causes the narrator to remark wryly that it's just as well that Hitler is taking care of the Jews, since Henrietta is now preoccupied with her own family concerns).

9. The subversive strategy of *écriture féminine* is for woman to "transform subordination into affirmation . . . to resubmit herself . . . to 'ideas' about her, elaborated in/by a masculine logic" (Irigaray 1985, 73–74). Kaja Silverman (1983, 189) notes that female sexuality is "a site where numerous discourses converge."

10. See Esther 2:7: "And he [Mordecai] brought up Hadassah, that is, Esther, his uncle's daughter; for she had neither father nor mother." The Midrash expands on this verse, telling us that through a miracle, Mordecai's breast supplied milk for Esther [Ginzberg, v. 4, 383, citing Tehillim 22, 192–93; Megillah 13a; Targum Esther and Esther Rabbah 2.7].

11. *Shoshanat yeriḥo* is the name of a flower from the Cruciferae family that grows wild in desert areas of the land of Israel; it is also the name of a kind of ulcer caused by the protozoon leishmania tropica, transmitted to human beings by the bite of the mosquito Phlebotomus or "sand fly"; the disease is found in Asia, Africa and the Middle East.

12. Compare this image of the opening of the body in Agnon's novel to the "rose-red wound" found in Franz Kafka's "A Country Doctor." The doctor is called to the bedside of a patient, whose wound discloses, on closer examination, "Worms, as thick and as long as my little finger, themselves rose-red." We see through the eyes of the ambivalent doctor, first-person narrator of the story, who oscillates in his relation to the patient, from keeping his distance to finally allowing himself to be placed in bed with the patient [1971, 220–25; 1946, 74–79]. "Rose" is also the name of the serving-girl in Kafka's story, who is forced to submit to a stable-groom's sadistic lust. "Rose" is used both to name the woman and to designate the wound. A similar complex of verbal connotations permeates *Shira: shoshanat yeriḥo* or "rose of Jericho" carries a positive aesthetic connotation at the same time that it names the disease which shows itself in Anita Brik's ulcerated jaw.

13. The Jerusalem doctor of the novel is modelled on Dr. Saul Adler of the Hebrew University, who actually carried out such an experiment [Schocken, 1978, 238].

14. Some of the ambiguities that attach to culture's definition of the feminine make themselves felt in Herbst's attraction to Shira, whose name means poetry and whose skin gives the appearance of early signs of leprosy (as, for instance, in the reference to her bruised cheek; see 1989, 108; 1979, 110).

15. The charge that leprosy was the disease of the Jews originated in ancient Egypt, in the accusation that the Israelites of the Exodus were lepers. It can be found in the "pseudoscientific paradigm" of 19th-century anti-Semitic discourse [Gilman 1985, 150–51].

16. In an exhaustive reading of the leprosy motif in *Shira,* Gershom Schocken [1978] identifies many of Agnon's German allusions, and supplies additional evidence of the workings of the leprosy motif. Schocken's own odyssey from Germany to Jerusalem helps the reader to understand his argument for reinserting Herbst's reunion with the infected Shira in the leprosarium as an "affirmative" ending to the novel. Schocken's reiteration of the importance of the leprosy motif and his editorial preference for the

embrace of disease constitute his use of the novel as part of his own response to German culture: the writer turns around and assigns value to the substance of the slurs that were perpetrated against him. In its own way, Schocken's essay is an accretion, a layer of history surrounding *Shira,* appropriating it while also submitting to it. His essay encloses itself within a double gesture of filial piety, opening with tribute to his father, the publisher, on the hundredth anniversary of his birth, and closing with notation of the date, the ninth of Av, solidifying the essay's link to Agnon.

17. As a parodic figure of the scholar, Herbst experiences a crisis of non-productivity that can be compared to the crisis of authority Flaubert depicts in *Bouvard et Pécuchet*. Robert Weimann speaks of Flaubert's novel as a "parable of appropriation," a story of the "attempt at both world-appropriating and text-appropriating action" that yields not "representativity but social isolation" [1988, 436]. It is this sort of self-reflectiveness in which "the writing represents the crisis of its own representativeness" [p. 439] that comes to mark the modernist text. Fuchs [1985, 58–59, 112–15] reads a severe irony in Herbst's inattention to his historical situation; she criticizes any attempt to suggest sympathy between Agnon and Herbst or to accept at face value the narrator's seeming neutrality, which she reads as an ironic pose. Her survey of the workings of irony is exhaustive and corrects any lingering tendencies to identify author, narrator and character, although it should not be taken to the opposite extreme, that is to the assumption of a fixed ironic distance that sustains detachment.

18. Herbst differs from other German Jews, who retain their primary and exclusive attachment to German culture; he moves between two cultures: "This scholar—born and educated in Germany, author of a six-hundred-page tome and many essays in German, who spoke German to his wife and most of his friends, who thought in German—when he was about to pour his lyrical musings into German verse, found neither the words nor the form. Herbst was caught between two tongues" [1989, 209; 1979, 210].

19. Consider, for example, this instance of the novel's analysis of the mentality of German Jews: "These people whose fathers and forefathers preferred the soil of Germany to that of the Land of Israel, loving Germany perhaps even more than the Germans did, felt the ground crumbling under them and could find no foothold anywhere in Germany" [1989, 38; 1979, 42].

20. In discussing Mendelssohn, Michael Meyer [1967, 22] highlights the conflict when he notes the "strange paradox that nascent German culture should have been championed by a Jew. What could be more ironic than the young bearded Moses, at the time only 'tolerated' in Berlin, audaciously criticizing Frederick the Great for writing poetry in French instead of German?" Philippe Lacoue-Labarthe and Jean-Luc Nancy [1990, 298–300] offer insight into the place of French within German national consciousness. They examine the relatively tenuous nature of German identity at the start of

modernity and show its dependency on French culture as a mediating term in a relationship to Greek antiquity.

21. Alexander Altmann was born in 1906; his father was a Hungarian-born rabbi who wrote on the history of the Jews of Salzburg and Trier and died in Auschwitz. Altmann served as a rabbi in Berlin and lectured on philosophy at the rabbinical assembly there; from Berlin, he went to Manchester, England and eventually to Brandeis University. His, then, is a history of the sort we find embedded in *Shira*.

22. The German-Jewish background of Agnon's wife, Esther Marx, should probably be taken into account here. In this respect, Dan Miron reads *Shira* as something of a geographical-cultural allegory in which Herbst is the meeting of eastern and western Jew, Professor Neu and Lisbet are Ashkenazi Jewry and Shira is "the totally godless and anarchistic representation of the East" [1977, 279–80].

23. On Nietzsche and the dichotomizing of Greek culture, see Philippe Lacoue-Labarthe and Jean-Luc Nancy, 1990. See also Thomas Mann's *Doctor Faustus,* as for example, in Zeitblom's reference to the "propitiatory entrance of the dark and uncanny into the service of the gods" [1948, 10].

24. Compare also: "He began to sort through familiar and unfamiliar books, with his eyes and with his hands. Some were books he had been looking for; some, he began to covet as soon as he saw them. If he had had seven eyes and ten hands at each of his fingertips, he would not have been able to satisfy his desires" [1989, 445; 1979, 434].

25. Frederick Grunfeld provides a series of portraits of twentieth-century German-Jewish intellectuals in *Prophets Without Honor,* that could house themselves with anecdotal ease in Agnon's novel. In what I find to be a striking parallel for Herbst's bibliophilia, Grunfeld offers the example of Karl Wolfskehl as one for whom living among books provided, in his own words, "a gently erotic atmosphere" like that of a harem [1979, 77]; Wolfskehl discovered the oldest German cradle song in a tenth-century manuscript which preserved the handwriting of a scribe who was apparently more comfortable writing Hebrew. This manuscript had been pasted into the binding of a medieval book discovered by a baptized Jewish scholar from Vienna in the 1850s; it had been dismissed as a fraud because of the connection of both manuscript and discoverer to Jews [Grunfeld 1979, 74–77].

26. Robert Alter [1989, 578–80] offers an interesting discussion of the three paintings, unusual references to visual art in Agnon, that recur in the novel; they consist of a painting by Böcklin, one by Rembrandt and one from the school of Breughel.

27. Consider, in this respect, Sarah Kofman's observations [1985, 32]: "The intimate, shameful secrets that Freud fears to expose to the public, because of the horror they are very likely to arouse, are thus inseparably

linked with his Jewishness and with femininity, with castration anxiety. In this sense, *The Interpretation of Dreams* is another Medusa's head."

28. Other related dreams: 1989, 281, 379, 427; 1979, 278–29, 373, 418.

29. Joseph Boone [1989, 167] asks: "And even when the male writer focuses on the 'feminine', might there be alternatives beyond 'appropriation'—instances, however rare, when he has let femaleness transform, redefine, his textual erotics, allowed himself *to be read through* femininity and femaleness, rather than become the authorizer speaking on behalf of it."

30. Luce Irigaray [1985, 133] observes: "Subjectivity denied to woman: indisputably this provides the financial backing for every irreducible constitution as an object: of representation, of discourse, of desire." The elusive body of the woman is the "place of slippage, that which cannot be captured by the sign" [Jardine 1985, 242].

31. Compare: "Thus, despite his arguments to the contrary, Montaigne's predicament is an amorous one, as is his discourse. Infinite, and without aim; filled to overflowing with its own emptiness and offering what it does not possess; disseminating the fragmented presence of the beloved" [Schlossman 1981, 905].

32. Revisions to the sections of the novel published in the late 1940s in *Ha'arets* show insertions that add ambiguity to this question of the meaning of Shira's name. For example, "Nadia that is Shira" (ms. p. 4) is revised to "Nadia that is Shira that is Nadia" (1979, 8). This reiterated wavering in the text seems almost to respond to the reader's efforts to dwell too exclusively on the ethereal aspects of Shira as a noun meaning "poetry" or "literariness." Nadia—*n-d-y-h*—is associated with the noun *n-y-d-h,* referring to the uncleanliness of women.

References

Aberbach, David. 1984. *At the Handles of the Lock: Themes in the Fiction of S. J. Agnon.* Oxford: Oxford University Press.

Abrams, M. H. 1953. *The Mirror and the Lamp: Romantic Theory and the Critical Tradition.* New York: Oxford University Press.

Agnon, S. Y. 1968. *Kol sipurav shel Sh. Y. 'Agnon.* [The Collected Stories of S. Y. Agnon]. 8 vols. Jerusalem and Tel-Aviv: Schocken.

____. 1968. *Kol sipurav.* [The Collected Stories]. Vol. 1, *Hakhnasat kalah.* [The Bridal Canopy]. Jerusalem and Tel-Aviv: Schocken.

____. 1968. *Kol sipurav.* [The Collected Stories]. Vol. 2, *Elu ve'elu.* [These and Those]. Jerusalem and Tel-Aviv: Schocken.

____. 1968. *Kol sipurav.* [The Collected Stories]. Vol. 3, *'Al Kapot haman'ul.* [At The Handles of the Lock]. Jerusalem and Tel-Aviv: Schocken.

____. 1968. *Kol sipurav.* [The Collected Stories]. Vol. 4, *Oreaḥ natah lalun.* [A Guest for the Night]. Jerusalem and Tel-Aviv: Schocken.

____. 1968. *Kol sipurav.* [The Collected Stories]. Vol. 5, *Tmol shilshom.* [Only Yesterday]. Jerusalem and Tel-Aviv: Schocken.

____. 1968. *Kol sipurav.* [The Collected Stories]. Vol. 6, *Samukh venir'eh.* [Nearby and Seen]. Jerusalem and Tel-Aviv: Schocken.

____. 1968. *Kol sipurav.* [The Collected Stories]. Vol. 7, *'Ad henah.* [Until Now]. Jerusalem and Tel-Aviv: Schocken.

____. 1968. *Kol sipurav.* [The Collected Stories]. Vol. 8, *Ha'esh veha'etsim.* [The Fire and the Trees]. Jerusalem and Tel-Aviv: Schocken.

____. 1968a. *A Guest for the Night.* Trans. Misha Louvish. New York: Schocken.

____. 1968b. *The Bridal Canopy.* Trans. I. M. Lask. New York: Schocken.

____. 1970. *Twenty-One Stories.* Ed. Nahum Glatzer. New York: Schocken.

____. 1970a. "Letter to Fishel Lachover." *Yedi'ot Genazim* 4: 587.

____. 1975. "Forevermore." Trans. Joel Blocker. In *Modern Hebrew Literature,* ed. Robert Alter. New York: Behrman.

____. 1976. *Me'atsmi le'atsmi.* [From Myself to Myself]. Jerusalem and Tel-Aviv: Schocken.

____. 1978. *Sefer, sofer, vesippur.* [Book, Writer, and Story]. Jerusalem and Tel-Aviv: Schocken.

____. 1979. *Shira.* Jerusalem and Tel-Aviv: Schocken.

____. 1979a. *Qorot bateynu.* [The Pillars of Our House]. Jerusalem and Tel-Aviv: Schocken.

____. 1983. *Esterleyn yeqirati: Mikhtavim 1924–1931.* [Estherlein My Dear: Letters 1924–31]. Ed. Emuna Yaron. Jerusalem and Tel-Aviv: Schocken.

____. 1984. "Knots Upon Knots." Trans. with an Afterword by Anne Golomb Hoffman. *Conservative Judaism* 37, iii: 38–42.

____. 1985. *A Simple Story.* Trans. Hillel Halkin. New York: Schocken.

____. 1987. *Sippure habesht.* [Tales of the Baal Shem Tov]. Jerusalem and Tel-Aviv: Schocken.

____. 1987a. *In the Heart of the Seas.* Trans. I. M. Lask. New York: Schocken.

____. 1989. *Shira.* Trans. Zeva Shapiro. New York: Schocken.

Alter, Robert. 1969. *After the Tradition: Essays on Modern Jewish Writing.* New York: Dutton.

____. 1971. "Agnon's Last Word." *Commentary* 51, vi: 74–81.

____. 1975. *Partial Magic: The Novel as a Self-Conscious Genre.* Berkeley: University of California Press.

____, ed. 1975a. *Modern Hebrew Literature.* New York: Behrman.

____. 1989. Afterword to *Shira,* by S. Y. Agnon. New York: Schocken.

Altmann, Alexander. 1985. "Moses Mendelssohn as the Archetypal German Jew." In *The Jewish Response to German Culture,* eds. J. Reinharz and W. Schatzberg. Hanover: University Press of New England.

Anderson, Chester G., ed. 1968. *James Joyce's A Portrait of the Artist as a Young Man.* New York: Viking.

Aphek, Edna. 1979. *Ma'arot milim: 'iyunim besignono shel Sh. Y. 'Agnon.*[Word Systems: Studies in the Style of S. Y. Agnon]. Tel-Aviv: Deqel.

Aschheim, Steven E. 1982. *Brothers and Strangers: The East European Jew in German and German-Jewish Consciousness, 1800–1923.* Madison: University of Wisconsin Press.

Babylonian Talmud. 1938. Ed. I. Epstein. London: Soncino.

Bakhtin, Mikhail. 1984. *Problems of Dostoevsky's Poetics.* Ed. and Trans. Caryl Emerson. Minneapolis: University of Minnesota Press.

____. 1987. *The Dialogic Imagination: Four Essays.* Ed. Michael Holquist. Trans. M. Holquist and C. Emerson. Austin: University of Texas Press.

Bakon, Yitzhak. 1968. *"'Al shnat 'aliyato shel 'Agnon la'arets ve'al hamista'ef mizeh."* [On the Year of Agnon's *Aliyah* and Its Ramifications]. *Hapo'el hatsa'ir.* 4/9/68.

Band, Arnold. 1968. *Nostalgia and Nightmare: A Study in the Fiction of S. Y. Agnon.* Berkeley: University of California Press.

____. 1967. *"Haḥeit ve'onsho be 'Tmol shilshom'."* [Sin and Its Punishment in "Only Yesterday"]. *Molad* 1: 75–81.

Bar-Adon, Aharon. 1977. *Sh. Y. 'Agnon uteḥiyyat halashon ha'ivrit.* [S. Y. Agnon and the Revival of the Hebrew Language]. Jerusalem: Bialik.

Barshai, Avinoam. 1988. *Dyoqno shel Shai Agnon: Haromanim shel Shai Agnon.* [Portrait of S. Y. Agnon: The Novels of S. Y. Agnon]. Ramat-Aviv: Everyman's University.

Barthes, Roland. 1975. *The Pleasure of the Text.* Trans. Richard Miller. New York: Hill and Wang.

____. 1977. *Image, Music, Text.* Trans. Stephen Heath. New York: Hill and Wang.

Barzel, Hillel. 1972. *Bein Agnon leKafka: Meḥqar umashveh.* [Agnon and Kafka: A Comparative Study]. Ramat-Gan: Bar-Ilan University Press.

____. 1975. *Sippure ahavah shel Sh. Y. Agnon: 'Iyune meḥqar.* [The Love Stories of S. Y. Agnon: Research Studies] Ramat-Gan: Bar-Ilan University Press.

Beit-Aryeh, Malachi. 1967. *Catalogue: Exhibition in Honor of S. J. Agnon.* Jerusalem: Jewish National and University Library.

Benveniste, Emile. 1971. *Problems in General Linguistics.* Trans. Mary Elizabeth Meek. Coral Gables: University of Miami Press.

Bernheimer, Charles and Claire Kahane, eds. 1985. *In Dora's Case: Freud—Hysteria—Feminism.* New York: Columbia University Press.

Biale, David. 1979. *Gershom Scholem: Kabbalah and Counter-History.* Cambridge, Mass.: Harvard University Press.

Bialik, Hayyim Nahman. 1939. *Aftergrowth and Other Stories.* Trans. I. M. Lask. Philadelphia: Jewish Publication Society.

____. 1963. *Kol kitvei Ḥ. N. Bialik.* [The Complete Writings of H. N. Bialik]. Tel-Aviv: Dvir.

____. 1975. "Revealment and Concealment in Language." Trans. Jacob Sloan. In *Modern Hebrew Literature,* ed. Robert Alter. New York: Behrman.

Bloom, Harold. 1973. *The Anxiety of Influence: A Theory of Poetry.* New York: Oxford University Press.

Boone, Joseph A. 1989. "Of Me(n) and Feminism: Who(se) is the Sex that Writes?" In *Gender and Theory,* ed. Linda Kauffman. New York: Blackwell.

Boyarin, Daniel. 1988. "Re-Citing the Torah." *Orim* 3, ii: 22–29.

Brenner, Yoseph Hayyim. 1971. *Breakdown and Bereavement.* Trans. Hillel Halkin. Ithaca: Cornell University Press.

____. 1972. *Shekhol vekishalon.* [Breakdown and Bereavement]. Tel-Aviv: Am Oved.

Brod, Max. 1963. *Franz Kafka: A Biography.* Trans. G. H. Humphreys and R. Winston. New York: Schocken.

Brooks, Peter. 1982. "Freud's Masterplot." In *Literature and Psychoanalysis: The Question of Reading: Otherwise,* ed. S. Felman. Baltimore: Johns Hopkins University Press.

____. 1984. *Reading for the Plot: Design and Intention in Narrative.* New York: A. A. Knopf.

Caron, Vicki. 1989. "The Ambivalent Legacy: The Impact of Enlightenment and Emancipation on Zionism." *Judaism* 38, iv: 502–16.

Casey, Edward S. and J. Melvin Woody. 1983. "Hegel, Heidegger, Lacan: The Dialectic of Desire." In *Interpreting Lacan,* eds. Joseph Smith and William Kerrigan. New Haven: Yale University Press.

Caws, Mary Ann. 1981. *The Eye in the Text: Essays on Perception, Mannerist to Modern.* Princeton: Princeton University Press.

Cassirer, Ernst. 1944. *Language and Myth.* Trans. Suzanne K. Langer. New York: Harper and Brothers.

Cervantes, Miguel de Saavedra. 1964. *Don Quixote.* Trans. J. M. Cohen. New York: Penguin.

Cixous, Hélène and Catherine Clément. 1986. *The Newly Born Woman.* Trans. Betsy Wing. Minneapolis: University of Minnesota Press.

Cnaani, David. 1971. *Shai 'Agnon be'al peh.* [S. Y. Agnon in Speech]. Merhavia.

Cohen, Israel, ed. 1968. *Sefer Buczacz: Matsevat zikaron leqehilah qedoshah.* [The Book of Buczacz: Memorial to a Holy Community]. Tel-Aviv: Am Oved.

Conrad, Joseph. 1983. *Heart of Darkness and the Secret Sharer.* New York: New American Library.

Curtius, Ernst Robert. 1953. *European Literature and the Latin Middle Ages.* Trans. Willard R. Trask. Princeton: Princeton University Press.

Davis, Robert Con. 1981. Introduction to *The Fictional Father: Lacanian Readings of the Text,* ed. R. C. Davis. Amherst: University of Massachusetts Press.

Deleuze, Gilles and Felix Guattari. 1986. *Kafka: Toward a Minor Literature.* Trans. Dana Polan. Minneapolis: University of Minnesota Press.

De Man, Paul. 1979. *Allegories of Reading: Figural Language in Rousseau, Nietzsche, and Proust.* New Haven: Yale University Press.

____. 1984. *The Rhetoric of Romanticism.* New York: Columbia University Press.

Derrida, Jacques. 1976. *Of Grammatology.* Trans. Gayatri C. Spivak. Baltimore: Johns Hopkins University Press.

____. 1978. *Writing and Difference.* Trans. Alan Bass. Chicago: University of Chicago Press.

____. 1981. *Dissemination* Ed. and Trans. Barbara Johnson. Chicago: University of Chicago Press.

____. 1982. *Margins of Philosophy.* Trans. Alan Bass. Chicago: University of Chicago Press.

____. 1987. "The Abyss and the Volcano: The Secularization of Language." Public lecture, City University Graduate Center (9/22/87).

Doane, Mary Ann. 1986. "The Clinical Eye: Medical Discourses in the 'Woman's Film' of the 1940's." In *The Female Body in Western Culture: Contemporary Perspectives,* ed. Susan R. Suleiman. Cambridge, Mass.: Harvard University Press.

Eco, Umberto. 1979. *The Role of the Reader: Explorations in the Semiotics of Texts.* Bloomington: Indiana University Press.

Faur, José. 1977. "Some General Observations on the Character of Classical Jewish Literature." *Journal of Jewish Studies* 37.

____. 1986. *Golden Doves with Silver Dots: Semiotics and Textuality in Rabbinic Tradition.* Bloomington: Indiana University Press.

Feierberg, Mordecai Zeev. 1958. *Ketavim* [Writings]. Tel-Aviv: Dvir.

____. 1973. *Whither? and Other Stories.* Trans. Hillel Halkin. Philadelphia: Jewish Publication Society.

Feldman, Yael. 1985. "How Does a Convention Mean? A Semiotic Reading of Agnon's Bilingual Key-Irony in *A Guest for the Night.*" *Hebrew Union College Annual* 56: 251–69.

____. 1987. "The Latent and the Manifest: Freudianism in *A Guest for the Night.*" *Prooftexts* 7: 29–39.

Felman, Shoshana. 1980."Turning the Screw of Interpretation." In *Psychoanalysis and Literature, The Question of Reading: Otherwise,* ed. Shoshana Felman. Baltimore: Johns Hopkins University Press.

____. 1985. *Writing and Madness (Literature / Philosophy / Psychoanalysis.)* Trans. M. N. Evans and S. Felman. Ithaca: Cornell University Press.

Flaubert, Gustave. 1976. *Bouvard and Pécuchet.* Trans. A. J. Krailsheimer. New York.

Flieger, Jerry Anne. 1983. "The Purloined Punchline: Joke as Textual Paradigm." In *Lacan and Narration: The Psychoanalytic Difference in Narrative Theory,* ed. Robert Con Davis. Baltimore: Johns Hopkins University Press.

Foucault, Michel. 1965. *Madness and Civilization: A History of Insanity in the Age of Reason.* Trans. Richard Howard. New York: Vintage.

Freud, Sigmund. 1974. *The Standard Edition of the Complete Psychological Works.* Trans. and Ed. James Strachey, with A. Freud, A. Strachey and A. Tyson. 24 vols. London: Hogarth.

____. [1900] Vol. 5, *The Interpretation of Dreams.*

____. [1905] Vol. 7, "Fragment of an Analysis of a Case of Hysteria."

____. [1905a] Vol. 7, "Three Essays on a Theory of Sexuality."

____. [1910] Vol. 11, "Leonardo da Vinci and a Memory of his Childhood."

____. [1912–13] Vol. 13, "Totem and Taboo."

____. [1919] Vol. 17, "The Uncanny."

____. [1920] Vol. 18, "Beyond the Pleasure Principle."

____. [1922] Vol. 18, "Medusa's Head."

____. [1923a] Vol. 19, "The Ego and the Id."

____. [1923b] Vol. 19, "The Infantile Genital Organization: An Interpolation into the Theory of Sexuality."

____. [1925] Vol. 19, "Note on a Mystic Writing-Pad."

____. [1927] Vol. 21, "Fetishism."

____. [1929] Vol. 21, "Civilization and Its Discontents."

____. [1931] Vol. 21, "Female Sexuality."

Fuchs, Esther. 1985. *Omanut hahitmamut: 'al ha'ironiah shel Shai 'Anon*[Cunning Innocence: On S.Y. Agnon's Irony]. Jerusalem: Geffen.

Gallop, Jane. 1988. "The American Other." In *The Purloined Poe: Lacan, Derrida and Psychoanalytic Reading,* eds. John P. Muller and William J. Richardson. Baltimore: Johns Hopkins University Press.

Gay, Peter. 1968. *Weimar Culture: The Outsider as Insider.* New York: Harper and Row.

____. 1978. *Freud, Jews and Other Germans: Masters and Victims in Modernist Culture.* New York: Oxford University Press.

Genette, Gérard. 1982. *Figures of Literary Discourse.* Trans. Alan Sheridan. New York: Columbia University Press.

Gilman, Sander. 1985. *Difference and Pathology: Stereotypes of Sexuality, Race, and Madness.* Ithaca: Cornell University Press.

____. 1986. *Jewish Self-Hatred: Anti-Semitism and the Hidden Language of the Jews.* Baltimore: Johns Hopkins University Press.

Ginzberg, Louis. 1968. *Legends of the Jews.* 7 vols. Philadelphia: Jewish Publication Society.

Goldenberg, Robert. 1984. "Talmud." In *Back to the Sources: Reading the Classic Jewish Texts,* ed. Barry Holtz. New York: Summit.

Goldner, Martin, ed. 1987. *Die Gabe: For Franz Rosenzweig on his 40th Birthday, 12/25/26.* New York: Leo Baeck Institute.

Gould, Eric, ed. 1985. *The Sin of the Book: Edmond Jabès.* Lincoln, Nebr.: University of Nebraska Press.

Green, Arthur. 1981. *Tormented Master: A Life of Rabbi Nahman of Bratslav.* New York: Schocken.

Grunfeld, Frederic. 1979. *Prophets Without Honor: A Background to Freud, Kafka, Einstein and Their World.* New York: Holt, Rinehart and Winston.

Haberman, A. M. 1969. *"R. Shalom Mordecai Czaczkes: Aviv shel R. Shmuel*

Yosef 'Agnon" [R. Shalom Mordecai Czaczkes: Father of R. Shmuel Yosef Agnon]. In *LeAgnon Shai: Devarim al hasofer usefarav* [To S. Y. Agnon: Words on the Writer and His Books], eds. Dov Sadan and Ephraim Urbach. Jerusalem: The Jewish Agency.

Hagar, Sara. 1978. "'*Tmol shilshom': Hithavut hamivneh veaḥduto*" ['Only Yesterday': Creation of the Structure and its Unity]. In *Shai 'Agnon: Meḥqarim ute'udot* [S. Y. Agnon: Studies and Documents], eds. Gershon Shaked and Rafael Veiser. Jerusalem: Bialik.

Halkin, Shimon. 1964. *"'Al 'Oreah natah lalun'."* In *Le'Agnon Shai: Devarim al hasofer usefarav* [To S. Y. Agnon: Words on the Writer and His Books], eds. Dov Sadan and Ephraim Urbach. Jerusalem: The Jewish Agency.

Handelman, Susan, 1982. *The Slayers of Moses: The Emergence of Rabbinic Interpretation in Modern Literary Theory.* Albany: State University of New York Press.

____. 1985. "Fragments of the Rock: Contemporary Literary Theory and the Study of Rabbinic Texts." *Prooftexts* 5:75–95.

Hartman, Geoffrey, 1985. "On the Jewish Imagination." *Prooftexts* 5, iii: 201–20.

____. and Sanford Budick, eds. 1986. *Midrash and Literature.* New Haven: Yale University Press.

Heller, Erich. 1975. *The Disinherited Mind: Essays in Modern German Literature and Thought.* New York: Harcourt, Brace and Jovanovich.

Hoffman, Anne Golomb. 1981. "Plotting the Landscape: Stories and Storytellers in Kafka's *The Castle.*" *Twentieth Century Literature* 27, iii: 289–307.

____. 1982. "Housing the Past in Agnon's *A Guest for the Night.*" *Prooftexts* 2: 265–82.

____. 1987. "'In Exile from the Palace of his Father': Dramas of Writing in the Fiction of S. Y. Agnon." *Hebrew Annual Review* 11:153–71.

____. 1988. "Inscription and Madness in *Tmol shilshom.*" In *S. Y. Agnon: Texts and Contexts.* Ed. Leon Yudkin. New York: Markus Wiener.

Holtz, Avraham. 1971. *"'Meshlemut le'avodah zarah': 'iyunim be 'pat slemah.'"* [From Wholeness to Idolatry: Studies in "A Whole Loaf"]. *Hasifrut* 3:295–311.

____. 1973. *"Hamashal hapatuaḥ kemafteaḥ le'sefer hama'asim' leShai 'Agnon."* [The Open Parable as Key to Agnon's "The Book of Deeds"]. *Hasifrut* 4: 298–333.

____. 1989. "S. Y. Agnon's *T'mol shilshom* as a Medical Record." *Koroth* 9, ix–x:629–49.

Horodetzky, S. A., ed. 1975. *Sefer shivḥe habesht.* [The Book of Praises of the Baal Shem Tov]. Tel-Aviv:

____. ed. 1922. *Sippure ma'asiyot.* Berlin: Einot.

Hsia, R. Po-chia. 1988. *The Myth of Ritual Murder: Jews and Magic in Reformation Germany.* New Haven: Yale University Press.

Idel, Moshe. 1988. *Kabbalah: New Perspectives.* New Haven: Yale University Press.

Irigaray, Luce. 1985. *This Sex Which Is Not One.* Trans. Catherine Porter, with Carolyn Burke. Ithaca: Cornell University Press.

Jabès, Edmond. 1963. *Le Livre des questions.* Paris: Gallimard.

____. 1964. *Le Livre de Yukel.* Paris: Gallimard.

____. 1967. *Yaël.* Paris: Gallimard.

____. 1969. *Elya* Paris: Gallimard.

____. 1972. *Aely.* Paris: Gallimard.

____. 1973. *(El, ou le dernier livre).* Paris: Gallimard.

____. 1976a. *Le Livre des ressemblances.* Paris: Gallimard.

____. 1976b. *The Book of Questions. Trans. Rosmarie Waldrop. Middletown, Conn.: Wesleyan University Press.*

____. *1977. The Book of Yukel.* Trans. Rosmarie Waldrop. Middletown, Conn.: Wesleyan University Press.

____. 1978. *Le Soupçon le désert.* Paris: Gallimard.

____. 1980a. *Du Désert au livre: entretiens avec marcel Cohen.* Paris: P. Belfond.

____. 1980b. *L'Inéffacable l'inaperçu.* Paris: Gallimard.

____. 1983. *The Book of Questions: Yael, Elya, Aely.* Trans. Rosmarie Waldrop. Middletown, Conn.: Wesleyan University Press.

____. 1984. *.El, or the Last Book.* Trans. Rosmarie Waldrop. Middletown, Conn.: Wesleyan University Press.

____. 1987. *The Book of Dialogue.* Trans. Rosmarie Waldrop. Middletown, Conn.: Wesleyan University Press.

Jakobson, Roman and Morris Halle. 1956. *Fundamentals of Language.* The Hague: Mouton.

Jakobson, Roman. 1960. "Closing Statement: Linguistics and Poetics." In *Style in Language,* ed. Thomas A. Sebeok. Cambridge, Mass.: Massachusetts Institute of Technology.

Janouch, Gustav. 1953. *Conversations with Kafka: Notes and Reminiscences.* Trans. Boronwy Rees. London: D. Verschoyle.

Jardine, Alice. 1985. *Gynesis: Configurations of Woman and Modernity.* Ithaca: Cornell University Press.

Jenny, Laurent. 1982. "The Strategy of Form." In *French Literary Theory Today.* Ed. Tzvetan Todorov. Cambridge: Cambridge University Press.

Joyce, James. 1968. *A Portrait of the Artist as a Young Man,* ed. C. G. Anderson. New York: Viking.

Joyce, James. 1986. *Ulysses.* Ed. H. W. Gabler, W. Steppe, C. Melchior. New York: Random House.

Kafka, Franz. 1946. *Das Urteil und andere erzählungen.* New York: Schocken.

____. 1964. *The Trial.* Trans. Willa and Edwin Muir. New York: Schocken.

____. 1971. *The Complete Stories.* Ed. N. Glatzer. New York: Schocken.

____. 1966. *Letter to his Father / Brief an den vater.* Trans. Ernst Kaiser and Eithne Wilkins. New York: Schocken.

____. 1977. *Letters to Friends, Family and Editors.* Trs. Richard Winston and Clara Winston. New York: Schocken.

Kauffman, Linda, ed. 1989. *Gender and Theory: Dialogues on Feminist Criticism.* Oxford: Blackwell.

Kirshenblatt-Gimblett, Barbara. 1982. "The Cut that Binds: The Western Ashkenazic Torah Binder as Nexus between Circumcision and Torah." In *Celebration: Studies in Festivity and Ritual,* ed. Victor Turner. Washington, D.C.: Smithsonian Institution Press.

Koelb, Clayton. 1987. "The Margin in the Middle: Kafka's Other Reading of Reading." In *Kafka and the Contemporary Critical Performance,* ed. Alan Udoff. Bloomington: Indiana University Press.

____. 1989. *Kafka's Rhetoric: The Passion of Reading.* Ithaca: Cornell University Press.

Kofman, Sarah. 1985. *The Enigma of Woman: Woman in Freud's Writings.* Trans. Catherine Porter. Ithaca: Cornell University Press.

Kristeva, Julia. 1986. *The Kristeva Reader.* Ed. Toril Moi. New York: Columbia University Press.

Kuk, Judith. 1973. *Rabbi Naḥman meBraslav: 'Iyunim besippurav.* Jerusalem.

Kurzweil, Baruch. 1970. *Masot al sipure Sh. Y. 'Agnon.* [Essays on the Stories of S. Y. Agnon]. Jerusalem: Schocken.

____. 1982. *"'Tmol shilshom.'"* [Only Yesterday]. In *Shmu'el Yosef Agnon: mivḥar ma'amarim 'al yetsirato* [S. Y. Agnon: A Selection of Articles on His Work], ed. H. Barzel. Tel-Aviv: Bar Ilan University Press.

Lacan, Jacques. 1977. *Écrits: A Selection.* Trans. Alan Sheridan. New York: Norton.

____. 1978. *The Four Fundamental Concepts of Psychoanalysis.* Trans. Alan Sheridan. New York: Norton.

____. 1982. "Desire and the Interpretation of Desire in *Hamlet.*" *Literature and Psychoanalysis: The Question of Reading: Otherwise,* ed. Shoshana Felman. Baltimore: Johns Hopkins University Press.

____. 1988. "Seminar on 'The Purloined Letter.'" Trans. Jeffrey Mehlman. In *The Purloined Poe: Lacan, Derrida and Psychoanalytic Reading,* eds. John P. Muller and William J. Richardson. Baltimore: Johns Hopkins University Press.

Lacoue-Labarthe, Philippe and Jean-Luc Nancy. 1990. "The Nazi Myth." *Critical Inquiry* 16, ii:291–312.

Laplanche, Jean and J. -B. Pontalis. 1973. *The Language of Psychoanalysis.* Trans. Daniel Lagache. London: Hogarth.

Lejeune, Philippe. 1982. "The Autobiographical Contract." In *French Literary Theory Today,* ed. Tzvetan Todorov. Cambridge: Cambridge University Press.

Levinger, Yaakov. 1966. *"He'arot leperush 'al 'Pat shlemah.'"* [Notes for an Interpretation of "A Whole Loaf"]. In *Le'Agnon Shai: Devarim 'al hasofer usefarav* [For S. Y. Agnon: Words on the Writer and His Books], eds. Dov Sadan and Ephraim Urbach. Jerusalem: The Jewish Agency.

Lieberman, Saul. 1950. *Hellenism in Jewish Palestine.* New York: Jewish Theological Seminary of America.

Macksey, Richard. 1983. "'Alas, Poor Yorick': Sterne Thoughts." In *Lacan and Narration: The Psychoanalytic Difference in Narrative Theory,* ed. R. C. Davis. Baltimore: Johns Hopkins University Press.

Mann, Thomas. 1927. *The Magic Mountain.* 2 vols. Trans. H. T. Lowe-Porter. New York: A. A. Knopf.

____. 1948. *Doctor Faustus.* Trans. H. T. Lowe-Porter. New York: A. A. Knopf.

____. 1952. *Buddenbrooks.* Trans. H. T. Lowe-Porter. New York: Random House.

____. 1963. *Death in Venice and Seven Other Stories.* Trans. H. T. Lowe-Porter. New York: Random House.

Mantel, Martin. 1977. *Rabbi Nachman of Bratzlav's Tales: A Critical Translation from the Yiddish with Annotations and Commentary.* 2 vols. Ann Arbor: University Microfilms.

Marcus, Steven. 1985. "Freud and Dora: History, Case History." In *In Dora's Case: Freud—Hysteria—Feminism,* eds. C. Bernheimer and C. Kahane. New York: Columbia University Press.

Messer-Davidow, Ellen. 1989. "The Philosophical Bases of Feminist Literary Criticisms." In *Gender and Theory: Dialogues on Feminist Criticism,* ed. Linda Kauffman. Oxford: Blackwell.

Meyer, Michael. 1967. *The Origins of the Modern Jew: Jewish Identity and European Culture in Germany, 1749–1842.* Detroit: Wayne State University Press.

Midrash Rabbah. 1983. Eds. H. Freedman and Maurice Simon. 10 vols. London: Soncino.

Miller, J. Hillis. 1977. "The Critic as Host." *Critical Inquiry* 3, iii: 439–448.

Mintz, Alan. 1980. "Agnon in Jaffa: The Myth of the Artist as a Young Man." *Prooftexts* 1:62–83.

____. 1989. *Banished From Their Father's Table: Loss of Faith and Hebrew Autobiography.* Bloomington: Indiana University Press.

Miron, Dan. 1977. "German Jews in Agnon's Work." *Leo Baeck Institute Yearbook*: 265–280.

____. 1987. "Domesticating a Foreign Genre: Agnon's Transactions with the Novel." Trans. N. Sokoloff. *Prooftexts* 7, i: 1–28.

Mitchell, Juliet. 1982. Introduction to *Feminine Sexuality: Jacques Lacan and the école freudienne,* eds Juliet Mitchell and Jacqueline Rose. New York: Norton.

Montaigne, Michel de. 1965. *The Complete Essays of Montaigne.* Trans. Donald M. Frame. Stanford: Stanford University Press.

Mosse, George. 1985. "Jewish Emancipation: Between *Bildung* and Respectability." In *The Jewish Response to German Culture,* eds. J. Reinharz and W. Schatzberg. Hanover: University Press of New England.

Muller, John P. 1983. "Language, Psychosis, and the Subject in Lacan." In *Interpreting Lacan,* eds. Joseph Smith and William Kerrigan. New Haven: Yale University Press.

___ and William J. Richardson, eds. 1988. *The Purloined Poe: Lacan, Derrida and Psychoanalytic Reading*. Baltimore: Johns Hopkins University Press.

Nahman of Bratslav. 1978. *The Tales*. Trans. and ed. Arnold J. Band. New York: Paulist Press.

___. 1983. *The Captive Soul of the Messiah: New Tales about Reb Nachman*. Trans. Howard Schwartz. New York.

[Rabbi] Nahman meBraslav. 1981. *Sippure ma'asiyot*. Ed. Yisrael Har. Jerusalem.

Nietzsche, Friedrich. 1987. *The Birth of Tragedy and the Genealogy of Morals*. Trans. F. Golffing. New York: Doubleday.

Olney, James, ed. 1980. *Autobiography, Essays Theoretical and Critical*.Princeton: Princeton University Press.

Pawel, Ernst. 1984. *The Nightmare of Reason: A Life of Franz Kafka*. New York: Farrar, Straus and Giroux.

Politzer, Heinz. 1966. *Franz Kafka: Parable and Paradox*. Ithaca: Cornell University Press.

Rawidowicz, Simon. 1974. *Studies in Jewish Thought*. Ed. Nahum Glatzer. Philadelphia: Jewish Publication Society.

Reed, T. J. 1974. *Thomas Mann and the Uses of Tradition*. Oxford: Clarendon.

Riffaterre, Michael. 1987. "The Intertextual Unconscious." *Critical Inquiry* 13, ii:371–85.

Robertson, Ritchie. 1985. *Kafka: Judaism, Politics, Literature*. New York: Oxford University Press.

Sachar, Howard. 1982. *A History of Israel: From the Rise of Zionism to Our Time*. New York: A. A. Knopf.

Sadan, Dov. 1959. *'Al Shai 'Agnon: Masah, 'iyun veḥeqer*. [On S. Y. Agnon: Essay, Inquiry and Research]. Tel-Aviv: Hakibbutz Hameuchad.

___. and Ephraim Urbach, eds. 1969. *Le'Agnon Shai: Devarim 'al hasofer usefarav*. [For S. Y. Agnon: Words on the Writer and His Books]. Jerusalem: The Jewish Agency.

de Saussure, Ferdinand. 1959. *Course in General Linguistics*. Eds. C. Bally, A. Sechehaye and A. Reidlinger. Trans. Wade Baskin. New York: The Philosophical Library.

Schlossman, Beryl. 1983. "From La Boétie to Montaigne: The Place of the Text." In *Lacan and Narration: The Psychoanalytic Difference in Nar-*

rative Theory, ed. R. C. Davis. Baltimore: Johns Hopkins University Press.

Schocken, Gershom. 1978. *"Motiv hatsara'at be'shira' ve'ad 'olam.'"* [The Leprosy Motif in "Shira" and "Forevermore"] In *Shai Agnon: Meḥqarim ute'udot* [S. Y. Agnon: Studies and Documents], eds. G. Shaked and R. Veiser. Jerusalem: Bialik.

Scholem, Gershom. 1954. *Major Trends in Jewish Mysticism.* New York: Schocken.

____. 1962. s. v. *Ba'al shem. Ha'entsiqlopedia ha'ivrit.* Jerusalem.

____. 1969. *On The Kabbalah and Its Symbolism.* Trans. Ralph Mannheim. New York: Schocken.

____. 1971. *The Messianic Idea in Judaism and Other Essays on Jewish Spirituality.* New York: Schocken.

____. 1972. "The Name of God and the Linguistic Theory of the Kabbalah." *Diogenes* 79: 59–80; 164–94.

Schwartz, Howard. 1982. "Rabbi Nachman of Bratslav: Forerunner of Modern Jewish Literature." *Judaism: A Quarterly Journal* 31, ii: 211–28.

Shaked, Gershon. 1971. *"Ḥelqat hasadah hanetushah."* [The Abandoned Part of the Field]. *Moznayim* 32:213–215.

____. 1973. *Omanut hasippur shel Agnon* [Agnon's Narrative Art]. Tel-Aviv: Sifriat Poalim.

____, and Rafael Veiser, eds. 1978. *Shai Agnon: Meḥqarim ute'udot.* [S. Y. Agnon: Studies and Documents]. Jerusalem: Bialik.

____. 1983. *Hasiporet ha'ivrit 1880–1980.* [Hebrew Fiction 1880–1980]. Vol. 2. Jerusalem: Hakibbutz Hameuchad and Keter.

____. 1986. "Midrash and Narrative: Agnon's 'Agunot.'" In *Midrash and Literature,* eds. Geoffrey Hartman and Sanford Budick. New Haven: Yale University Press.

____. 1987. *The Shadows Within: Essays on Modern Jewish Writers.* Philadelphia: Jewish Publication Society.

____. 1987a. "Portrait of the Artist as a Young Neurotic." *Prooftexts* 7:41–52.

____. 1989. *Shmuel Yosef Agnon: A Revolutionary Traditionalist.* New York: New York University Press.

Shumway, David. 1989. "Solidarity or Perspectivity?" In *Gender and Theory: Dialogues on Feminist Criticism,* ed. Linda Kauffman. Oxford: Blackwell.

Silverman, Kaja. 1983. *The Subject of Semiotics.* New York: Oxford University Press.

Smith, Joseph, and William Kerrigan, eds. 1983. *Interpreting Lacan.* New Haven: Yale University Press.

Sokel, Walter. 1973. "Franz Kafka as a Jew." *Leo Baeck Institute Yearbook* 18: 223–28.

Sokoloff, Naomi. 1984. "Metaphor and Metonymy in Agnon's *A Guest for the Night.*" *AJS Review* 9, i.

____. 1988. "Feminist Criticism and Hebrew Literature." *Prooftexts* 8: 143–56.

Sophocles. 1954. *Oedipus the King.* Trans. David Grene. In *Three Tragedies,* eds. David Grene and Richmond Lattimore. Chicago: University of Chicago Press.

Stanton, Domna C. 1986. "Difference on Trial: A Critique of the Maternal Metaphor in Cixous, Irigaray, and Kristeva. In *The Poetics of Gender,*ed. Nancy K. Miller. New York: Columbia University Press.

Starobinski, Jean. 1980. "The Style of Autobiography." In *Autobiography, Essays Theoretical and Critical,* ed. J. Olney. Princeton: Princeton University Press.

Stern, David. 1984. "Review of Susan Handelman, *The Slayers of Moses.*"*Prooftexts* 4:193–204.

____. 1985. "Literary Criticism or Literary Homilies? Susan Handelman and the Contemporary Study of Midrash." *Prooftexts* 5:96–103.

____. 1988. "Midrash and Indeterminacy." *Critical Inquiry* 15, i: 132–61.

Sterne, Laurence. 1925. *The Life and Opinions of Tristram Shandy, Gentleman.* New York: Liveright.

Tishby, Isaiah, ed. 1948. *Mishnat haZohar.* [The Teaching of the Zohar]. Jerusalem: Bialik.

Tomashevsky, Boris. 1971. "Literature and Biography" [1923]. In *Russian Poetics: Formalist and Structuralist Views,* eds. Ladislav Matejka and Krystyna Pomorska. Cambridge, Mass.: Harvard University Press.

Veiser, Raphael. 1988. *"Mamashut ubedayon bebiographiah shel 'Agnon"* [1980]. [Reality and Fiction in the Biography of Agnon]. In *Dyoqno shel Shai 'Agnon: Haromanim shel Shai 'Agnon* [Portrait of S. Y. Agnon: The Novels of S. Y. Agnon], ed. Avinoam Barshai. Tel-Aviv: Everyman's University.

Weigand, Hermann J. 1965. *The Magic Mountain: A Study of Thomas*

Mann's Der Zauberberg. Chapel Hill: University of North Carolina Press.

Weimann, Robert. 1988. "Text, Author-Function, and Appropriation in Modern Narrative: Toward A Sociology of Literature." *Critical Inquiry* 14, iii:431–47.

Wieder, N. 1957. "'Sanctuary' as a Metaphor for Scripture." *The Journal for Jewish Studies* 8, iii–iv:165–75.

Wilden, Anthony. 1968. "Lacan and the Discourse of the Other." In Jacques Lacan, *The Language of the Self: The Function of Language in Psychoanalysis.* Trans. Anthony Wilden. Baltimore: Johns Hopkins University Press.

Wilson, Edmund. 1947. *The Wound and the Bow: Seven Studies in Literature.* New York: Oxford University Press.

Wineman, Aryeh. 1978. "The Metamorphosis of a Hasidic Legend in Agnon's *'Al even aḥat.'*" *AJS Review* 3:197–201.

Yaron, Emuna. 1978. "*'Shira': pereq menusaḥ qodem.*" ["Shira": Draft of an Early Chapter]. In *Shai Agnon: Meḥqarim ute'udot* [S. Y. Agnon: Studies and Documents], eds. Gershon Shaked and Rafael Veiser. Jerusalem: Bialik.

____. 1979. Afterword to *Shira,* by S. Y. Agnon. Jerusalem and Tel-Aviv: Schocken.

Zoïla, Adolfo Fernandez. 1978. *Le Livre, Recherche autre d'Edmond Jabès.* [The Book: Research on Edmond Jabes]. Paris: J. M. Place.

Index